Introduction to Networking Using NetWare (4.1x)

Second Edition

Nancy B. Velasco

Upper Saddle River, New Jersey
Columbus, Ohio

tion Data

Introduction to networking using NetWare 4.1x/Nancy B. Velasco.—2nd ed.
   p. cm.
Includes index.
ISBN 0-13-010570-8
   1. NetWare. 2. Operating systems (Computers) 3. Local area networks (Computer
networks) I. Title.

QA76.76.O63 V42 2001
005.7′1369—dc21   99-086776

Vice President and Publisher: Dave Garza
Editor in Chief: Stephen Helba
Assistant Vice President and Publisher: Charles E. Stewart, Jr.
Production Editor: Alexandrina Benedicto Wolf
Production Supervision: Carlisle Publishers Services
Design Coordinator: Robin G. Chukes
Cover Designer: Dean Barrett
Cover art: FPG International
Production Manager: Matthew Ottenweller
Marketing Manager: Barbara Rose

This book was set in Times by Carlisle Communications, Ltd. It was printed and bound by R.R. Donnelley &
Sons. The cover was printed by Phoenix Color Corp.

Notice to the Reader: All product names listed herein are trademarks and/or registered trademarks of their
respective manufacturer.

The publisher and the authors do not warrant or guarantee any of the products and/or equipment
described herein, nor has the publisher or the authors made any independent analysis in connection with any
of the products, equipment, or information used herein. The reader is expressly advised to adopt all safety
precautions that might be indicated by the activities and experiments described herein. The reader assumes
all risks in connection with such instructions.

10 9 8 7 6 5 4 3 2 1
ISBN 0-13-010570-8

PREFACE

Introduction to Networking Using NetWare (4.1x), Second Edition, is an essential guide for anyone new to networking or anyone needing a quick refresher or overview. It is also an excellent resource for people who do not have weeks to sift through technical manuals and traditional networking books. This book, written in a down-to-earth, concise style, seeks to speed up the learning process and improve retention of the concepts learned.

Networking is no longer something of the future. In our mobile society, networking ties together people from all walks of life. Within a company, networking enables workers to communicate without even leaving their desks; thus the term *paperless society* came into vogue. Networks allow users to share hardware and software, which cuts down on the expenditures of the company. Networking also allows users to share customer databases, thus cutting down on repetitiveness and increasing accuracy. Novell NetWare® currently ranks as the network operating system that many companies choose to implement at the installation site. Personnel who can work with a local area network (LAN) to set up user accounts, troubleshoot, and manage day-to-day tasks are a valuable asset to a company. The goal of this book is to help the readers do just that—by providing the resources that they need to excel in their careers.

Some of the important features of this book are as follows:

- *Introduction to networking components, jargon, and common usage.* This discussion looks at the ingredients for making a small-size LAN and introduces terms commonly used in the networking industry.
- *Setting up and managing the user's workstation.* This book covers how the local operating system (such as DOS) and the network operation system (NOS) interrelate. It discusses the steps needed to set up a workstation on the network and to log into the network. It also covers a helpful review of Windows Explorer® used at the local level.
- *Novell® Directory Services (NDS).* Working with files and directories is at the heart of NetWare; thus this book emphasizes this area. This book explores the structure of Novell Directory Services, gives helpful suggestions on setting up and managing the NDS, and explores many utilities required for such management.
- *Managing user accounts and providing for security.* Setting up users on the network, assigning rights, and taking other safeguard measures are important to the network's overall security and daily operation. This book explores various utilities available for managing the network.
- *Communicating and printing.* This book looks at ways of communicating on the network and also discusses printer setups and the printing of reports.
- *Automating the user's work environment.* This book explains how to create login scripts and work with drive mappings.

This text is introductory in nature; therefore, with the exception of the NetWare 4.11 Server Installation instructions given in Appendix A, the material presented is applicable to both NetWare 4.10 and NetWare 4.11. The key addition added in NetWare 4.11 relates to setting up web access, which is beyond the scope of this book.

Network Courtesy

As with most industries, the networking profession has a code of conduct that is unspoken yet expected of all users on the system. Review the following courtesy rules before starting your networking adventure:

1. Administrators need to find out from users what their needs are. Administrators should politely explain that they want to ensure that the network working environment is sufficient for all users.
2. Administrators need to let the users know that they are available if problems are encountered, especially problems with accessing software and updating customer accounts.
3. Administrators need to follow up with users of new accounts to ensure that those users are not experiencing any problems with the system. If they are experiencing problems, the administrator should find the cause and the solution for each problem. Sometimes, it may be necessary to increase rights in a given directory, but this should be done cautiously.
4. All users should remember to respect other users' workspace "bubble" when sending messages. Users should keep messages on a professional level and avoid cluttering up other users' screens with unnecessary messages.

Network Setup

This book takes into consideration that the reader is an end user. In addition, the text acquaints readers with the responsibilities and tasks required of an administrator. For training purposes, it is advisable to set up home directories for each user under a main directory called VOL1:USERS. This will help the labs run consistently. Readers should have access to a NetWare 4.x network and workstations that are running Windows. Chapter 2 provides an overview of Windows Explorer, and Chapter 3 reviews frequently used DOS commands. Chapter 4 walks through setting up workstations, and Chapter 5 explains how to set up user accounts.

Acknowledgments

First of all, I thank my husband, Tito, for his constant support and patience. Second, thanks to my son, Tito Jr., who served as an inspiration. It was during my maternity leave that I wrote the first edition of this book. I thank the many networking students who helped to pilot test the early drafts of the first edition manuscript and gave much valuable feedback. I also thank all the staff and faculty at Computer Learning Center for their support, input, and encouragement. I am very thankful for the opportunity to work at Evangelical Christian Credit Union as a supervisor in the Information Systems Unit. I would like to say thank you to Alan Weisenberger and Vincent Keys for their leadership and for giving me the chance to grow and learn more. Thanks to my IS front office staff for their dedication and support as we tackled computer challenges together. Thanks to Charles Stewart and Alex Wolf for their dedication and professionalism in getting this book ready for the readers. I wish to acknowledge the staff at Carlisle Publishers Services, particularly Kathy Davis for her work in this edition.

I thank Marcy Shanti of Novell, Inc. for granting me permission to use material from Novell. Novell, Netware, and Groupwise are registered trademarks; Novell BorderManager and Zenworks are trademarks of Novell, Inc. in the United States and other countries. Screen shots from Netware, © 1983–1999, Novell, Inc. All rights reserved. Reprinted and used with permission.

Finally, I thank the following reviewers of the first and second editions for their insightful suggestions: Susan Meardon, Wake Technical Community College; Robert P. Diffenderfer, DeVry Institute of Technology; John Hilby, Perry Technical Institute; and Jim Barlow, Computer Learning Center.

Technical Advisor

Very special thanks go to my technical advisor for the first edition of this book, Marc A. Busch, Enterprise Certified NetWare Engineer/Certified NetWare Engineer/Certified NetWare Administrator. During the writing of the first edition he served as the vice president of the Orange County Network Professional Association and was lead CNE instructor at Computer Learning Center. Mr. Busch answered numerous networking questions and examined the manuscript's technical content.

In loving memory of my parents
Ida Mae Blackmon
and
Tollie Zack Blackmon
who taught me to value the learning
opportunities that come my way
and to enjoy life
and the Creator of life

CONTENTS

Part I Getting Started   1

Chapter 1 / LAN Basics   2
Local Area Networks (LANs)   3
Key Components of a LAN   4
    Component 1: File Server   4
    Component 2: Network Operating System
        (NOS)   5
    Component 3: Workstations   6
    Component 4: Local Operating System
        (LOS)   6
    Component 5: Network Interface Card (NIC)   6
    Component 6: Cables or Media   7
Communication Protocols and Access Methods   7
    Carrier Sense Multiple Access/Collision Detection
        (CSMA/CD) or Contention   8
    Polling   8
    Token Passing   8
Working with Cabling   9
    Topologies   9
LAN versus Other Platforms   11
Interconnectivity   11
    Bridge   11
    Gateway   12
    Terminal Emulation   12
    Host and Client   12

**Chapter 2 / Windows Review and Directory
Management   15**
Windows Explorer Basics   16
    Launching Windows Explorer   16
    Software Installations   17
    Creating a Directory Folder   17
    Copying One File   18
    Copying Multiple Files   21
    Moving Files   22
    Renaming a File   22
    Properties   22
    Quick Tips   24
Physical, Logical, and Search Drives   24
    Physical Drives   24

Logical Drives and Drive Mapping   26
Search Drives   27
Life Span of Logical and Search Drive
    Mappings   28
Special Mapping Options   30
    Deleting Map Assignments   30
    Using the NEXT Option   30
    The Disappearing Act!   31
    Assigning Drive Maps Using Windows Explorer   31
Directory Structure   32
    LOGIN   33
    PUBLIC   35
    SYSTEM   35
    MAIL   35
    DELETED.SAV   35
The PUBLIC Directory: User Access   36
Directory Rights   36

Chapter 3 / DOS Review   40
Introduction   41
Internal DOS Commands   41
    DIR, COPY, ERASE, and TYPE   41
    TIME, DATE, and CLS   42
    Make Directory (MD)   42
    Change Directory (CD)   43
    Remove Directory (RD)   43
    PATH   44
External DOS Commands   44
    ATTRIB   45
    BACKUP and MSBACKUP   45
    Delete Tree (DELTREE)   47
    EDIT   47

Part II Setting Up the
Network Environment   53

**Chapter 4 / Setting Up the NetWare
Workstation   54**
Preparing the Workstation   55
    Creating Workstation NetWare Client
        Diskettes   55

Installing the NetWare Client at the
Workstation   56
The Login Process   58
Common Error Message Associated with Attaching
and Logging In   59
"File Server Not Found" or "Invalid Drive
Specifcation"   60
"Access Denied" or "Intruder Detection
Lockout"   61
NetWare Directory Services (NDS) Tree Further Clari-
fication   61
Context   61
Verifying and Changing the Context   62
Login Results Screen   63
Customizing the Login Process   63
Network Neighborhood   63
Placement of the Login Shortcut   70

**Chapter 5 / Introduction to NWADMIN, Creating
Users and Groups   75**
NetWare Administrator (NWADMIN)   76
Netware Directory Services (NDS) Tree   78
Creating Organizational Unit Objects   78
User Leaves   80
Creating Groups   81
Assigning Users to Groups   83
Assigning Security Access   84
Viewing Trustee Rights   85
Changing Trustee Assignments   86
Adding Trustee Assignments   87
Understanding the Rights   87

Chapter 6 / Setting Up Accounts Using NetAdmin   90
The NetAdmin Account   91
Setting Up the Account and Viewing Existing
Accounts   91
Placement of User Accounts   91
Managing Objects   92
Changing the Context   93
Selecting the Object   95
"Actions for User" Menu   95
Viewing or Editing Rights to Files and
Directories   97
Viewing or Editing the Trustee of This Object   97
Notes Regarding Rights   100
Working with Help   100
Manage According to Search Pattern   100

Part III Common Tasks   107

Chapter 7 / NETUSER Utility   108
NETUSER Options   109

Printing   109
Network Printers   110
Printer Port   110
Assigning a Port for Network Use   110
Check Jobs Waiting to Print   110
Messages   111
Send Messages to Groups   111
Send Messages to Users   111
Set Receive Message   111
Drives   112
Drive Mappings   112
The Purpose of Logical Drives   112
NETUSER and Drive Mapping   113
Logical Drives   113
DOS PATH Command   114
PATH versus Search Mapping   115
Attachment   115

Chapter 8 / FILER Utility   118
FILER   119
Select Current Directory   119
Manage Files and Directories   120
Change the Directory Path to a Different Level   120
Manage One or More Subdirectories   121
Manage One or More Files   121
View and/or Set Directory Information   122
Assign Trustees and Their Rights Using the
"Directory Information" Screen   123
Manage According to Search Patterns   124
Exclude Directory Pattern   125
Include Directory Pattern   125
Exclude and Include File Patterns   125
File Search Attributes   125
Directory Search Attributes   125
View Volume Information   126
Work with Deleted Files   126
Salvage Deleted Files   126
Purge Deleted Files   126
Set Default FILER Options   127
Set Default Options   127
Confirm Deletions   127
Confirm File Copies   127
Confirm File Overwrites   128

Chapter 9 / Command Line Utilities   136
Command Line Utilities Basic Commands   137
Routine System Command Line Utilities   137
LOGIN   137
LOGIN/NS   137
LOGIN SERV2/USERXX   138
LOGOUT   138
LOGOUT SERV2   138

SYSTIME SERV2   138
SETPASS   138
SETPASS SERV2/   138
NVER   138
NPATH   138
Communicating on the Network   139
NLIST USER   139
WHOAMI   139
WHOAMI/ALL   139
SEND "How About Lunch?" TO USER11;
    SEND "Can Someone Help Me?" TO
    LANCLASS   141
SEND/A=C   141
SEND/A=N   141
SEND/A   141
Managing Directories with Command Line
    Utilities   141
MAP G:=SERV1_VOL1:USERS\USER05; MAP
    S4:=SERV1_SYS:APPS\WP   141
MAP INS S4:=SERV1_SYS:APPS\WP   141
MAP DEL G: 141
MAP N SERV2/ABC_SYS:APPS\PR
    OJECTS   141
MAP S16:=ABC_SYS:APPS\DB   143
RENDIR USER\USER05\PRACTICE
    USER\USER05\KEEPIT   143
RIGHTS ABC_SYS:USERS\USER05   143
RIGHTS SERV1_SYS:APPS\WP /T   143
RIGHTS SERV1_SYS:APPS\WP /I   144
RIGHTS ABC_SYS:APPS\WP\TUTORS\
    SPECIAL REFCEW
    /NAME=INSTRUCTA,USERXX   145
FLAG H:*.*RO /S /DO   145
Managing Files with Command Line Utilities   145
NDIR   145
NMENU MYMENU   145
NCOPY G:MYTEST.TXT A:MYTEST.
    BAK   145
NCOPY H:*.* I:*.* /S   146
PURGE H:*.*   147
PURGE H:*.* /S   147
FLAG ABC_SYS:USERS\USER01\MYTEST.
    TXT RO /F0   147
Controlling Printing with Command Line
    Utilities   149
CAPTURE B=SINGERS C=2 FF L=1
    Q=PRINTQ_1 S=SERV1 TI=15 AU
    NOTI   150
PSC PS=PS0 STAT   152
NPRINT H:MYTEST.TXT Q=PRINTQ_0
    B=NANCY FF   152

Part IV Printing   155

Chapter 10 / Managing Printers Using NWADMIN   156
Understanding Printing Concepts   157
    Local versus Network Printers   157
    Four Special Objects Required for Printing   157
    Submitting a Print Request   157
    Waiting in the Print Queue Line   158
    The Printer   158
    The Print Server   159
    Completing the Circle   159
    Important Documentation   159
Printer Setups and Management   159
    Creating Print Queue Leaf Objects   159

Chapter 11 / Print Utilities   169
Exploring Print Utilities   170
PRINTDEF   170
    Print Devices   170
    Print Forms   171
    Change Current Context   172
PRINTCON   172
    Edit Print Job Configuration   172
    Select Default Print Job Configuration   173
    Change Current Object   173
    Using the Print Job Configuration   173
PCONSOLE   173
    Print Queues   175
    Print Queue Information   175
    Specifying File to Print   176
Changing Print Parameters   177
    Status   178
    Print Queue ID   179
    Queue Users   179
    Operators   179
    Print Servers   180
    The "Printers" Screen   180
    Service Modes for Forms   181
Special Notes Regarding Printers   183

Part V Safeguarding the LAN   195

Chapter 12 / LAN Security, Safeguards, and Troubleshooting   196
LAN Security   197
Account Restrictions   197
    Login Restrictions   198
    Password Restrictions   199
    Network Address Restrictions   200
    Login Time Restrictions   200
    Volume/Space Restrictions   200

Directory Trustee Assignments and LAN Security   201
Trustee Directory Rights   201
Passwords and LAN Security   202
Virus Threat   202
Safeguards and Troubleshooting   203
    Troubleshooting   203
    Uninterruptible Power Supply (UPS)   204
    Backups   204
System Fault Tolerance   204
    SFT I   204
    SFT II: Disk Mirroring and Duplexing   205
    SFT III: Two Servers and Server Mirroring   205

Part VI   Automation   209

Chapter 13 / Login Scripts   210
Login Script Files   211
    Container Login Script   211
    Profile Login Script   212
    User/Personal Login Script   213
    Default Login Script   213
Creating and Locating the Login Script   214
Common Login Script Commands   214
    WRITE Command   215
    Sounding Alerts Command   215
    DISPLAY Command   217
    INCLUDE Command   217
    Executing .EXE, .COM, and .BAT
        Commands   217
    Changing Default Drives   217
    Conditional Instructions   217
    Running Programs upon Exiting   217
    Executing Internal DOS Commands   218
    Mapping   218

Chapter 14 / Menus   221
NetWare Menus   222
Rights Required to Create Menus   222
Requirements for Running a Menu   223
Advantages to Using Menus   223
Sample Menu   224
    Executing a Menu   225
    EXEC Command   225
Automating a Menu   226

Part VII   Exploring Software   231

Chapter 15 / Selecting Software   232
Selecting and Buying Software   233
Determining How Many Workstations Can Use
    Software   233
    Software Metering   234
    Why Is Software Metering Important?   234

Deciding Where to Purchase Software   234
Determining Software's Use   235
    Word-Processing Software   235
    Spreadsheet Software   235
    Database Management Software   235
    Desktop Publishing Software   236
    Accounting Software   236
    Modem Software   236
    Integrated Packages   236
    Computer-Aided Design and Computer-Aided
        Mapping Software   236
    Education Software   236
Deciding What Software to Buy   237
Finding Further Information on Software   237
    Magazines   237
    User Groups   237
    Bulletin Board Services   238
    The Internet   238
    Computer Stores   238
    Libraries   238
    Software Manufacturers   238

Appendix A / Server Installation   241
Partitioning the Hard Drive   241
Format Drive C   242
Special DOS Files   242
CD-ROM Driver   243
Edit Confi.Sys   243
The Network Interface Card (NIC)   244
Installing IntranetWare 4.11   245

Appendix B / For Further Learning   249
Magazines Relating to Networking   249
Magazines Relating to Computers in General   249
Interesting Web Sites on the Internet   250

Appendix C / Error Messages   251
Bad Command or File Name   251
Directory Could Not Be Located   251
File Cannot Be Copied onto Itself   251
Invalid Drive Specification   251
Path/File Access Error   252
The Command Line Syntax Is Invalid   252
Your Current Context Is ABC_CO.CONSULTANTS;
    The User Does Not Exist in the Specified Context;
    Access Has Been Denied   252
Your Current Context Is ABC_CO.CONSULTANTS;
    Access Has Been Denied   252

Glossary   253

Index   258

GETTING STARTED

This section introduces basic networking concepts and presents a review of Microsoft Windows Explorer®, used locally at the workstation, and DOS commands encountered most often on the network.

CHAPTER ONE   LAN Basics

CHAPTER TWO   Windows Review and Directory Management

CHAPTER THREE   DOS Review

CHAPTER ONE

LAN BASICS

INSPIRING MOMENT

Today's rapidly growing networking infrastructures consist of everything from interoffice means for communicating via electronic mail (e-mail), to the sharing of sophisticated software (programs), the sharing of hardware (equipment), and connecting to the outside world by means of the Internet. Just a few years ago, companies for the most part relied on photocopying memos and mass distributing them to in-house staff, in box slots and the like. Today, if the e-mail system goes down, the result can be confusion and loss of productivity. People rely on the company e-mail system for communicating information and staying in touch. They depend on it for setting, scheduling, and being reminded of appointments, special tasks, and events. Most e-mail systems today keep a record of which users have actually opened the electronic message that was sent, so the sender knows exactly the date and time that the memo was read. Managers, supervisors, and team leaders can use e-mail to inform team members of the objectives of the day, or the objectives for a group project. Instead of chasing people in the hallways, they can leave an e-mail message. Also, computer workstations can be set up to notify users when they log in that they have mail. It can also inform them throughout the day when new messages arrive.

QUESTIONS FOR THOUGHT

Can you imagine group scheduling where everyone in the group does not have to be present at a meeting? Would you like to know exactly who has and has not read your e-mail messages? How far have we come at lessening the amount of photocopy machine jams, phone tag, missed appointments, and expensive group meetings? If used properly, the e-mail systems found in organizations today can greatly help improve efficiency, communication, and productivity. Yet, the reverse is also true. If organizations fail to control how e-mail is used, then staff could end up wasting man-hours of time with reading unimportant e-mails.

CHALLENGE

Does your network have an electronic messaging system installed? If so, ask your network administrator or other personnel how to use it. Become familiar and adhere to any protocols regarding the use of the e-mail system. With a little practice, you can send e-mail messages and appointments to your associates. What are some ways that you could improve your productivity and business communications through the use of an e-mail system?

CHAPTER OBJECTIVES

After finishing this chapter, you should be able to:

1. Define *local area network* and list the benefits involved in using a LAN.
2. Identify the key components of a LAN: a file server, a network operating system (NOS), workstations, a local operating system (LOS), network interface cards (NICs), and cables.
3. Explain how a workstation attaches to the NetWare network and identify key files required.
4. Define *communication protocol* (access method) and list the popular types.
5. Define *topology* and list the popular types.
6. Discuss interconnectivity and its importance, and define common terms found in connecting different platforms together.

LOCAL AREA NETWORKS (LANS)

This chapter assumes that the Novell NetWare operating system is already installed on the file server, and that the LAN is up and running. (For help on installation, consult your Novell documentation manuals.)

Local area networks (LANs) allow computer users to share resources and communicate together, thus saving time and money and improving efficiency. Users share hardware resources such as printers, plotters, fax/modems, CD-ROMs, and storage devices. They share software applications for word processing, spreadsheet management, database management, desktop publishing, computer-aided design, accounting, financial management, and so forth. Perhaps the most common service is to share data such as customer, employee, or vendor databases.

Without a LAN environment, users constantly run back and forth physically from station to station. With a LAN, improved communication, through sending short messages, e-mail, faxes, and even files of information, leads to more informed workers who can make better decisions and accomplish more.

A LAN is a way in which several computers can connect together in short proximity (normally within a building); share resources such as software, hardware, and data; and communicate together. The key word is *connectivity;* in a LAN, the personal computers are all connected together to share resources and communicate.

To provide access to a LAN and maintain security, accounts are created. Without an account, you cannot use a LAN. To set up accounts, you should have access to the ADMIN account or have been assigned ADMIN-equivalent privileges. In a class setting, this may not be possible. As a student, though, you can view many of the settings of your own account, which should give you an ample opportunity to learn. The only restriction is that you cannot change the settings.

LAN security is a prime reason for assigning trustee directory rights and for setting up accounts. With proper training and care in deciding who should gain access to various

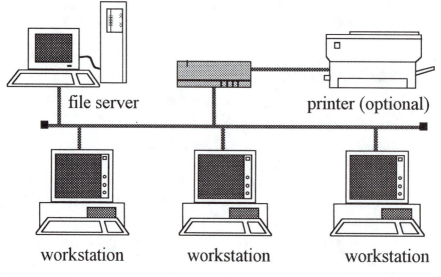

FIGURE 1.1
Key components of a local area network.

parts of software and data, you can set up and manage accounts to help the company or organization with controlling and sharing of the resources on the LAN.

The network administrator oversees the day-to-day operation of the network. By setting up and managing user accounts, controlling security, creating comfortable work environments with tools such as menus and login scripts, making sure the printers are set up and working, maintaining server backups, and monitoring network performance, the network administrator makes sure that the users can work on the LAN easily and efficiently.

KEY COMPONENTS OF A LAN

LAN components include a file server, the network operating system (such as Novell® NetWare), workstations, local operating systems for the workstations (such as DOS), **network interface cards** (NICs), cables, and possibly other hardware such as printers, fax machines, and hubs (see Figure 1.1). A basic knowledge of how these components function together makes working on the LAN more meaningful.

Component 1: File Server

The **file server** is the heart of the LAN (see Figure 1.2). Its purpose, as its name implies, is to serve the workstation files and other resources as requested. Keep in mind that the software and data that are to be shared among different users are normally stored on the file server's hard drive(s) or on a disk subsystem connected to the file server (a disk subsystem consists of a housing unit that holds additional drives). Because many users will share resources from the file server, it's important to keep it as secure as possible. Locking it in a closet or restricted computer room is one way to secure it.

DOS partition
contains the C: drive

NetWare partition
contains volumes
such as SYS: and VOL1:

FIGURE 1.2
Typical hard drive set up for a file server.

The file server is a personal computer that has a minimum of 8 megabytes (MB) of random-access memory (RAM). Ideally, the file server will have upward of 16 MB of RAM. The hard drive of the file server will be shared by the users; therefore, it's wise to invest in as large of a hard drive as an organization can afford.

A dedicated file server constantly acts as a servant to the workstations by sharing resources and serving files. A nondedicated file server only acts as a servant part of the time; the rest of the time, it doubles as an ordinary workstation where a user can work on a software application. Novell NetWare 4.1x only runs in dedicated mode. Earlier versions of NetWare, such as release 2.15c, allow for nondedicated operation.

Component 2: Network Operating System (NOS)

Personal computers (PCs) speak the **local operating system** (DOS, Windows 95/98/NT) language, whereas the file server speaks or uses the **network operating system** (NOS) to operate and perform day-to-day functions or tasks. Novell NetWare is a common NOS. The file server is booted like a DOS-based PC; the hard drive itself is set up differently, however. The file server's hard drive has a minimum of two partitions or sections. One partition is referred to as a DOS partition, and it contains the files necessary for booting. It also contains SERVER.EXE, which, when executed, starts the network. (SERVER.EXE is normally found in a subdirectory called C:-NWSERVER.) The DOS partition contains divisions called drives such as C: and D:. The file server's other partition is known as a non-DOS NetWare partition. Rather than being called drives, the divisions of the NetWare partition are known as volumes, such as SYS: and VOL1:. When the file server is activated and the network is brought up by executing the SERVER.EXE file, the colon prompt (:) appears on the file server's screen. The colon prompt denotes that the file server is ready to receive keyboard instructions from the file server console and that it speaks NOS language, namely, Novell Net-Ware 4.1x. (This is similar to having a C:\> prompt at the workstation indicating that the station is ready for instructions and that DOS is the local operating system.) Network drives, which are normally letters F: through Z:, are covered in more detail in Chapter 2.

Component 3: Workstations

The **workstation** is usually a personal computer on which a user logs in. Note that in a LAN environment, distributed processing rather than centralized processing is used. In a mainframe or midrange platform, the actual processing takes place at the main unit, not at each workstation. The stations are therefore often referred to as *dumb terminals* because they do not have central processing units (CPUs). In a LAN platform environment, however, the workstations do have CPUs and process their own work. Once software (or data) has been requested from the file server, it is loaded into the RAM of the workstation for the actual processing. Because the processing power is scattered among different workstations on the LAN, the term used is *distributed processing.* In a mainframe or midrange environment, however, because the processing is sent to one main place, the term used is *centralized,* or *shared, processing.* Because the file server's hard drive and/or disk subsystem may be shared by all users, some companies and organizations eliminate the drives on the workstation. Under such circumstances the network interface card (NIC) would contain a special chip known as a boot PROM (programmable read-only memory) for getting the workstation started. The boot PROM contains instructions to allow the workstation to boot, or get started. Some companies have workstations fully equipped with floppy drives, hard drives, and perhaps even tape drives. In such cases, the workstation would boot up by running instructions found in three special files on drive C:'s root directory: COMMAND.COM, IO.SYS, and MSDOS.SYS. With more recent versions of DOS and Windows, the workstation may even have a fourth boot-up file that controls file compression. If drive A: has a disk in it and the drive door is closed, then the system would try to find the three files required for booting in drive A: instead of in the hard drive C:. The booting or start-up process loads the local operating system (LOS) so that the workstation can function.

Component 4: Local Operating System (LOS)

To operate a personal computer, you must first start it using an operating system software such as DOS (disk operating system) or Windows. The following DOS files are needed to boot your system: IO.SYS, MSDOS.SYS, and COMMAND.COM (see Figure 1.3). Note that IO.SYS and MSDOS.SYS do not appear in a normal directory listing because they are hidden. These three files collectively are often referred to as *system files.* The computer itself is just a machine; it needs software (instructions) to operate. Operating system software such as DOS provides the instructions needed for day-to-day operations. When referring to software or hardware items specifically for the workstation, the word *local* is used. In this discussion, booting and operating the workstations are the goals of the **local operating system.**

Network drives (F: through Z:) are discussed in Chapter 2. The first network drive is accessible only after the workstation attaches to the network. The user must log in to access the remaining drives.

Component 5: Network Interface Card (NIC)

Each computer on the LAN, including all workstations and the file server, must have an **NIC (network interface card).** An NIC is the hardware that allows the computer to receive and send messages. An NIC is sometimes referred to as an adapter. The NIC is controlled

system files on disk (hard drive or floppy)	when the computer starts, these system files go to the computer's memory	the prompt appears on the screen

COMMAND.COM
IO.SYS
MSDOS.SYS

random-access memory

C:\> = local drive
F:\> = network drive

FIGURE 1.3

by a software program called a LAN driver. The LAN driver is normally provided by the NIC manufacturer. Novell provides a copy of some of the more standard LAN drivers; these come with the workstation installation software provided with your NOS.

Component 6: Cables or Media

Cables also referred to as **media,** connect all the workstations and the file server together. There are various cabling systems available today. Some of the more well-known types are coaxial (base band and broad band), twisted pair (shielded and unshielded), and fiber-optic cables. The type of cable chosen depends on cost factors, electrical interference around the LAN, the experience of the person installing the cabling, and, in some cases, the topology, or cable layout, chosen.

Twisted pair cabling is fairly inexpensive and is easy to install, but it provides the least resistance to electrical interference. The most commonly expressed forms of twisted pair cabling are unshielded twisted pair (UTP) and shielded twisted pair (STP). STP provides some extra protection against electrical interference. Coaxial cabling is in the middle; it offers a fair amount of resistance to electrical interference, costs a little more than twisted pair, and is somewhat more difficult than twisted pair to install. Fiber-optic cabling is at the high end of the scale in terms of its ability to withstand electrical interference, its high cost, and the need for a highly skilled person to install it. Cabling is also referred to by some as media, because it is the *media* through which signals and pieces of software and data are sent.

COMMUNICATION PROTOCOLS AND ACCESS METHODS

Protocols refer to the procedures or rules. For example, there are rules regulating how data packets are sent across the LAN. When a software application or data file is sent from the file server to the workstation, it must be sent in small pieces called data packets. The most popular protocols are **carrier sense multiple access/collision detection (CSMA/CD),** also known as contention; polling; and token passing.

Carrier Sense Multiple Access/Collision Detection (CSMA/CD) or Contention

The **carrier sense multiple access/collision detection (CSMA/CD)** protocol is commonly used with a bus topology. The workstation's NIC card must look to see if the channel (cable path) is busy before sending anything to the file server. If more than one workstation sends at the same time, and there is a "data collision," however, this is detected by the network, and the workstations' NICs will resend.

This procedure takes place behind the scenes; other than perhaps noticing slower sending or receiving, the user may be unaware of these events. On most systems, this happens at such a high rate of speed that it is doubtful the user will notice. The advantages of CSMA/CD are that it is straightforward to install, is cost effective, and has normally high throughput. The disadvantages are that time delays may occur in a busy LAN environment and that during busy traffic times bottlenecks may occur from several workstations sending at one time.

Collisions are common in CSMA/CD environments. They occur as traffic increases on the network, yet users continue operating as usual. When there is a crash, people sometimes refer to it as a collision.

Note: A collision and a crash differ in that a collision usually does not affect LAN operations, whereas with a crash, the entire LAN does not function (in other words, the LAN is down). Networks that use the CSMA/CD access method are often referred to as belonging to the "Ethernet" family.

Polling

With the **polling** protocol, more processing power on the part of the file server is required. The file server checks with each workstation, one by one, to see if there are any requests or commands that need processing. The star topology normally uses the polling protocol. The advantages of polling are that there is more control by the file server and that the amount of throughput is consistent. The disadvantage is that the file server's CPU has to work harder.

Token Passing

In the **token-passing** protocol, a token is passed throughout the LAN from workstation to workstation. Imagine a small elevator going up and down between floors in a tall building. There is only room for one passenger in this tiny elevator. If the elevator is already occupied, however, the would-be next passenger can press a button to indicate that he or she would like to ride next. After dropping off the current passenger, the elevator would then go to the floor from which that next request came. Similarly, on a network that uses token passing, the workstation waits until an electronic box (signal) called a token comes around. If the electronic token does not have any pending requests being processed, the station can put an instruction, such as "retrieve a file," into the token. If the token is already full, the workstation's NIC will simply tag the token to indicate that it needs to place an instruction

FIGURE 1.4
Bus topology.

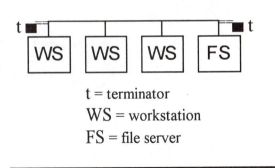

t = terminator
WS = workstation
FS = file server

when available. The token passes between the workstation and the file server. The file server carries out the instructions and relays the answer back to the requesting workstation.

WORKING WITH CABLING

Topologies

Topology refers to how the cables are arranged, or the cable layout. Popular topologies are bus, ring, star, mesh, and hybrid.

In a ***bus topology*** (see Figure 1.4), workstations are normally connected in a straight line, one after the other. Each end of the line is capped off with a *terminator,* one at either end; this marks the end of the bus segment.

In a ***ring topology*** (see Figure 1.5), workstations are connected in a circular pattern with the file server also attached to the circle. The ends of the circle normally connect to the file server.

FIGURE 1.5
Ring topology.

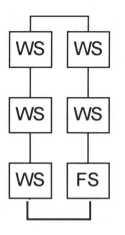

WS = workstation
FS = file server

FIGURE 1.6
Star topology.

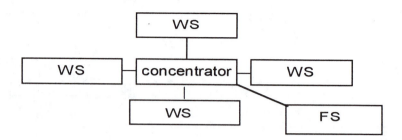

WS = workstation

concentrator = connection box

FS = workstation

In a *star topology* (see Figure 1.6), the file server is in the center and each workstation connects to a box connected to the file server.

In a *mesh topology* (Figure 1.7), each computer, including the file server, is connected together with cables. The connections are considered point to point.

In a *hybrid topology,* various topologies are integrated together to best meet the needs of the installation site.

Each topology has its advantages and disadvantages. The advantage of the bus and ring topologies is that they require less cabling than other methods; therefore, they are less expensive. Their disadvantage is that to add or remove workstations, someone must bring down the file server first. Thus, no one can use the LAN while this type of maintenance takes place. With star and ring topologies, on the other hand, each of the workstations has its own cable; therefore, someone may add or remove workstations without taking down the file server. Their disadvantage is that the amount of cabling required is significantly more than with the bus or ring topologies; therefore, they are more expensive to use than other methods.

FIGURE 1.7
Mesh topology.

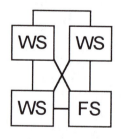

WS = workstation

FS = file server

LAN VERSUS OTHER PLATFORMS

In a LAN environment, each workstation's CPU does its own work. This type of environment has traditionally been known as distributed or decentralized processing, which is different from a standard mainframe or midrange environment. For example, in a normal midrange environment, workstations do not process their own work. Programs are submitted from the workstations to a central location, commonly called a data center. The main CPU for this type of environment is shared among several workstations. This type of processing is referred to as centralized processing. The advantage to working in a LAN environment where decentralized processing occurs is that the user does not have to submit programs for processing; the programs are processed right at the user's station.

INTERCONNECTIVITY

Before LANs became popular, companies invested considerable money into personnel, hardware, and software resources for mainframe and midrange computers. Many companies are still buying these larger-size computers. A need has arisen for interconnecting midrange, mainframes, and PCs found together on a LAN. Thus the term *interconnectivity* is used.

In general, **interconnectivity** means the connecting of computers on more than one platform. Platforms are characterized as consisting of different kinds of computers running under different operating systems. This section discusses several common terms associated with interconnectivity.

The term *downsizing* became very popular in the early 1990s as companies cut their budgets and reduced their work forces. Downsizing made LANs more popular. Mainframes, with all their workstations, were generally more expensive to buy and maintain than a LAN system consisting of PCs. Improved speed and performance of CPU chips also influenced the move toward LANs. Hard drives capable of storing 1 gigabyte (GB) of data also have influenced buying decisions.

Instead of having to buy both workstations for LANs and dumb terminals for the mainframe or midrange platforms, companies are now using gateways and terminal emulation. Through this technology, PCs can communicate both to the file server on the LAN and to the other platform (mainframe or midrange), thus saving a company or organization the cost of the dumb terminal and the space needed for additional equipment. Gateways have an advantage over terminal emulation and represent a newer technology. With a gateway, any workstation already on the LAN can communicate with the other platform. With terminal emulation, each workstation must have its own special emulation card and appropriate software, as well as a separate cable connecting it to the other platform.

Bridge

A bridge is a method of using special hardware and software to allow two LANs to connect together. Two major types of bridges exist, internal and external. With internal bridging, one file server contains two NICs. Each NIC connects to a separate LAN. With external bridging, a dedicated PC connected to the backbone contains two NICs, each connected to a separate file server and associated LAN, using special Novell bridging software to connect the two separate LANs.

Gateway

A gateway is a method of using special hardware and software to connect dissimilar platforms, such as a LAN and a mainframe or midrange computer.

Terminal Emulation

Terminal emulation consists of a special computer card and software that allows a PC to act like a dumb terminal for purposes of communicating to the host computer in a centralized processing–type platform.

Host and Client

In a bridge or gateway environment, the host is the platform that provides requested data and the client is the platform that receives the data. For example, if your workstation (hooked up to the LAN) makes a request through the gateway for some customer data records stored on the mainframe, the LAN then serves as the client and the mainframe as the host.

SUMMARY

A LAN consists of different components that work together to allow for the sharing of data and software and hardware resources and to facilitate communication. Putting these components together first requires deciding on the topology or layout of cables (bus, ring, star, or hybrid), cabling type (twisted pair, coaxial, or fiber-optic cables), the protocol or sending procedures (polling, CSMA/CD, or token passing), the local operating system (such as DOS or Windows), and the network operating system (such as Novell NetWare 4.1x). Making these decisions requires both practice and training. The lab at the end of this chapter takes a firsthand look at workstation installation and logging in to the network.

EXERCISES

1. Define the following:
   a. LAN
   b. file server
   c. workstation
   d. NIC
   e. media
   f. network operating system
   g. local operating system
   h. topology

    i. protocol

    j. terminal emulation

    k. bridge

    l. gateway

    m. downsizing

    n. system files

    o. dumb terminals

    p. distributed processing

    q. shared processing

    r. CSMA/CD

    s. polling

    t. token passing

    u. bus topology

    v. ring topology

    w. star topology

    x. mesh topology

    y. hybrid topology

    z. interconnectivity

2. What do the following stand for?

    a. LAN

    b. NIC

    c. NOS

    d. LOS

    e. UTP

    f. STP

    g. CSMA/CD

3. List the components making up a LAN.

4. Name four topologies and list the advantages and disadvantages of each.

5. Name three protocols and list the advantages and disadvantages of each.

6. What are some reasons for having a LAN?

7. Your company is very concerned about having to add or delete workstations periodically throughout the day and has asked you to recommend the cabling type and the topology for the LAN. The cost of cable is very high in your area. What do you recommend and why?

8. You work for a company that is surrounded by high-power electrical lines. Throughout the company, computer files have been damaged, and engineers suspect that this may be the result of having the wrong cable type installed. What do you recommend, and why do you think the engineers came to the conclusion mentioned?

LAB #1A

Become familiar with your organization's network infrastructure.

1. Draw a picture to illustrate the overall layout of the network.
2. After drawing this picture, refer back to this chapter's discussion, and identify the type of topology and protocols used on the network.
3. Identify the network operating system used.
4. Identify the local operating system used.
5. List at least two key software applications shared on the network.
6. List at least two hardware components shared on the network.

LAB #1B

Call or visit a different organization in your area that also uses networking. Describe the network infrastructure of this organization.

LAB #1C

Visit a library or your organization's data center and browse through magazines. Locate and possibly photocopy pictures of the LAN components discussed in this chapter. In particular, find pictures of the following items: a file server, a network printer, your ideal workstation, an NIC, RAM, twisted pair cabling, coaxial cabling, fiber-optic cabling, and a hub. Note any discoveries that you personally made through this adventure.

CHAPTER TWO

WINDOWS REVIEW AND DIRECTORY MANAGEMENT

INSPIRING MOMENT

Congratulations on your new position! You now work for a company that has an average-size network consisting of somewhere between 30 and 100 users, a handful of printers, and a file server or two. But the people normally available to answer questions are out of the office all week, attending a networking conference. In this networking environment, you sometimes feel lost and are not sure of the location of different directories. You do not know how much access you have to various directories. Once logged into the network, you find that moving around in the system takes time. You are not as familiar with Windows Explorer and you have a limited understanding of the overall directory structure for your network.

QUESTIONS FOR THOUGHT

What should you do? How do you feel? If you have users for whom you are also responsible, what should you do? How do you think they feel?

CHALLENGE

Read this chapter carefully for tips on exploring your LAN setup and hints on moving around the LAN quickly. Once you have a feel for the directory structure of your network, sketch a layout of it and keep it on file for easy access. (You may even want to keep it next to you. You should usually make two copies, one for the lab documentation file or binder and one for daily referral and use.) If you manage other users, give them a copy of your layout and highlight the areas with which they work. You will find that paper documentation saves time, even in this so-called paperless society.

CHAPTER OBJECTIVES

After finishing this chapter, you should be able to:

1. List the directories that appear as a result of installing NetWare and become familiar with the contents of each directory.
2. Discuss recommended directory tree setup.

3. Review Windows Explorer as it relates to directories and files.

4. Recognize the difference among local, logical, and search drives and know NetWare's limitations.

5. Explain what mapping does and how to set up, view, and use maps to aid in moving from one directory to another.

WINDOWS EXPLORER BASICS

Windows Explorer allows you to create and manage directory structures. Therefore, it is crucial that you become comfortable with moving about and using Windows Explorer. This chapter reviews the basic operations that go hand and hand with network management.

Launching Windows Explorer

One of the quickest ways to get to Windows Explorer is simply to point and right mouse click the word "Start" located in the lower left corner of the screen. As illustrated in Figures 2.1 and 2.2, doing so brings up Windows Explorer.

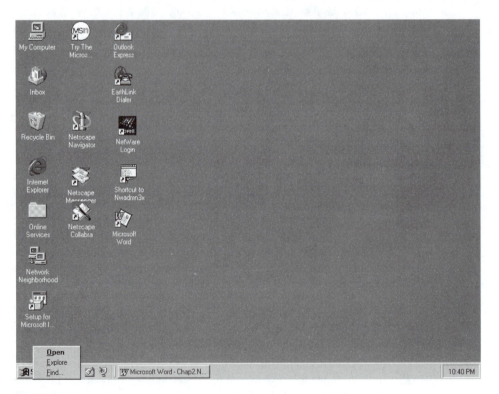

FIGURE 2.1
Launch Explorer ® by right clicking on "Start," then left clicking on "Explore."
Source: Screen shot reprinted by permission from Microsoft Corporation.

FIGURE 2.2
Windows Explorer appears after you point and right mouse click on "Start," then "Explore."
Source: Screen shot reprinted by permission from Microsoft Corporation.

Notice that the Explorer window is divided into two sides. The left side represents the folder or directory structure view; the right side depicts what is contained in the currently selected folder (directory). In Explorer, directories are represented by folders. Clicking on a folder visible in the left side of Explorer's window causes the contents of the folder to be listed on the right (Figure 2.3).

Software Installations

Most software applications sold today come with a setup or installation program. Some installation programs will automatically create a directory on your hard drive or onto the file server's hard drive without prompting you. However, most will stop and ask you where you would like the new software application installed. Once you have indicated the directory in which you would like to place the new software, most installation programs will check to see if that particular directory folder already exists. If not, it will ask you if you want the directory to be created.

Creating a Directory Folder

What happens during this directory creation process? How are directories manually created in Explorer?

FIGURE 2.3

Clicking on a folder visible on the left side causes its contents to be listed on the right.

Source: Screen shot reprinted by permission from Microsoft Corporation.

1. In order to create a directory, first point and click the mouse where you want the directory created. Keep in mind that the directory folder will be created at the next lower level of where you click. For example, find and click on the directory entitled MY DOCUMENTS. By doing so, you are indicating that the position for the new folder is immediately inside and under MY DOCUMENTS.
2. Next, from the top menu line, select "File," "New," "Folder." (Click on "Folder.") In Figure 2.4 you will notice that by default the directory folder is named NEW FOLDER. Assign the directory folder a particular name by simply typing over the highlighted default name—in this case, NEW FOLDER (Figure 2.5).

Copying One File

1. When you click on one of the folders on the left side of the screen, the contents of the folder appear on the right side of the screen (Figure 2.6).
2. On the right side of the screen, right click on a file that you would like to copy. Select "Copy" from the menu that appears (Figure 2.7).
3. On the left side, scroll down or up the screen until you locate the folder or drive that you would like to receive the new copy. Right click on the folder or drive and choose "Paste."

FIGURE 2.4

To create a new directory folder in Explorer, click on "File," "New," "Folder."
Source: Screen shot reprinted by permission from Microsoft Corporation.

FIGURE 2.5

Type over the NEW FOLDER text to assign a directory folder name.
Source: Screen shot reprinted by permission from Microsoft Corporation.

FIGURE 2.6
The contents of the CHAPTERS folder appear on the right.
Source: Screen shot reprinted by permission from Microsoft Corporation.

FIGURE 2.7
Right click on the name of the file you wish to copy and left click on "Copy."
Source: Screen shot reprinted by permission from Microsoft Corporation.

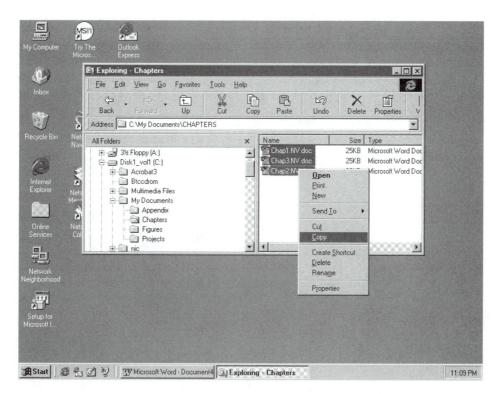

FIGURE 2.8
Click on the first file, then Shift click on the last file, then right click on the highlighted region.
Source: Screen shot reprinted by permission from Microsoft Corporation.

Copying Multiple Files

1. To copy more than one file at the same time, open the folder containing the files that you wish to copy.
2. On the right side of the screen, click on the first file you would like to copy.
3a. Next, if the remaining files to copy are all positioned immediately below the first one in the directory list, then scroll down the window, and stop when you get to the last file. Now hold down the Shift key and click on the last file in the list that you would like to copy (Figure 2.8). The files should now be highlighted.

   or

3b. If the files are not next to each other in the list, you may select each one of them separately by holding down the Control (Ctrl) key and clicking on each file that you want to include (Figure 2.9).
4. Once they are selected, you may right click anywhere in the highlighted region and choose "Copy" from the menu that appears.
5. Next, scroll up or down the left side of the window and right click on the folder or the drive into which you would like to copy the new files. Select "Paste" from the menu that appears (Figure 2.10).

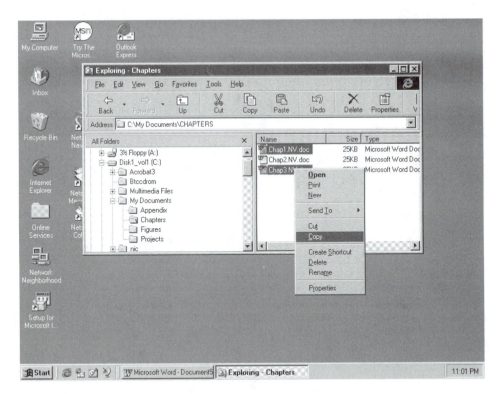

FIGURE 2.9
Use Ctrl click to select files not in sequence, then right click to select the "Copy" operation.
Source: Screen shot reprinted by permission from Microsoft Corporation.

Moving Files

To move a file to a new folder or drive, the steps are identical to the copy steps noted previously, except select "Cut" instead of "Copy" from the menu that appears when you right click on the files in question. All other steps are the same.

Renaming a File

To change a file's name, simply right click on the name. Select "Rename" from the menu that appears. The file's current name is now highlighted. You may type over it with the new name and press the Enter key.

Properties

While in Explorer, right click on one of the file or folder names. Select "Properties" to find out pertinent information such as who owns the files, what are the current attributes (Figure 2.11), and what access rights have been assigned (Figure 2.12). Notice that the properties for

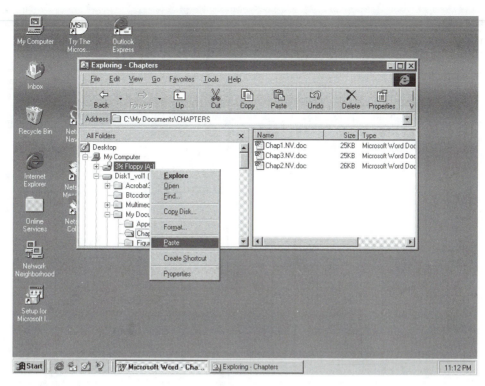

FIGURE 2.10
Paste the file to its new location.
Source: Screen shot reprinted by permission from Microsoft Corporation.

FIGURE 2.11
Right click and choose "Properties," then click on "NetWare File" to see ownership and attributes.
Source: Screen shot from NetWare, ©1983-1999, Novell, Inc. All rights reserved. Reprinted and used with permission.

Server.doc Properties

General | Summary | Statistics | NetWare File | NetWare Rights

SERVER.DOC

Name Space:	DOS
Owner:	Admin.ABC_CO
Size:	44.00KB (45,056 bytes)
Creation Date:	Saturday, June 19, 1999 3:47:58 PM
Access Date:	Saturday, June 19, 1999
Last Update:	Saturday, June 12, 1999 8:00:06 AM
Last Archive:	Never Archived

Attributes:
- [ ] Read-only
- [✓] Archive
- [ ] Sharable
- [ ] Transactional
- [ ] Purge Immediate
- [ ] Hidden
- [ ] Rename Inhibit
- [ ] Delete Inhibit
- [ ] Copy Inhibit

OK | Cancel | Apply

FIGURE 2.12
Right click, then choose "Properties" followed by the "NetWare
Rights" tab to see who has access.
Source: Screen shot from NetWare,
©1983-1999, Novell, Inc. All rights
reserved. Reprinted and used with
permission.

a file on the local drive C: (Figure 2.13) are different than those of a file on a network drive (Figure 2.14). This is because files on the network are normally used by more than one user; thus there is a need for security. The security is in place to lessen the chance of unauthorized use of files and directories.

Quick Tips

To edit a text file, you may use Wordpad or Notepad. You can get to either by clicking on "Start," then "Programs," then "Accessories." However, this takes a few mouse clicks. They also may be executed by clicking on "Start," then clicking on "Run," typing in "Word-pad" or "Notepad," then clicking on "OK."

PHYSICAL, LOGICAL, AND SEARCH DRIVES

Physical Drives

In order to start exploring the directory structure, we need to assign some drive letters to point to some key directories on the network. On your local workstation, drive letters refer to actual physical devices. Drive C:, for example, may be used to reference your hard drive. Drive D: may be used for referencing a CD-ROM drive. On the network, the main physical drive divisions are the partitions. NetWare volume names, in our case SYS: and VOL1:, are assigned to these partitions for identification purposes. (It is possible to assign a volume name to more than one partition. This is called *spanning volumes* and is beyond the scope of this text.)

FIGURE 2.13
This is an example of what is located under the properties of a local file.
Source: Screen shot reprinted by permission from Microsoft Corporation.

FIGURE 2.14
This is an example of properties for a network file.
Source: Screen shot reprinted by permission from Microsoft Corporation.

FIGURE 2.15
Drive mappings allow the user to move from one directory to another. *Source:* Screen shot reprinted by permission from Microsoft Corporation.

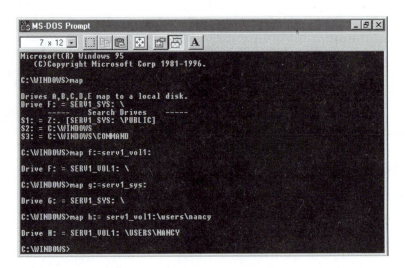

Logical Drives and Drive Mapping

Assigning drive letters to directories with the NetWare volume is called *drive mapping*. Maps serve to give directions on how to get from one place to another. Similarly, LAN mappings allow the user to move from one directory to another. In Figure 2.15, notice the MAP commands the user has typed in at the DOS command prompt.

The MAP command is used by itself to help the user identify what map drives are currently in memory.

```
C:\WINDOWS>MAP
```

Next, we will assign the F: drive letter to the VOL1: directory. Since the users will work from VOL1: primarily, it makes sense to assign F:, which is the first available drive letter. Notice that SERV1, our server name, is specified. This is required in a multiserver environment. It is optional in a single-server environment.

```
C:\WINDOWS>MAP F:=SERV1_VOL1:
```

Once the drive letter F: has been assigned to the file server's volume VOL1:, we can move there quickly by typing F: and pressing Enter at the DOS command prompt (Figure 2.16). Next, let's map the SYS: volume as drive G:. The network administrator will need access to SYS: quite often.

```
C:\WINDOWS>MAP G:=SERV1_SYS:
```

To move to this location on the server, once the drive assignment has been made, simply type G: and press the Enter key (Figure 2.17). Next, to make it easier for the user, Nancy, to find her user data files on the network, we are going to associated drive letter H: to her home directory. Instead of having to open each of the subdirectories USERS and NANCY to get to the data on the network, the user will just need to go to drive H:.

```
C:\WINDOWS>MAP H:=SERV1_VOL1:\USERS\NANCY
```

FIGURE 2.16

Typing F: from the DOS command prompt takes the user to VOL1:.
Source: Screen shot reprinted by permission from Microsoft Corporation.

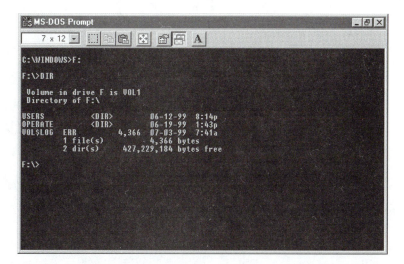

FIGURE 2.17

Typing G: from the DOS command prompt takes the user to the SYS: volume.
Source: Screen shot reprinted by permission from Microsoft Corporation.

Again, we can move there by typing in H: and pressing the Enter key. Notice that the USERS directory is located inside of the volume VOL1:. The NANCY directory is located inside of the USERS directory (Figure 2.18).

In working on the network you should notice three types of drive letters: physical local drives, logical network drives, and network search drives. As mentioned earlier, the hard drive C: found on the local workstation is physical. Drive maps are logical, meaning they are not a physical hardware device. Rather, they simply point the way to a directory on the network file server's volume.

Search Drives

Look back at Figure 2.15. Drive Z: is by default already directed to point at the PUBLIC directory. Notice also that the MAP command executed without error though the command itself is not located in the C:\WINDOWS directory. This is because drive Z: is a search drive

FIGURE 2.18
Typing in H: and pressing Enter
takes the user, Nancy, to her home
directory.
Source: Screen shot reprinted by
permission from Microsoft Corporation.

assignment. Search drives are very similar to the DOS or Windows PATH command. PATH aids the computer in finding .EXE, .COM, and .BAT files. We do not need to change to the PUB-LIC directory in order to execute the MAP command. That's because this command is housed in the PUBLIC directory, which has been assigned as a search drive. Users share applications that are stored on the file server's hard drive. Search drives are convenient in that they allow users to run applications without having to search through various directories to find them.

S1: is commonly mapped to the SYS:PUBLIC directory, and this particular MAP command is placed in the system login script by the LAN administrator or, as in this case, by default during the server installation process. Notice that S1: instructs the computer where to search first if .EXE or .COM files do not reside in the current directory.

When the user or LAN administrator assigns map S1:, the computer assigns the letter Z: to it. The computer starts with Z: and goes backward through the alphabet as needed until the letter K: is reached (Figure 2.19). Normally, the maximum number of search drives is 16 (Z: to K:). Users must first use a MAP command for each search drive map that they wish to use. This is unlike the DOS or Windows PATH command, where multiple directories may be specified on one line.

The MAP command for assigning the PUBLIC directory as the first search location would look like this:

```
MAP S1:=SERV1_SYS:PUBLIC
```

Life Span of Logical and Search Drive Mappings

The map stays in effect until the user enters a command to change it or executes the LO-GOUT command. Mapped drives, also known as network drives, do not stay permanently. Login scripts often contain map commands; this way, the computer system sets up the map every time the user logs in. MAP commands can also be entered at the prompt. Users often map to their home directories (a private directory that houses a user's data).

Mapping is an action. When the network operating system (NOS) encounters a MAP command, the system maps out, or executes, the instruction to create a drive pointer for a

Network drives from F: - Z:

F:
G:
H:
I:
J:
K:
L:
M:
N:
O:
P:
Q:
R:
S:
T:
U:
V:
W:
X:
Y:
Z:

Search drives from Z: - K:

Z:
Y:
X:
W:
V:
U:
T:
S:
R:
Q:
P:
O:
N:
M:
L:
K:

Local drives from A: - E:

A:
B:
C:
D:
E:

FIGURE 2.19
Logical network drives versus search drives.

FIGURE 2.20
The assignment for drive H: has changed to SERV1_VOL1:.
Source: Screen shot reprinted by permission from Microsoft Corporation.

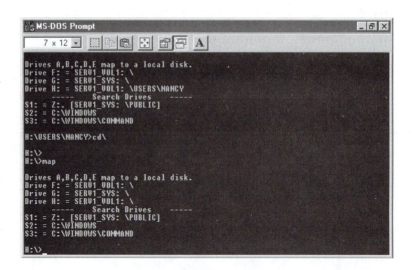

```
MS-DOS Prompt                                                    _  ☐ ✕
  7 x 12  ▾   ☐ ☐ ☐ ☒ ☐ ☐ A
Drives A,B,C,D,E map to a local disk.
Drive F: = SERV1_VOL1: \
Drive G: = SERV1_SYS: \
Drive H: = SERV1_VOL1: \USERS\NANCY
        -----     Search Drives     -----
S1: = Z:. [SERV1_SYS: \PUBLIC]
S2: = C:\WINDOWS
S3: = C:\WINDOWS\COMMAND

H:\USERS\NANCY>cd\

H:\>
H:\>map

Drives A,B,C,D,E map to a local disk.
Drive F: = SERV1_VOL1: \
Drive G: = SERV1_SYS: \
Drive H: = SERV1_VOL1: \
        -----     Search Drives     -----
S1: = Z:. [SERV1_SYS: \PUBLIC]
S2: = C:\WINDOWS
S3: = C:\WINDOWS\COMMAND

H:\>_
```

particular directory path. A map is simply a pathway built by the NOS. This pathway leads to a particular directory specified in the MAP statement. This pathway is labeled with a drive name, also called a drive pointer.

Warning: It's easy to change the path assignment for a logical drive letter. In Figure 2.20 the logical drive mapping for H: has been changed with the use of the change directory (CD) command. Instead of pointing to the home directory for the user, Nancy, it now points directly to VOL1:.

SPECIAL MAPPING OPTIONS

Deleting Map Assignments

Sometimes it is necessary to delete or get rid of mapping assignments. NetWare provides a DEL (delete) option for the MAP command that takes care of this rather simply. For example, to delete the map assignment for G:, simply key in the following:

```
MAP DEL G:
```

(Note: It is advisable to type "map" by itself first to verify which drive letter you wish to delete.)

Using the NEXT Option

When creating map assignments, the user normally specifies which drive letter should be assigned. By using the NEXT option, the user is asking the network operating system to see what the next available drive letter is and then make the assignment using that letter. In the following example, notice two things: the letter N does not have a colon after it and there is no equal sign. In this example, a map assignment is made to the next available letter for the directory FUNSTUFF:

```
MAP N SERV1_VOL1:USERS\FUNSTUFF
```

FIGURE 2.21
The description for F: drive is very long.
Source: Screen shot reprinted by permission from Microsoft Corporation.

To find out which drive letter actually gets assigned in this case, the user may key in "map" by itself after the assignment has been made.

The Disappearing Act!

In Figure 2.21, on the left side, notice the drive letter assignments. Notice that though we have not used the CD command or any other related commands, the H: drive is once again pointing at VOL1:. Drive Map assignments do not hold long term when assigned through the DOS command prompt. Drive map assignments are commonly initiated either through Windows Explorer or through the NetWare login scripts.

Assigning Drive Maps Using Windows Explorer

To assign a network logical drive map using Windows Explorer, follow these steps:

1. Go to Windows Explorer.
2. Identify the directory path that you need to assign a drive letter.
3. From the Windows Explorer menu, click on "Tools," then "Map Network Drive" (Figure 2.22).
4. In the dialog box, select the drive letter that you wish to assign.

FIGURE 2.22
Click on "Tools," then "Map Network Drive" to assign a drive letter in Windows Explorer.
Source: Screen shot reprinted by permission from Microsoft Corporation.

5. In the path prompt line, enter the direction for locating the directory. Notice the syntax for this. The syntax used here follows the UNC method, better known as the Universal Naming Convention (Figure 2.23).
6. Also located in the dialog box is the "Reconnect at Logon" option. If this option box is checked, then every time you start Windows, the drive maps will be created automatically by the system.

Assigning network drive mapping inside of login scripts will be discussed in Chapter 10.

DIRECTORY STRUCTURE

Now that the SYS: and VOL1: volumes have been mapped properly, in this section we will look at their contents (Figure 2.24).

Because file servers allow for the sharing of files, it is crucial that the directories that house the files are managed properly and wisely. In this section, NetWare and other directories and how to map to them are explored.

When NetWare is installed, several directories appear as a result: LOGIN, PUBLIC, SYSTEM, MAIL, DELETED.SAV, DOC, DOCVIEW, MHS, and ETC. These directories provide the foundation for the directory structure. These reside on the file server's hard

FIGURE 2.23
Select a drive letter, and enter the UNC path to association with the directory in question.
Source: Screen shot reprinted by permission from Microsoft Corporation.

drive in the disk partition entitled SYS:VOLUME. In NetWare, the main divisions on the disk drive are called *volumes.* Directories reside in volumes.

LOGIN

The LOGIN directory contains the files SLIST.EXE and LOGIN.EXE. When logging into a LAN, DOS users must first go through the LOGIN directory. For example, at the F:\> prompt, enter "LOGIN USER01." Here, LOGIN is a command instructing the computer to run a program called LOGIN.EXE, and USER01 acts as a parameter needed by the program to verify that a particular user is authorized to use the system (Figure 2.25). The LOGIN.EXE program also checks the security data found in the Novell Directory Services (NDS) to make sure that the user is allowed to log in and meets any requirements to do so. SLIST.EXE is used to find a list of file servers available. SLIST stands for "server list."

If you are using Client32, then your login files reside locally under C:\NOVELL\CLIENT32 (Figure 2.26).

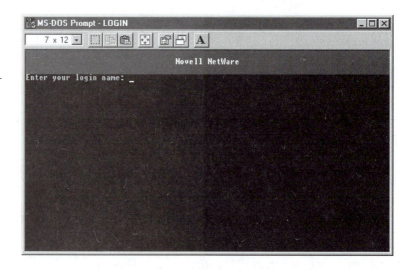

FIGURE 2.24
Using Windows Explorer you can view the directory structure for SYS: and VOL1:.
Source: Screen shot reprinted by permission from Microsoft Corporation.

FIGURE 2.25
The DOS login screen executed from the F:\LOGIN directory.
Source: Screen shot reprinted by permission from Microsoft Corporation.

FIGURE 2.26
Client32 login files are located under C:\NOVELL\CLIENT32.
Source: Screen shot reprinted by permission from Microsoft Corporation.

PUBLIC

The PUBLIC directory is used often. It contains NetWare user commands and utilities. Everyone with a LAN account normally has access to this directory, unless for some reason the LAN administrator has taken the rights away (Figure 2.27).

SYSTEM

The SYSTEM directory houses supervisory commands and utilities. Users normally do not have access to this directory.

MAIL

The MAIL directory is left over from prior versions of NetWare in which user ID directories were located here. The user ID directories used to contain the user's login script. This directory is here for backward compatibility.

DELETED.SAV

The DELETED.SAV directory contains files that were previously deleted and have been salvaged. The directory in which they were originally stored no longer exists.

```
F:\PUBLIC>dir *.exe/w

Volume in drive F is SYS
Directory of F:\PUBLIC

BREQUEST.EXE    BREQUTIL.EXE    BROLLFWD.EXE    CX.EXE          LOGIN.EXE
NDBCNVT.EXE     NLIST.EXE       NPATH.EXE       RCONSOLE.EXE    TYPEMSG.EXE
ATOTAL.EXE      AUDITCON.EXE    CAPTURE.EXE     COLORPAL.EXE    FILER.EXE
FLAG.EXE        LOGOUT.EXE      MAP.EXE         MENUCNVT.EXE    MENUEXE.EXE
MENUMAKE.EXE    MENURSET.EXE    NCOPY.EXE       NCUPDATE.EXE    NDIR.EXE
NETADMIN.EXE    NETUSER.EXE     NPRINT.EXE      NPRINTER.EXE    NVER.EXE
PARTMGR.EXE     PCONSOLE.EXE    PRINTCON.EXE    PRINTDEF.EXE    PSC.EXE
PURGE.EXE       RENDIR.EXE      RIGHTS.EXE      SEND.EXE        SETPASS.EXE
SETTTS.EXE      SYSTIME.EXE     UIMPORT.EXE     WHOAMI.EXE      WSUPDATE.EXE
WSUPGRD.EXE     NWADMIN.EXE     WBROLL.EXE      WNDBCNVT.EXE

     49 file(s)    13,268,003 bytes
                   64,831,488 bytes free
```

FIGURE 2.27
PUBLIC directory .EXE files.

THE PUBLIC DIRECTORY: USER ACCESS

As mentioned, PUBLIC is commonly used on the network, and everyone with an account has access to it. In Figure 2.27, the executable files (.EXE) located in the PUBLIC directory are listed for reference. These executable files are commonly known as utility files, or menu utilities and command line utilities (CLUs). They will be explored in more detail throughout the text.

DIRECTORY RIGHTS

Users must be granted permission to directories to use, modify, or make files in them. Granting permission is commonly called assigning rights. Rights are discussed further in Chapters 5 and 8.

When assigning rights, do not give users too many rights to the main directories. Avoid assigning rights that give users the power to create, delete, or modify in these directories. In addition to the main directories, some companies add others. Normally, applications branch off from one or two directories, and user home directories branch off a directory called USERS (see Figure 2.28). To create subdirectories, use the Windows Explorer NEW FOLDER command or NetWare's FILER menu utility. (FILER is discussed in Chapter 6.)

With the NetWare LAN system, the directory structure consists of the file server name (optional unless working in a multiserver environment), the volume name, and the directory name, in that order.

FIGURE 2.28

System-related directories are grouped together under SYS:. User-related directories reside under VOL1:.

Source: Screen shot reprinted by permission from Microsoft Corporation and © 1983-1999, Novell, Inc. All rights reserved. Reprinted and used with permission.

SUMMARY

Practice using Windows Explorer until you can comfortably browse, delete, create, and move files and directories. Search drives help users run programs without having to change directories. Logical network drives aid in the process of moving from one drive to the next. Local drives at the workstation normally consist of the letters A: to E:.

EXERCISES

1. Define the following:
    a. salvaged files
    b. utility files
    c. local drive
    d. network drive
    e. search drive
2. List at least four tasks that Windows Explorer allows you to accomplish.
3. What is a quick way to get into Windows Explorer?

4. How would you indicate that you would like to do something to multiple sequential files in Windows Explorer?

5. How would you indicate that you would like to do something to multiple scattered files in Windows Explorer?

6. Compare the differences and similarities of local, logical network, and search network drives.

7. List the main directories of NetWare. What purpose does each directory serve?

8. How would you create the following directories?

   a. SERV1_VOL1:USERS\JOE

   b. SERV1_VOL1:APPS\WP

   c. SERV1_VOL1:UTIL\CHKDRV

9. How would you map to USER01 through USER03 directories?

10. How would you make a search map to DB if it resides under APPS? (See Figure 2.28.)

11. Are maps permanent? If not, what suggestions can you make to overcome this limitation?

12. What type of information does the "Properties" selection give for a particular file?

13. Why is it important to assign directory rights to users?

LAB #2A

This lab presents a hands-on application of directory management. In this lab, you will create a directory tree, organize files in the tree, and gain experience working with creating, revising, and printing maps.

1. Make the following directory tree structure *under your home directory.*

QTR1			QTR2			QTR3			QTR4		
JAN	FEB	MAR	APR	MAY	JUN	JUL	AUG	SEP	OCT	NOV	DEC

2. Check to see which drive letters are available:

   `F:\>`**MAP**

   If a printer is available, print your map for handy reference:

   `F:\>`**MAP** > **PRN**

3. Next, assign map drive letters for each month in your tree structure. Be careful not to key in a letter already in use. For example,

   `F:\>`MAP I:=SERV1_VOL1::USERS\USER01\QTR1\JAN

   (See your instructor or LAN administrator for help in choosing your directory path.)

4. Double check your map when you are done:

   `F:\>`**MAP**>**PRN**

5. Test your map by changing to each directory. Simply type in the letter you assigned, type a colon, and press Enter. Do this for each directory:

   `F:\>`I:

You should see the prompt on your screen change to indicate that your computer is now pointing to a different directory. For example,

```
I:\USERS\USER01\QTR1\JAN>
```

6. Friends of yours will be visiting you in January. Make a note of it in the appropriate directory. Make sure to print the note. *Hint:* Use NotePad or WordPad to enter the text, then save it to the I: drive or from a DOS prompt do the following:

```
F:\>I:"enter"
I:\USERS\USER01\QTR1\JAN>EDIT VISIT.TXT
```

There are a few ways to print your file:

   a. While in the DOS editor, choose "Print" from the file menu.

   b. From the prompt, use the DOS TYPE command:

```
I:\USERS\USER01\QTR1\JAN>TYPE VISIT.TXT>PRN
```

   c. From the prompt, use NetWare's NPRINT command:

```
I:\USERS\USER01\QTR1\JAN>NPRINT VISIT.TXT Q=PRINT_Q1
```

   d. From NotePad or WordPad, click on "File," then click "Print."

   PRINTQ_1 is an example of a print queue name. A print queue is a waiting line for jobs that need to be printed. See your LAN administrator or an instructor for the names of available print queues.

7. You just found out that there will be a sale on lawn furniture in May. Make a note of it under May. Make sure to print the note when done.

8. December is your vacation. Make and print a note.

LAB #2B

1. In Windows Explorer, create three subdirectories under your home directory. Call them A, B, and C, respectively.
2. Rename each of these directories to EXPLORER, DIRS, and QUEST, respectively.
3. Inside of directory EXPLORER, create a text file to summarize what you have learned in practicing using Windows Explorer.
4. Print the text file.
5. Inside of directory DIRS, create a text file to summarize what you have learned about directory management.
6. Inside of directory QUEST, create a text file that contains at least one question that you would like answered regarding what you are learning.
7. Inside your home directory, create a new directory called ALL.
8. Copy the files contained in the other three directories to the ALL directory.
9. Create another directory called PART. Copy the first and last file contained in the ALL directory to the PART directory. (Remember the Ctrl key!)
10. Delete the EXPLORER directory.
11. Delete just the file found in the DIRS directory.
12. Rename the file found in the QUEST directory.

CHAPTER THREE

DOS REVIEW

INSPIRING MOMENT

Many users log onto the network that you manage daily. Recently, you've noticed that many users have difficulty managing their workstations at a local level. You are constantly assisting users with copying files, managing them, and creating directories. You often spend hours just trying to fix problems associated with mistakes. Sometimes the workstations fail to boot up (start) properly. Also, you notice that users in general are not aware of the importance of making backups.

QUESTIONS FOR THOUGHT

Do you think that users should be exposed to a short training seminar in the use of DOS commands? If so, which commands would you include? How strong is your own knowledge of DOS? Are you comfortable managing files and directories in a DOS environment? What can you do to improve any weaknesses you or the users have in this area?

CHALLENGE

Read through this chapter and understand how each command works, but don't stop there. Learning the key DOS commands is not enough. Experiment, explore, and practice using each command. If you find that users need help in this area, hold a seminar to introduce them to the commands, or produce a handbook where you explain the various commands in your own words. Also, many good software tutors exist in this area; consider using one.

CHAPTER OBJECTIVES

After finishing this chapter, you should be able to:

1. Identify commonly used internal and external DOS commands and distinguish among them.
2. Manage files by creating, viewing, editing, erasing, changing attributes, and printing them.
3. Manage subdirectories by creating directories, performing directory searches, moving around in the system, performing routine backups, and removing directories.

4. Initialize a floppy disk and turn it into a system boot disk.

5. Use the PATH command to instruct the local operating system where to look for executable files.

6. Demonstrate the use of the DOS wild cards ? and *.

7. Use the DOS editor to create and edit files.

INTRODUCTION

A good working knowledge of the disk operating system (DOS) is essential before launching an exploration of networking. This chapter is a brief review of some of the commands and concepts of DOS.

DOS has two parts, internal and external. Those commands that may be performed once the computer has been booted up (without having to access a DOS subdirectory or DOS disk) are referred to as internal commands. External DOS commands are programs.

INTERNAL DOS COMMANDS

The following are commonly used internal DOS commands:

DIR
COPY
TIME
DATE
CLS
TYPE
ERASE
MD
CD
RD
PATH

DIR, COPY, ERASE, and TYPE

The DIR, COPY, ERASE, and TYPE commands allow users to manage and work with files located on storage devices found at the workstation or on the network. (The user must be granted permission to use network storage devices. This is discussed in Chapters 6, 8, and 12.) The DIR, COPY, and ERASE commands may look different with the addition of the wild cards ? and *.

DIR *.EXE This command shows a directory of all files with the extension of .EXE (executable files).

DIR TEST?.BAT This command shows a directory of all files with the first four letters "TEST." The next, or fifth, character can be anything, and the extension ends with .BAT (batch files).

DIR TEST?.* This command shows a directory of all files with the first four letters "TEST." The next, or fifth, character can be anything, and the extension ends with anything.

COPY *.* B: This command copies all files from the current directory to the B: drive.

COPY C:\DATA\WPDATA\SJONES.LTR B: This command copies a file called SJONES.LTR that is currently in a subsubdirectory on the C: drive C:\DATA\WPDATA and puts the copy in the B: drive. Normally, subsubdirectories are just called subdirectories.

ERASE *.* This command erases all files from the current directory.

ERASE C:\DATA\WPDATA*.TXT This command erases all files from the C:\DATA\WPDATA subdirectory that end with the extension .TXT (text files).

TYPE C:\DATA\WPDATA\SJONES.LTR >PRN This command simply instructs the computer to print the contents of the file called SJONES.LTR that is located in the subdirectory C:\DATA\WPDATA. The >PRN pipe option is used to redirect output to the printer. You can also use >PRN on other commands that give an output to the screen such as DIR >PRN. If you just want to see the work on the screen, simply leave off >PRN. If you are going to use the >PRN option in a LAN environment, that option is normally accompanied by the CAPTURE NetWare command (discussed in Chapter 9). Your LAN administrator can preprogram the CAPTURE command for you for now.

TIME, DATE, and CLS

The following internal commands cover basics of computer use.

TIME This command simply lets you see the current time setting and change it as needed. Note that the computer time is in military format; therefore, 1:00 P.M. is entered as 13:00. (You do not start over counting until you reach midnight, or 24:00.)

DATE This command allows you to change the current date on your computer. Many computers have built-in computer clocks, so the use of this command is not always necessary. Sometimes, however, it is needed to fool the computer into thinking that today is either an earlier or later date than it actually is. Changing the date becomes necessary when working report-printing programs that rely on the system date. For example, when sending a mailing to 100 customers, you might want to have the letters dated next Monday to allow time to finish the in-house processing and would change the date accordingly.

CLS This command simply allows you to clear the screen. This is handy when you want to erase whatever is on your screen quickly.

Make Directory (MD)

The following examples illustrate how the make directory (MD) command is used to create directories and subdirectories.

MD REPORTS This command makes a subdirectory inside the current directory and calls it REPORTS. *Note:* Because no drive name or backslash is given, the subdirectory is made inside the current directory.

MD \REPORTS This command makes a subdirectory from the current default drive. The slash indicates an immediate subdirectory off the root directory.

MD D:\REPORTS This command specifically requests the computer to make a subdirectory in drive D:, right off the root, and call it REPORTS.

MD D:\REPORTS\NEWS This command makes a subdirectory called D:\REPORTS\ NEWS. The subdirectory D:\REPORTS must have already been created for this command to work properly; otherwise, you will get an error message.

Change Directory (CD)

The following examples illustrate how the change directory (CD) command is used to move to a different subdirectory or to move all the way back to the root directory of the drive. If the prompt on the screen reads C:\>, the local operating system is currently pointing to (looking at) the root directory or the C: drive.

CD This command instructs the computer to change to the root directory in the current drive.

CD REPORTS This command instructs the computer to change to the subdirectory REPORTS that is inside the current directory.

CD \REPORTS This command instructs the computer to change to the subdirectory REPORTS that is off the root directory of the current drive.

CD D:\REPORTS This command instructs the computer to change to the directory D:\REPORTS. (Be careful how you interpret this command.)

Remove Directory (RD)

The following examples illustrate how the remove directory (RD) command is used to get rid of unwanted subdirectories.

RD REPORTS This command removes a subdirectory from inside the current directory. The subdirectory removed was called REPORTS. Because no drive name or backslash is given, the subdirectory is removed from inside the current directory (if it exists). The subdirectory REPORT must not contain any files or other subdirectories inside or an error message will appear on the screen and the subdirectory will not be removed.

RD \REPORTS This command removes a subdirectory from the current default drive. The slash indicates an immediate subdirectory off the root directory. As with the prior example, the subdirectory REPORT must not contain any files or subdirectories inside or an error message will appear on the screen and the subdirectory will not be removed.

RD D:\REPORTS This command specifically requests the computer to remove a subdirectory in drive D:, right off the root. The subdirectory removed was called REPORTS, given that it contained no other files or subdirectories inside.

PATH

The PATH command can help decrease the chances of receiving error messages by assisting the LOS and NOS in finding executable files. This command is discussed in more detail in Chapter 7.

PATH C:\;C:\DOS;C:\BATCH   If you issue an instruction to the computer to run an executable file (.EXE or .COM) or a batch file (.BAT) and the file name is not found, this command tells the computer to look elsewhere for it before giving an error message. In this case, the computer would first look in the root directory C: for the requested file. If it is not found there, the computer will look in the subdirectory C:\DOS. If it still is not found, the computer will look in the subdirectory C:\BATCH. If it still is not found, the computer will then display an error message.

External Dos Commands

The word *commands* in referring to external DOS commands is a little deceiving. Actually, the external part of DOS is made up of programs. But the ease in using the programs leads many, if not most, people to call them commands.

The external part of DOS is not loaded into random-access memory (RAM) when you boot your computer. Unlike the internal part of DOS, the individual programs are loaded into RAM off your DOS subdirectory or DOS floppy disk on an as needed basis, whenever you decide to run an external DOS program.

Several programs make up external DOS, such as the following:

ATTRIB

BACKUP

CHKDSK

COMP

DISKCOPY

EDIT

EDLIN

FDISK

FORMAT

GRAPHICS

LABEL

MIRROR

MODE

RESTORE

SYS

TREE

UNDELETE

UNFORMAT

XCOPY

Some of these commands are discussed as follows.

ATTRIB

ATTRIB allows a user to view or modify characteristics of one or more files. These file characteristics are called attributes; attributes are also known as flags. The ATTRIB command is used to view and turn the different attribute flags on and off. Two of the most commonly used attributes, read only and hidden, are illustrated in this section. An additional attribute, archive needed, is discussed in the backup section.

The ATTRIB command is used to flag files located on the workstation's floppy and hard drive(s), but it is not used for files located on network drives controlled by the file server. To flag files located on a network drive controlled by the file server, use the Net-Ware command FLAG, which is discussed in Chapter 9.

*ATTRIB +H *.EXE*   This command instructs the computer to hide all the files in the current subdirectory that end with .EXE.

*ATTRIB +R *.TXT*   This command instructs the computer to allow the files to be read but not modified.

ATTRIB +H /S   This command instructs the computer to hide all files in all subdirectories under the current directory.

*ATTRIB –H *.EXE*   This command removes the hide attribute that was applied earlier (the minus sign reverses the operation).

ATTRIB   The command ATTRIB by itself will list the attributes of all the files in the current directory.

BACKUP and MSBACKUP

It's important to have backups of your directories and files. Hard drives have been known to crash occasionally, computer viruses have been known to invade and destroy or damage files, and users have been known to accidentally erase or unwantingly change file contents. BACKUP (for MS-DOS version 5.0 and prior) and MSBACKUP (for MS-DOS versions 6.x) allow users to take preventative measures by securing a backup copy of their files.

MSBACKUP (for MS-DOS version 6.x)   The MSBACKUP command instructs the local operating system to run the Microsoft backup program and bring up the menu for it. These are the steps for menu selections when making backups.

Step 1   Getting into backup:

MSBACKUP   Go to Microsoft backup

Alt b   Select "Backup"

Step 2   Indicate which files are going to be backed up:

Alt k   Backup From

⇓   Press the Arrow Down key to select the drive letter corresponding to where your files are currently located. Press the Enter key.

⇓ Alt n   Highlight a directory or file that you want to back up, and hold down Alt and press n for its inclusion.

Alt e   Alt e allows you to edit your list of selected files for backup. Tab over to OK when done and press Enter.

Repeat the two steps, ⇓ Alt n and Alt e, until all directories and files to be backed up have been selected.

Step 3   Select the type of backup desired:

Alt y   Backup Type

Choose from the following:

Alt f   Full

Alt i   Incremental

Alt d   Differential

The local operating system places (or turns on) an attribute of "archive needed" to a file when the file is modified or newly created. The archive needed attribute is treated as a flag used to control the backup process, depending on which backup type (listed above) is selected.

If the full backup type is selected, all the selected files, even if the archive needed flag is not turned on, are backed up. Once the backup is completed, the archive needed flags, if they exist, are removed. This is the most common backup type.

If the incremental backup type is selected, the selected files are only backed up if the archive needed flag is on. Once the backup is completed, the archive needed flags are removed.

If the differential backup type is selected, the selected files are only backed up if the archive needed flag is on, just as in incremental backups. Once the backup is completed, however, the archive needed flags are not removed. Some data-processing professionals use this option for daily backups because they like a complete backup of all changes at the end of the week. The incremental backup type is used at the end of the week to ensure that the archive needed flags are removed.

Step 4   Specify where the backups are to go:

Alt a   Select "Backup To" (you choose where to place the backups)

Alt a (floppy drive)   Select your particular floppy drive (press Enter to confirm)

(floppy drive)

or

Alt d   "MS-DOS Drive and Path" (press Enter to confirm)

(hard drive path)   Enter the path for your hard drive. For example, [D:\BACKUP . . . .]

Step 5   Include any special options desired:

Alt o   Options

There are a variety of special settings available. We will accept the defaults; press Enter to continue.

Step 6   Start the backup process:

Alt s   Start Backup

The backup should proceed. If it does not allow you to select "Start Backup," either you skipped a step or you chose incremental or differential backup type and no archive needed attributes were found on the files selected.

Step 7   Close the backup menu screen:

Alt q   Quit

Step 8   Save the backup settings:

Alt f   File

Alt a   Save Setup As

Enter a file name such as YOURNAME.SET and press Enter to confirm.

Step 9   Exit Microsoft Backup

Alt f   File

Alt x   Exit

BACKUP C:*.* A: /S /L   This backup command will instruct the computer to back up all files in the C: drive. The A: means that the A: drive is the target.

Delete Tree (DELTREE)

The delete tree command (DELTREE) can be best compared to a tree trimmer. When a tree trimmer cuts off a tree branch, any attached smaller branches get discarded also. Similarly, when the local operating system executes the DELTREE program, any subdirectories inside the directory in question are removed.

DELTREE C:\TEMP   This command deletes the subdirectory called C:\TEMP along with any subdirectories or files that are located inside.

EDIT

The DOS EDIT program is actually referred to as the DOS editor. It allows an opportunity to create text files, batch files, and so forth. It is not as sophisticated as a word processor, because it was not designed for creating reports and other business type documents. The DOS editor is better used for viewing, creating, and editing files used by the local operating system or by NOS.

To use EDIT follow these steps.

Step 1   Verify the PATH: Because EDIT is a DOS program, it resides in the DOS directory. Verify that the DOS directory is being referenced in the PATH command:

```
C:\>PATH
```

The DOS directory path should be listed:

```
PATH = C:\;C:\DOS;C:\WINDOWS;C:\NWCLIENT
```

Step 2   Run the EDIT program and indicate the file name:

```
C:\>EDIT A:\MYTEST.BAT
```

Step 3   Key in the contents for the file in the EDIT entry screen (called the editor):

REM *****Sample batch file for changing the time and date*****

@ECHO OFF

TIME

DATE

CLS

Step 4   Exit and save your work:

Hold down Alt and press "F" for file.

Press "X" for exit.

Confirm that you want to save changes.

Step 5   Test your work:

View it: `C:\>TYPE A:\MYTEST.BAT`

Print it: `C:\>TYPE A:\MYTEST.BAT>PRN`

Run it: `C:\>A:\MYTEST.BAT`   (Do this step only if applicable.)

FORMAT   The FORMAT program initializes a new disk for saving work. The FORMAT command sets up the directory entry table (DET), defines the tracks (concentric circles) and sectors (segments of tracks), and checks for bad spots on the disk. Disks usually come preformatted.

The FORMAT A: command initializes the floppy disk in drive A: for the storing of files. The FORMAT A: /S command initializes the floppy disk in drive A: for the storing of files. It also transfers system files to the disk, making it a bootable disk.

Once the format operation and system file transfer process is complete, the floppy disk can be used to boot the computer. It's a good idea to make a floppy bootable disk and keep it stored in a safe place in case the boot files on the hard drive become damaged.

MSD Microsoft Diagnostics   Sometimes error messages alert the user that the operating system could not find a particular hardware device, such as a mouse, an NIC, or a printer. MSD is useful in accessing which hardware devices the system is recognizing and how such devices are being referenced.

MSD   This command brings up a menu-oriented screen that allows you to view hardware and memory configurations for a particular workstation.

SUMMARY

This chapter reviewed basic internal and external DOS commands. If you want to specialize in networking, you must become comfortable with DOS or whatever operating system is going to be accessed. If you know how to manage files and directories, the workstations for whose operation you are responsible should experience few problems and run more smoothly.

EXERCISES

1. Define the following:

   a. internal DOS

   b. external DOS

   c. computer time (military time)

   d. path

   e. root directory

2. What happens when >PRN is added to the end of a TYPE command?
3. Which DOS commands are commonly used to manage and work with files?
4. Which DOS commands are commonly used to manage and work with directories?
5. To view the names of the files located on the A: drive, what command would you enter?
6. To copy a file called PROJECT1.TXT currently located in the path C:\LAN and store the new copy in the root directory of A:, what command should you enter?
7. To create a subdirectory on the A: drive called WORK, what command should you enter?
8. You changed your mind after question 7 and now wish to move PROJECT1.TXT from the root directory of the A: drive and place it in the newly created directory called WORK. What commands can you use to accomplish this?
9. How would you create the following directory tree structure?

```
                Daisies
C:\Flowers——Tulips        Miniature
                Marigolds——Regular
                            Giant
```

10. If you key in the command DELTREE A:\MARIGOLDS, what are the results?
11. To hide the PROJECT1.TXT file currently in the WORK subdirectory on the A: drive, what command should you use?
12. Explain the benefit of using the PATH command.
13. Explain the difference among full, differential, and incremental backups.
14. Why are backups important?

LAB #3

Part 1   Using DOS at the Workstation Level

This lab allows you to explore uses for DOS at your own workstation. The more you practice, the more comfortable you will become with DOS. After completing this lab, you should have an understanding of how to initialize a floppy disk, copy files to it, create new files in subdirectories, edit an AUTOEXEC.BAT, and print.

1. Use the DIR command to view the directories on your workstation's hard drive:

   ```
   C:\>DIR/P
   ```

   Write down the path needed to access your DOS directory.

2. Display all the files located in the root directory of drive C: that end with the .BAT extension:

`C:\>`**DIR *.BAT**

3. Display the contents of your computer's AUTOEXEC.BAT file:

`C:\>`**TYPE AUTOEXEC.BAT**

Do you see the PATH command listed? Does it reference the DOS subdirectory as you indicated in your answer to step 1?

4. Format a new floppy disk for saving your work. Also make it bootable:

`C:\>`**FORMAT A:/S**

5. Make a subdirectory on drive A: and call it NOTES:

`C:\>`**MD A:\NOTES**

6. Use the DOS EDIT program to create a short text file:

`C:\>`**EDIT A:\NOTES\INTDOS.TXT**

Key in your thoughts about internal DOS and enter a list of the internal DOS commands discussed in Chapter 1.

Exit the EDIT program by holding down Alt and pressing "F" for file, then press "X" for exit. Confirm that you want to save changes.

7. Copy the AUTOEXEC.BAT and CONFIG.SYS files to your floppy disk:

`C:\>`**COPY AUTOEXEC.BAT A:**
`C:\>`**COPY CONFIG.SYS A:**

8. With your floppy disk still in the computer, reboot your computer. Your computer should be booting from the files in drive A:. To test this, modify the AUTOEXEC.BAT file located on the A: drive to display your notes:

`C:\>`**EDIT A:\AUTOEXEC.BAT**

Make sure you specify A:\ or you will be editing the AUTOEXEC.BAT on drive C: instead. Add this line to the bottom of the AUTOEXEC.BAT file:

TYPE A:\NOTES\INTDOS.TXT

If the printer is available, key the line in as follows:

TYPE A:\NOTES\INTDOS.TXT>PRN

Reboot your computer to test your changes. If all the steps were done correctly, your workstation should boot up from the floppy disk in drive A:. It then should proceed to run your newly edited AUTOEXEC.BAT, which displays your notes and prints them.

Part 2   Using DOS Commands on the Network

In this lab, you explore how DOS commands can also be used on the network. As you will soon discover, the commands work in the same way, with two exceptions: (1) The drive letters correspond to network drives, and (2) you must have been granted permission to use the files and directories on the network.

1. Log in following the steps used in the login lab found in Chapter 1.
2. At the F:\> prompt, view the names of the directories found on the network:

    F:\>**DIR/P**

3. Do you see the subdirectory called PUBLIC listed in the directory? (If not, see the following notes for additional instructions.) Change to the PUBLIC directory:

    F:\>**CD PUBLIC**

4. Your prompt should now show that you are at the PUBLIC directory. Once again view the directory:

    F:\PUBLIC>**DIR/P**

5. You explored several DOS commands in this chapter; let's see which ones will work here. Try to create a new file:

    F:\PUBLIC>**EDIT NEWFILE.TXT**

    Type in a short text such as your name. Exit and save your work. Oops! You have not been granted permission to add new files to the PUBLIC directory.

    The PUBLIC directory, although accessible to everyone on the LAN, has security applied to it that prevents you from altering or adding to the contents of the subdirectory. This is discussed more in Chapters 6, 8, and 12. DOS commands do work on the network, however, provided that you have been granted permission to work with the files and directories in the way you are attempting.

6. To further illustrate that you can use DOS commands while on the network, explore the COPY command. Key in the following command:

    F:\PUBLIC>**COPY LOGOUT.EXE A:**

    You just instructed the computer to copy the file LOGOUT.EXE from the PUBLIC directory to your floppy drive.

    Verify that the COPY command was successful:

    F:\PUBLIC>**DIR A:\LOGOUT.EXE**

    The file name LOGOUT.EXE should appear on your screen. (If the system just logged you out when you tried, log back in and try again. Most likely you forgot to type DIR before the word LOGOUT.)

    You really do not need the LOGOUT.EXE file on your floppy disk; you can erase it from the floppy disk now:

    F:\PUBLIC>**ERASE A:\LOGOUT.EXE**

SETTING UP THE NETWORK ENVIRONMENT

Part II helps users learn the administrative side of networking, including workstation setups and setting up users and groups.

CHAPTER FOUR   Setting Up the NetWare® Workstation

CHAPTER FIVE   Introduction to NWADMIN, Creating Users and Groups

CHAPTER SIX   Setting Up Accounts Using NETADMIN

SETTING UP THE NETWARE WORKSTATION

INSPIRING MOMENT

Congratulations on your decision to learn networking! It's perhaps unlike anything you have ever set out to learn or accomplish before. Learning networking requires being able to comprehend and analyze small details: how-to steps, new vocabulary words, key concepts, and important relationships. It also requires being able to see the big picture: understanding structures, flow, and both the administrative and end-user side of the networking infrastructure. By the mere fact that you are reading this book, you have made a certain amount of commitment in this regard.

QUESTIONS FOR THOUGHT

Have you ever set out to learn something new, wondering as to the level of difficulty facing you? Have you ever thought that a particular subject may be too hard to master? Have you ever been afraid of learning something new?

CHALLENGE

Give yourself more than just a chance; decide that you will solidly set forth on this new learning adventure. Set forth unswervingly committed to learning, understanding, and mastering networking. These goals are far different than just going through the motions of memorizing, trying to "fit in," and just seeking to pass a class. Learning, understanding, and mastering are inner drives that when taken seriously make those initial fears seem unimportant. Learning networking requires approaching problems with an open mind and being willing to get back up if you make a mistake. It requires a great deal of patience with both self and others. The learning process also requires that you practice and apply new material. If you are not ready to commit to these challenges, and if the drive is not there, then close this book and find that which you really want to do! On the other hand, if you are ready for this adventure, fear not. You can do it!

CHAPTER OBJECTIVES

1. Walk through the process of creating workstation NetWare Client diskettes.
2. Describe the process of installing the NetWare Client at the workstation.

3. Explain the 1-2-3 processing of the login request.

4. Discuss the meaning of *context*.

5. Introduce Novell® Directory Services and explain how it provides setup support for each company's unique hierarchical structure.

6. Explore Network Neighborhood and walk through how to customize the login process.

PREPARING THE WORKSTATION

Before any computer can operate in the network environment, key pieces of software are loaded onto the hard drive and a series of configuration steps are performed. You may already be aware that your computer requires special operating system software for booting (starting) and running. Similarly, software is required to allow for connecting the workstation to the network. Special software is required for announcing to the network that someone would like to log in and use the services provided. The special software in this case is the NetWare Client; the network is Novell NetWare 4.11; and that someone is, in networking terms, the end user. The following section explores setting up the workstation with the NetWare Client and configuring it to attach to the network. Setting up and configuring the Novell NetWare server is covered in Appendix A for those desiring to explore this process. As you study the process of setting up the workstation, seek not to memorize the steps. Rather, grasp the overall process and be comfortable walking through the steps for setting up the NetWare Client.

Creating Workstation NetWare Client Diskettes

1. From the server's system colon prompt, load the INSTALL.NLM.

```
SERV1:LOAD INSTALL.NLM
```

2. From the "Installation Options" menu, select "Product Options".

3. From the "Other Installation Actions" menu, select "Choose an Item or Product Listed Above".

4. The first time you create NetWare Client diskettes in this manner, you will need to select "Create Client Installation Directories on Server".

5. Next, indicate that the client files you wish to copy are on CD. To do this, put the NetWare 4.11 operating system CD into the CD-ROM drive of the server, press the F3 function key, specify the path, and press the Enter key.

Specify a directory path:

```
D:\PRODUCTS\NW411\INSTALL\IBM\DOS\XXX\ENGLISH
```

Note: If you happen to get a warning message regarding the CD-ROM's ability to access the files, select "Continue and Access the CD-ROM". It will most likely still work.

6. From the "Indicate Which File Groups You Want Installed" screen, select "WIN95 (English) Client Install Area (17MB)" by pressing the space bar. Press F10 to continue.

7. The appropriate client files are copied into the

   `SYS:\PUBLIC\CLIENT\WIN95\IBM_ENU.`

   Note: The client setup files get updated periodically. Visit Novell's support web site at http//:www.support.novell.com to download newer client files.

8. Now that the client installation directory has been created on the server, you can make client install floppy diskettes for use to set up the individual workstations.
9. From the "Other Installation Items/Products" menu screen, once again select "Choose an Item or Product Listed Above".
10. From the "Other Installation Items/Products" screen, arrow down and select "Make Diskettes".
11. Next, you are prompted for the path from which to install the client. You could actually indicate the path on the CD again. However, suppose that you no longer have the CD-ROM drive loaded with the appropriate CD. For this reason, we will press F3 and select the directory path on the server that contains the client installation files.

    Specify a directory path:

    `SYS:\PUBLIC\CLIENT\WIN95\IBM_ENU`

12. The next screen prompts you with a message, "Indicate Which File Groups You Want Installed." For our example, press the space bar next to "Create Windows 95 English Diskettes (7 diskettes) 10 MB." Press F10 to accept the selection.
13. Follow the directions on the screen. Put a label on the first floppy disk and title it "Net-Ware Client 32 for Windows 95 Disk 1 - Setup (SETUP1)." Place the disk in drive A: and press the Enter key to continue. In like manner, label each disk and insert when directed following the on-screen directions. The NetWare Client disks are listed as follows in the order that they are created. You may wish to label the floppy disks beforehand in order to save some time.

    NetWare Client 32 for Windows 95 Disk 1 - Setup (SETUP)

    NetWare Client 32 for Windows 95 Disk 2 (DISK2)

    NetWare Client 32 for Windows 95 Disk 3 (DISK3)

    NetWare Client 32 for Windows 95 Disk 4 (DISK4)

    NetWare Client 32 for Windows 95 Disk 5 (DISK5)

    NetWare Client 32 for Windows 95 LAN Driver 16 Disk (LANDRV16)

    NetWare Client 32 for Windows 95 LAN Driver 32 Disk (LANDRV32)

14. Once the disks have all been created, you may escape out of the INSTALLATION utility.

Installing the NetWare Client at the Workstation

Once the NetWare Client disks have been created, they are then used to prepare the workstation for connecting to the network. The following steps allow for installing the NetWare Client software and configuring the workstations.

1. Put the NetWare Client for Windows 95 Disk 1 (SETUP) in drive A:.
2. Launch the start-up program by clicking on the Windows "Start" button, selecting "Run," typing in A:\SETUP.EXE as shown in Figure 4.1, and pressing the Enter key.

FIGURE 4.1
From the "Run" line, execute the
client SETUP.EXE
Source: Screen shot from NetWare,
© 1983-1999, Novell, Inc. All rights
reserved. Reprinted and used with
permission.

FIGURE 4.2
By selecting "Yes," you are agreeing to Novell Terms and Conditions.
Source: Screen shot from NetWare,
© 1983-1999, Novell, Inc. All rights
reserved. Reprinted and used with
permission.

3. After reading through the Novell Terms and Conditions, select "Yes" to note your ac-
   ceptance (Figure 4.2).
4. The "NetWare Client 32 Installation" opening screen appears (Figure 4.3). Click "Start"
   to continue.
5. If you are prompted to put in your Windows 95 or other operating system CD, do so and
   click on the "OK" button.
6. Follow the directions on the screen. You will be prompted to put in the next NetWare
   Client 32 diskette (Figure 4.4). Follow the on-screen directions to continue feeding in
   the disks.
7. After the appropriate files have been copied, you will be given the option to reboot and
   take defaults, or to customize (Figure 4.5). For this example, we will choose the "Reboot" option.
8. For customization and fine-tuning specialized to your network environment, please consult with the network administrator at your organization. For those wishing to further
   customize their NetWare Client, you may either click on "Customize" at this time, or
   you may choose to customize later using the Network Neighborhood shortcut located on
   the workstation's desktop. Customizing through Network Neighborhood is further discussed later in this chapter.
9. To conclude the NetWare Client 32 installation, click on "Reboot." Make sure to take
   the floppy disk out of the disk drive and store the disks for safekeeping.

FIGURE 4.3
The "NetWare Client 32 Installation" opening screen appears.
Source: Screen shot from NetWare, © 1983-1999, Novell, Inc. All rights reserved. Reprinted and used with permission.

FIGURE 4.4
You will be prompted to put in the next NetWare Client diskette.
Source: Screen shot from NetWare, © 1983-1999, Novell, Inc. All rights reserved. Reprinted and used with permission.

FIGURE 4.5
At this point the NetWare Client 32 basic install is complete.
Source: Screen shot from NetWare, © 1983-1999, Novell, Inc. All rights reserved. Reprinted and used with permission.

The Login Process

Once your network is set up and running correctly, the login process is fairly easy. After the workstation client software has been installed, make sure you have identified under which position each particular workstation will log in; this is called the *context*. Next, you will need to determine when to run the login request. Do you want it to prompt you for the log-in request when the workstation boots up, or do you want to double click on a shortcut that would then allow your login request to occur? Finally, you have the processing of the login request. Just remember 1-2-3: (1) context, (2) launching the login request prompt, and (3) processing the login request.

Context   You can think of context as positioning. In this case, at what position in the network structure do you wish to log in? During the server installation process, an initial default context was assigned. For our example, the default context is ABC_CO. ABC_CO is also the name of our tree. Normally the tree name corresponds to the name of the organization. The tree name is the root or the starting place for the hierarchical structure of our network. This hierarchical structure is referred to as NetWare Directory Services (NDS)™. Each item in the structure, such as a user's account, a printer, a file server, or a group, is referred to as an *object*. These objects are organized in an upside-down tree formation, the tree name being the name of the organization. The branches off of the main tree, or organization, could be the departments within the organization. With NetWare you may create container objects, just as an organization can have departments within it. An organization in NetWare may have organizational units within it too. In the case of larger organizations, the first level of branches may include divisions or different facilities under one organization. For example, a company having 50 divisions scattered throughout the state may well have 50 branches in NDS under the organization level itself. For simplicity's sake, we are going to assume this company has one location, and we are going to log in with the context of ABC_CO. Therefore, we will be fine with the default settings. Later in this chapter, we will learn to specify a different context.

Launching the Login Request Prompt   To launch the login process, you will need to run the executable file that was automatically installed as a result of going through the workstation client setup. By default, in Windows, the login shortcut is placed under "Start," "Programs." To get there, follow these steps (Figure 4.6):

1. Click on "Start."
2. Click on "Programs."
3. Click on "Novell."
4. Click on "NetWare Login."

Processing the login Request   You should now see the login screen as shown in Figure 4.7. Enter your login name and password. Notice that your password does not appear on the screen for security reasons. Once you have typed your login name and password correctly, you may click on "OK." The request will now be sent to the file server to verify and authenticate that the requested login name with the associated password has permission to log into this particular server, at this particular time of day, at this particular workstation, and at the context (position) requested.

COMMON ERROR MESSAGE ASSOCIATED WITH ATTACHING AND LOGGING IN

The first level of security on a Novell Netware system is the login name and password level. A user may receive an error message when attempting to log in. Some key error messages associated with attaching and logging into the network are discussed as follows.

FIGURE 4.6
The login shortcut is located under "Start," "Programs."
Source: Screen shot reprinted by permission from Microsoft Corporation and NetWare, © 1983-1999, Novell, Inc. All rights reserved. Reprinted and used with permission.

FIGURE 4.7
Enter your user name and password to log into the network.
Source: Screen shot from NetWare, © 1983-1999, Novell, Inc. All rights reserved. Reprinted and used with permission.

"File Server Not Found" or "Invalid Drive Specification"

Most LAN troubleshooting problems are associated with cabling and connections. "File Server Not Found" or "Invalid Drive Specification" usually indicates that the workstation could not get a good connection to the network. If this happens, double check the cabling. Check the connection leading to the user's workstation and the connection leading from the workstation going toward the file server (this may be at a concentrator or hub). Make sure the cable is plugged in all the way. If this does not work, the cable may need replacing. Test the workstation with a cable known to work, or test the suspected bad cable using a cable-testing device. A whole row of stations getting the same error message usually indicates that the point at which the stations meet, the *hub* or *concentrator,* has a weak connection or that the power to the hub or concentrator is not turned on. If all the workstations connected to the same file server are getting the same error message, then check the *backbone* cabling (the main cable leading from the file server and going throughout the network). If the backbone is not the problem, perhaps the file server is down or has some other problem. Check the file server itself. If needed, call your network engineer to assist you.

"Access Denied" or "Intruder Detection Lockout"

"Access Denied" generally means that either your login name or password is keyed in incorrectly. Notice that the error message itself has a level of security to it. It doesn't tell you which is incorrect, your login name or your password. If the network administrator has the feature called "Intruder Detection" turned on, however, then the message "Access Denied" will change to "Intruder Detection Lockout" if the login name is correct and the wrong password has been entered more than the number of allowable attempts set by the administrator. The number of allowable attempts set by the administrator is referred to as login attempts allowed.

NETWARE DIRECTORY SERVICES (NDS) TREE-FURTHER CLARIFICATION

As mentioned earlier, one benefit of having a LAN is sharing of resources. With Novell NetWare 4.1x,[®] these resources are tracked in a global, distributed, hierarchical database known as Novell[®] Directory Services (NDS). The NDS is actually a database that represents all the resources on the network in question.

When logging into the network, the user is actually logging into the NDS. The NDS also proves helpful for controlling security, addressed in Chapter 12.

The NDS is organized in an upside-down, treelike fashion with the "roots" of the tree located at the top. Off the root is normally found a container used for grouping and organization. There are different types of containers. If a company or organization is very large, doing business worldwide, then the type of container that attaches to the root is most likely a "country" container ("C="). For our examples, we will use a simple, medium-sized company. Therefore, our first container will be an "organization" container ("O="). For further clarity, we will divide our organization into departments, or "organizational unit" ("OU=") containers. The inside of each department's organizational unit containers will represent the actual resources. Resources may be a user, print queue, file server, volume, and so forth. Resources represented in this way are referred to as *leaves.*

Context

Before logging in, make sure the networks operating system knows which organization container you are attempting to access and which organizational unit container you wish to log into. This current location in the tree where you are known as the *current context.* Check the current context by using the "cx" (context) command:

```
F:\>cx
```

It may be easier to go to the root fist. If you did not get a rely message of "[root]," then use the "cx ." command to move down the tree. (*Note:* There is a space between the "cx" and the "."; if you do not use the space, you will get an error message saying that you issued a bad command.)

```
F:\>cx .
```

Note: Add one dot for each level you wish to move down.

Once at the root, specify your particular context. Keep in mind that the organization goes last. Remember, it's an upside-down tree.

```
F:\>cx .ou=acct .o=abc_co
```

or

```
F:\>cx .acct.abc_co
```

Notice that the second example uses a shortcut known as *typeless naming. Hint:* Once you figure out the right context and logging-in procedure for your account, write it down. These notes will come in handy until you commit the steps to memory.

Now you're ready to log in.

Verifying and Changing the Context

You may want to verify that you are logging in at the right context (or position). You may return to the login screen and click on the "Connection" tab (Figure 4.8). Notice that there are three blanks for specifying the name of the tree, the server, and the context that you wish to log into. For our example, we are logging into the tree ABC_CO. We only have one server, SERV1. Conceivably you could have multiple servers at your organization. For the context, to keep it simple, we are logging in at the root. Now, if your organization had chosen to break down the NDS structure by departments and implement organizational units in the tree, then you would type in something like ACTNG.ABC_CO as the context. Notice that the organizational unit name goes before the tree name, and that a period serves as a separator.

FIGURE 4.8
Use the "Connection" tab to verify or change the context.
Source: Screen shot from NetWare, © 1983-1999, Novell, Inc. All rights reserved. Reprinted and used with permission.

FIGURE 4.9
You may see the "Login Results" screen.
Source: Screen shot from NetWare, © 1983-1999, Novell, Inc. All rights reserved. Reprinted and used with permission.

Login Results Screen

Once the login process is complete, you may see the "Login Results" screen (Figure 4.9). Depending on how your Network Neighborhood (located on the workstation's desktop) is configured, this screen either stays up until you close it, or it may be set to continue on without remaining on the screen. Notice that the "Login Results" screen verifies that the user was permitted to log into the NDS in the context (position) requested. This is noted by the line that reads "You are attached to server SERV1" as illustrated in Figure 4.9. This screen also provides the results of the login scripts executed. Login scripts are discussed in Chapter 11.

CUSTOMIZING THE LOGIN PROCESS

There are three types of customization to address: (1) customization from the login screen itself, (2) customizing through the Network Neighborhood, and (3) customizing where the login shortcut is placed on the workstation. We just looked at customizing from the login screen itself (Figure 4.8). In this section, we will look at the other two customizations.

Network Neighborhood

This section does not cover every aspect of Network Neighborhood. The details of Network Neighborhood vary greatly depending on the hardware and software contained on the workstation and the server. This is simply a starting point, an introduction to beginning networking students.

1. Located on the desktop you will find Network Neighborhood. If you right click on this icon, you will see a small menu as depicted in Figure 4.10; select "Properties".
2. Once "Properties" has been selected, you should see the "Network Configuration and Identification" screen. This is like a summary screen for your network setup at the workstation level. Notice that it identifies that we are using the Novell NetWare Client 32. In Figure 4.11's example, we also have a modem installed on this particular workstation. The network interface card (NIC) is a Realtek RTL8019 plug and play model.

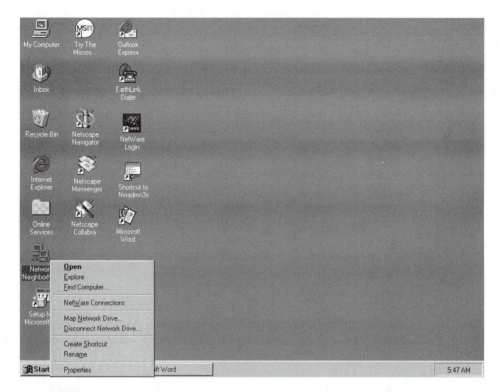

FIGURE 4.10
Right click on "Network Neighborhood" to get to "Properties."
Source: Screen shot reprinted by permission from Microsoft Corporation.

We are using the IPX protocol (rule) for sending and receiving computer bytes across the network. It is conceivable to have more than one type of network that the station logs into. Novell NetWare is set as our primary network.

3. Notice in Figure 4.11 that "Novell NetWare Client 32" is highlighted. Clicking on the "Properties" button at this point brings up the "Novell NetWare Client 32 Properties" screen as shown in Figure 4.12. From here you can customize the login process in a similar manner as shown earlier in Figure 4.8 from the "Connection" tab when the login screen pops up. For this example, our preferred server is SERV1. Our preferred tree is ABC_CO, and our first network drive letter is F:.

4. Also under the "Novell NetWare Client 32 Properties" screen you have three other tabs that may be selected to further customize the login process. Clicking on the "Login" tab reveals at which position you wish to log in. In our example (Figure 4.13), we are logging in directly to the tree level (ABC_CO).

5. The "Default Capture" tab assigns printing defaults. For our example (Figure 4.14), we would like to receive just one copy of each item printed, and we would like the forms to advance to the next page once the printing is complete. Notice that the "Enable banner" box is not checked. Checking the banner box results in an identifier page to be generated between reports. If you choose to print banners to separate reports, you may also type in two default lines for it to print on the banners.

FIGURE 4.11
The "Network Configuration and Identification" screen appears when "Properties" is selected.
Source: Screen shot from NetWare, © 1983-1999, Novell, Inc. All rights reserved. Reprinted and used with permission.

FIGURE 4.12
The "Novell NetWare Client 32 Properties" screen allows you to customize the login process.
Source: Screen shot from NetWare, © 1983-1999, Novell, Inc. All rights reserved. Reprinted and used with permission.

FIGURE 4.13
The "Login" tab allows you to specify the login position.
Source: Screen shot from NetWare, © 1983-1999, Novell, Inc. All rights reserved. Reprinted and used with permission.

Novell NetWare Client 32 Properties

Client 32 | Login | Default Capture | Advanced Settings

☑ Display connection page
  ◉ Log in to tree
  ○ Log in to server   ☐ Bindery connection
  ☑ Clear current connections

☑ Display script page
  Login Script: [   ]
  Profile Script: [   ]
  ☐ Close script results automatically   ☑ Run scripts

☐ Display variables page
  %2 [   ]   %3 [   ]
  %4 [   ]   %5 [   ]

☑ Save settings when exiting Login

[OK]   [Cancel]

FIGURE 4.14
"Default Capture" allows you to customize the printing process.
Source: Screen shot from NetWare, © 1983-1999, Novell, Inc. All rights reserved. Reprinted and used with permission.

Novell NetWare Client 32 Properties

Client 32 | Login | Default Capture | Advanced Settings

Output Settings
  Number of copies: [1]
  ☑ Form feed
  ☐ Enable tabs   Number of spaces: [8]

Banner Settings
  ☐ Enable banner
      1st banner name: [   ]
      2nd banner name: [   ]

Other Settings
  ☐ Hold   ☐ Notify
  ☑ Auto endcap   ☐ Keep
  Seconds before timeout: [0]

[OK]   [Cancel]

FIGURE 4.15
The "Advanced Settings" tab allows for further customization of the workstation.
Source: Screen shot from NetWare, © 1983-1999, Novell, Inc. All rights reserved. Reprinted and used with permission.

6. The "Advanced Settings" tab allows you to further customize the NetWare workstation. In Figure 4.15, "Search Dirs First" set to "on" results in having subdirectories listed first and file names listed last in directory listings. The other items listed under the "Advanced Settings" tab are beyond the scope of this text. Select "OK" to return to the "Network Configuration and Identification" screen.

7. Next, from the "Network Configuration and Identification" screen. select our network interface card "Realtek RTL8019," and click on "Properties" (Figure 4.16). This allows us to view and modify the configurations for the NIC.

8. The "Driver Type" tab allows us to indicate whether the NIC is sending and receiving in 16- or 32-bit format. In our example, we are using the driver capable of sending at either 32- or 16-bit format (Figure 4.17).

9. The "Bindings" tab allows for specifying which protocols (or sending and receiving rules) are applicable for our network environment. We will take all the defaults for this section as determined automatically during our NetWare Client setup (Figure 4.18). Clicking on "OK" takes us back to the "Network Configuration and Identification" screen.

10. Finally, the "Identification" tab located on the "Network" screen allows us to identify our computer name, workgroup, and a brief description if desired (Figure 4.19). Be aware that other software applications make use of this information. For example, LAN management software tools may pull from these fields for each workstation to establish an inventory database of workstations on the network. Do not confuse this with the login ID. This particular identification applies to the workstation. The login names apply to the users. Thus, some organizations prefer to put a

FIGURE 4.16
Select the network interface card
(NIC) and click on "Properties."
Source: Screen shot from NetWare,
© 1983-1999, Novell, Inc. All rights
reserved. Reprinted and used with
permission.

FIGURE 4.17
The NIC can recognize both 32- and
16-bit data formats.
Source: Screen shot from NetWare,
© 1983-1999, Novell, Inc. All rights
reserved. Reprinted and used with
permission.

FIGURE 4.18
Bindings specify which protocols
are appropriate for our network.
Source: Screen shot from NetWare,
© 1983-1999, Novell, Inc. All rights
reserved. Reprinted and used with
permission.

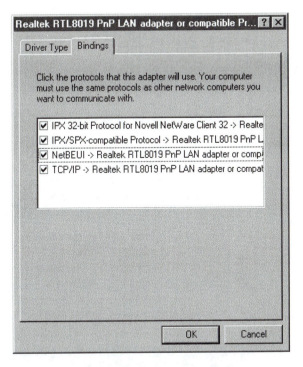

FIGURE 4.19
The "Identification" tab identifies
this workstation on the network.
Source: Screen shot from NetWare,
© 1983-1999, Novell, Inc. All rights
reserved. Reprinted and used with
permission.

computer number or some other workstation ID in the location that says "Computer name." In our example, users have their own workstation, so the person's name is entered. Clicking "OK" confirms all changes made in this section. Depending on the modifications entered, you may be prompted to restart the workstation before the changes will go into effect.

Placement of the Login Shortcut

The placement of the login shortcut determines when the login process is started. If the shortcut is placed in the STARTUP directory, then as soon as the workstation boots up and the Windows operating system is started, the user will be prompted to log in. If instead of placing the shortcut in the STARTUP directory, it's placed on the desktop or under programs, then the user may execute it at will.

Default Placement of the Shortcut   If you browse through the C:\WINDOWS directory structure using Windows Explorer, you will see that by default the shortcut is located in C:\WINDOWS\Start Menu\Programs\Novell (Figure 4.20). Recall from Figure 4.6 that we initially launched the NetWare login by clicking on "Start," "Programs," "Novell," and then "NetWare Login." This default requires users to select the shortcut before they are prompted to log in. Also, the shortcut is buried.

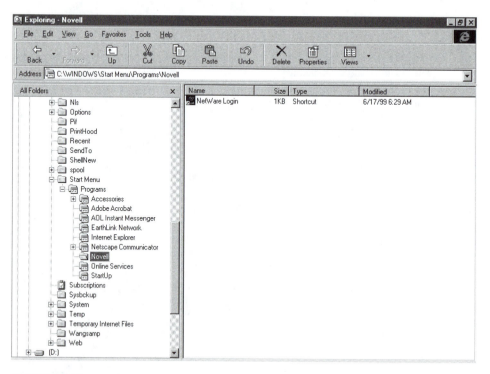

FIGURE 4.20
The NetWare login shortcut is located under C:\WINDOWS\Start Menu\Programs\Novell by default.
Source: Screen shot from NetWare, © 1983-1999, Novell, Inc. All rights reserved. Reprinted and used with permission.

FIGURE 4.21 Copy the shortcut to prepare for placing it elsewhere.
Source: Screen shot from NetWare, © 1983-1999, Novell, Inc. All rights reserved. Reprinted and used with permission.

Placing the Shortcut on the Desktop One approach is to place the shortcut on the desktop. One way to accomplish this is to follow these steps:

1. Right click on the shortcut and select "Copy" (Figure 4.21).
2. Minimize all open windows.
3. Right click on the desktop and select "Paste" (Figure 4.22).
4. The shortcut is now on the desktop (Figure 4.23).

Automatically Launching the Login Process Placing the shortcut on the desktop makes it easier for the user to find the shortcut. Many organizations prefer to have the login process happen automatically when the user logs in. This is accomplished by copying the shortcut and placing it in the STARTUP directory:

1. Once again locate the shortcut either on the desktop or in Windows Explorer.
2. Right click on the login shortcut and select "Copy."
3. Next, in Windows Explorer, go to the STARTUP directory located at C:\WINDOWS\ Start Menu\Programs\StartUp. Right click inside of this directory and select "Paste".
4. The shortcut should now appear in this directory (Figure 4.24). The next time the computer is started, the user will be prompted automatically to log in.

FIGURE 4.22
Right click on the desktop and select "Paste" to place the shortcut.
Source: Screen shot reprinted by permission from Microsoft Corporation.

FIGURE 4.23
The shortcut is now on the desktop.
Source: Screen shot reprinted by permission from Microsoft Corporation.

FIGURE 4.24
Place the NetWare login shortcut in the STARTUP directory to allow it to automatically start.
Source: Screen shot reprinted by permission from Microsoft Corporation.

SUMMARY

By installing the NetWare Client software on the workstation and properly configuring the Network Neighborhood, the station can connect to the network. This is provided that the cabling and the network interface card are installed and working correctly and that the file server has been properly set up and configured, and is working correctly. The login process allows the end users to identify themselves to the network.

EXERCISES

1. Define the following:
   a. NetWare Client
   b. Logging in
   c. Context
   d. NDS tree
   e. Launching
   f. Shortcut placement

2. What does NDS stand for?
3. Explain the overall process required for creating the NetWare Client diskettes.
4. Explain the overall process required for installing the NetWare Client.
5. List the three things you should remember about processing the login request.
6. What is the purpose of organizational units?
7. In this chapter, ABC_CO is the name of our tree. Explain what this means.
8. The Sales Division is an example of what type of object?
9. Draw a picture to illustrate the following context location: MARY.ACTNG.ABC_CO.
10. What happens if the "Enable banner" box is checked under the "Default Capture" tab located in Network Neighborhood?
11. What is the purpose of the "Driver Type" tab found in Network Neighborhood?
12. What is the result of having "Search Dirs First" set to on, and which tab of Network Neighborhood lets you set this?

LAB #4A

Walk through the steps noted in this chapter to create the NetWare Client diskettes.

LAB #4B

Walk through the steps noted in this chapter for installing the NetWare Client.

LAB #4C

Create a fictitious company. On paper, design an NDS tree to correspond with the company you just invented.

CHAPTER FIVE

INTRODUCTION TO NWADMIN, CREATING USERS AND GROUPS

INSPIRING MOMENT

You recently started working at your first position as a network administrator, and it has been brought to your attention that the company is growing. How will you learn the names of so many people? Who does what? What are the names of the departments in this company and who works in each department? You really want each person to feel special. You would like to call each by name and become aware of their computing needs. It has also been brought to your attention that you are responsible for reshaping and organizing the network user accounts.

QUESTIONS FOR THOUGHT

Is the current network structure of user accounts well planned? Is it easy to find particular user accounts and manage them? Does the overall structure of the network reflect the company's actual physical makeup? If you had the opportunity to plan, organize, and create the structure for user account management, what would it look like? Would it be organized and well managed?

CHALLENGE

Before beginning the account setup process on a new network, first draft out the plan on paper and seek to customize it to the organization's physical structure. When you begin a new position in the network arena of an organization, first look at the overall structure of the network. Seek to grasp an understanding of the bones or skeleton, so to speak, by understanding the principles underlying how the network has been set up.

CHAPTER OBJECTIVES

After finishing this chapter you should be able to:

1. Further explore the concept of NDS trees. Explain the purpose of organizational units, and distinguish between container objects, and user and group leaf objects.
2. Discuss the purpose of NetWare Administrator (NWADMIN), where it's located, and basic usage.

3. Become aware of Internet support for NetWare.

4. Walk through the steps for creating organizational unit objects, user accounts, and groups.

5. Explore steps involved in assigning users to particular groups.

6. Discuss the concept of "context sensitive" names.

ADMINISTRATING THE NETWORK

Before we can really explore the subject of setting up users and groups, you need to become more familiar with the NDS tree, objects, leafs, and how these are represented in NWADMIN. By having a firm understanding of these concepts, you can better manage and work with the network.

NETWARE ADMINISTRATOR (NWADMIN)

NWADMIN is an executable located in the SYS:PUBLIC directory (Figure 5.1). Yes, end users have access to NWADMIN; however, the access is limited. End users may view information regarding their own accounts and directories to which they have been assigned rights. Administrators and administrator equivalents have full access to NWADMIN. This

FIGURE 5.1
NWADMN3X.EXE is the actual NWADMIN executable located in SYS:PUBLIC.
Source: Screen shot reprinted by permission from Microsoft Corporation.

utility allows the administrator to create and manage users, groups, printers, and the Group-Wise e-mail. (GroupWise is purchased separately.)

You should be aware that Novell makes changes to NWADMIN periodically to improve or enhance performance. When this occurs, the administrator will want to download the newer NWADMIN executable, along with applicable instructions. Before installing the newer NWADMIN, however, it is important to read the documentation file that comes with it and the Technical Information Document (TID). Currently, download files are available through the Internet at the web site http://www.support.novell.com. This web site is a valuable resource for the network administrator (Figure 5.2). In addition to downloadable files, you can also find useful information about error messages encountered on the network, network concepts, and new updates on networking.

When you download the NWADMIN executable, the file name will not be NWADMIN.EXE. For example, it may read NWADMN3X.EXE. Just to make life more manageable, even if the executable is called NWADMN3X.EXE, "techies" still refer to the executable as NWADMIN when discussing it with beginners and laypersons and among themselves.

NWADMIN can get very technical, very quickly, which is not the goal of this text. Therefore, we will primarily concentrate on setting up users and groups for our discussion. We will return to NWADMIN in Chapter 7 to discuss printer setups, and in Chapter 6 as we look at network security.

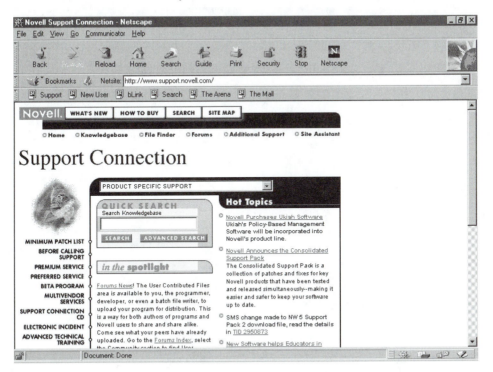

FIGURE 5.2

Go to http://www.support.novell.com to find valuable resources regarding NetWare.

Source: Screen shot from NetWare, © 1983-1999, Novell, Inc. All rights reserved. Reprinted and used with permission.

NETWARE DIRECTORY SERVICES (NDS) TREE

In Figure 5.3, you will see that our tree structure begins with ABC_CO. This is the root of the tree. Notice that our tree is being held to the ceiling by ABC_CO. (Please note that our tree grows upside down!) Notice that there are only leaf objects—users (Admin, Nancy, and TJ), a server (SERV1), and drive volumes (SERV1_SYS and SERV1_VOL1)—inside the tree at this point. In Figure 5.4, you will notice a list of available objects for NDS. Consider these similar to building blocks that the LAN administrator defines to form the organizational structure of the network.

Creating Organizational Unit Objects

In Figure 5.5, our network is reorganized. It now has a tree branch, much like a fork in the road, or a branch of an organization's hierarchical chart. The ABC Company is divided into two divisions: the Sales Division and the Service Division. Since these divisions have different departments inside of them, we represent Sales and Service as organizational units. To create an organizational unit, proceed with the following steps:

1. Bring up NWADMIN.

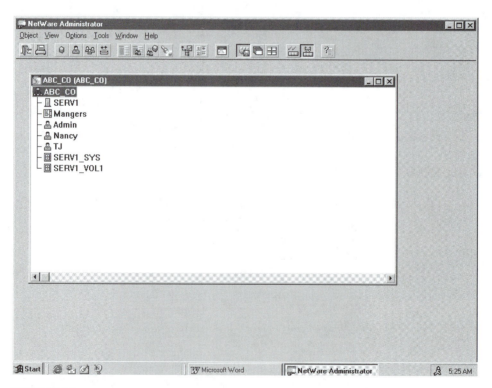

FIGURE 5.3

NWADMIN stands for NetWare Administrator.

Source: Screen shot from NetWare, © 1983-1999, Novell, Inc. All rights reserved. Reprinted and used with permission.

FIGURE 5.4

This is a list of available NDS objects.

Source: Screen shot from NetWare, © 1983-1999, Novell, Inc. All rights reserved. Reprinted and used with permission.

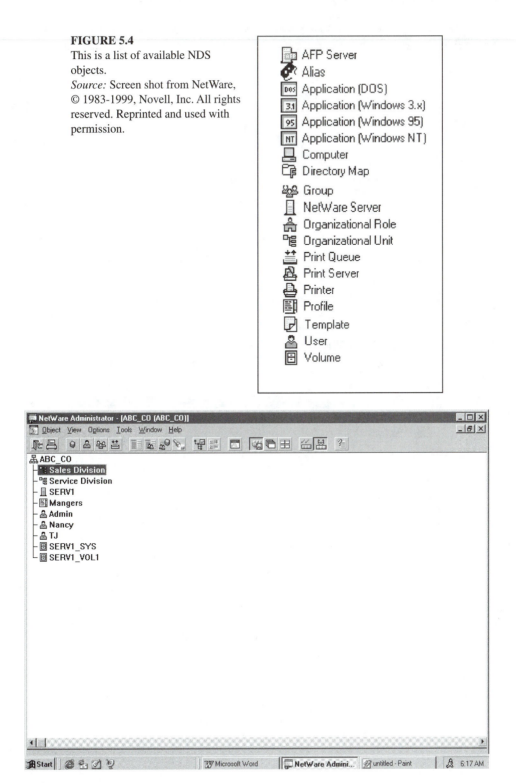

FIGURE 5.5

Organizational units allow for defining distinct divisions within the NDS tree.

Source: Screen shot from NetWare, © 1983-1999, Novell, Inc. All rights reserved. Reprinted and used with permission.

2. Click on the portion of the tree in which you want the new object or leaf to reside. In our example, we click on ABC_CO because Sales and Service are divisions springing off from the root.

3. From the NWADMIN menu, select "Object," then select "Create." You should then be prompted for the type of object (Figure 5.4). Choose "Organizational Unit."

4. When prompted to do so, supply a name for the organizational unit. In our case, we are using Sales Division and Service Division.

These steps would need to be repeated for each organizational unit in the network.

User Leaves

Now that we have organizational units, we may put each user account inside of its appropriate division by following these steps (Figure 5.6):

1. Click on the position of the NDS tree where you want the users to reside. We would like to create the users that reside in the Sales Division, so we click on the "Sales Division" organizational unit object.

2. From the NWADMIN main screen, click on "Object," then click on "Create." This time, select "**User**" (Figure 5.4). You will be prompted to identify the user.

FIGURE 5.6
Inside of the organizational unit, create user and group leaf objects.
Source: Screen shot from NetWare, © 1983-1999, Novell, Inc. All rights reserved. Reprinted and used with permission.

3. Complete the identification screen as shown in Figure 5.7. Notice that you have the option of creating a home directory. This is highly recommended. Just briefly consider some of the reasons for creating a home directory at this point in the account setup process:

    a. A home directory is a subdirectory on the network in which the users have been personally assigned rights and where they can save their work.

    b. If you specify that you wish to create the home directory at this point in the new account setup, then the subdirectory for the user's home directory will be created automatically.

    c. If you choose to create a home directory through the identification screen, the appropriate rights are automatically assigned for the user being created.

4. On the identification screen, check the box for "Create Home Directory." Next, click on the directory tree icon. In our case, we are selecting SERV1_VOL1:\USERS as the location for our home directory.

5. Once the home directory path has been selected, fill in the name of the subdirectory for this particular user to have access to. In our example, we key in "Sandy."

6. Normally we would checkmark "Define additional properties" and continue our way through the various portions of setting up the account. We will return to this in other chapters in this text, so for now you may choose to checkmark "Create another user" or to click on the "Create" button.

7. The user's account is now created. Please be aware that this account has no password yet. This is addressed when we discuss security in Chapter 6. (You may choose to glance at the section regarding passwords in Chapter 6 at this time.)

Creating Groups

Now that we have created our organizational units, Sales Division and Service Division, we may create groups. In an organization, NetWare groups may be created for each department.

FIGURE 5.7
Identify the user.
Source: Screen shot from NetWare, © 1983-1999, Novell, Inc. All rights reserved. Reprinted and used with permission.

FIGURE 5.8
Our Service Division has three groups inside of it.
Source: Screen shot from NetWare, © 1983-1999, Novell, Inc. All rights reserved. Reprinted and used with permission.

For example, in Figure 5.6, Accounting, Client Sales, Group Sales, and Public Relations are all departments located in our Sales Division. Our Service Division has three departments inside of it: the Research and Development Group, the Repair Group, and the Warranty Group (Figure 5.8). Notice that the groups for the Sales Division are on a separate branch of our NDS tree than the Service Division. This is one of the strengths of the NDS tree structure; it can be shaped to fit the organization's hierarchical or physical location structure. In our ABC Company example, organizational units are container objects, distinct branches inside of which group and user leaf objects reside.

The following steps take you through the process of creating a group inside of the Sales Division's organizational unit container. We will create the Accounting group leaf object here.

1. Go into NWADMIN and open up the Sales Division container object by double clicking on it (if it's not already open).
2. From the NWADMIN menu, select "Object," then select "Create." You should then be prompted for the type of object (Figure 5.4). Choose "Group."
3. When prompted to do so, supply a name for the group. In our case, we are adding a new group, Marketing.
4. You may also click the "**Define additional properties**" check box (Figure 5.9).

FIGURE 5.9
Specify the name for the new group object.
Source: Screen shot from NetWare, © 1983-1999, Novell, Inc. All rights reserved. Reprinted and used with permission.

FIGURE 5.10
You will need to click the "Add" button in order to assign users to the group.
Source: Screen shot from NetWare, © 1983-1999, Novell, Inc. All rights reserved. Reprinted and used with permission.

These steps would need to be repeated for each group in the Sales Division. After creating all the groups for the Sales Division, you would then double click on "Service Division" to expand the tree and add group leaf objects inside of it.

Assigning Users to Groups

The next part of setting up our NDS tree structure involves specifying which users are members of which groups. Up to this point we have created our NDS tree's branches, or organizational units, Sales Division and Service Division. We have created group leaf objects, our departments, for each of our divisions, inside of their respective organizational unit containers. We have also created user leaf objects inside of the divisions. However, the system has no way of knowing, as of yet, which users go inside of which groups. Follow these steps to accomplish group membership assignments:

1. Locate the group object in the NDS tree and double click on it.
2. The group window will appear; click on the "Members" button.
3. Click on the "Add" button to indicate that you want to add members (Figure 5.10).

FIGURE 5.11
Select multiple scattered user objects by holding down the Ctrl key and clicking.
Source: Screen shot from NetWare, © 1983-1999, Novell, Inc. All rights reserved. Reprinted and used with permission.

4. Select the members you wish to include in the group. Remember you may select more than one member by holding down the Ctrl key as you click (Figure 5.11). If the names are adjacent you may hold down the Shift key and click the first member name, then click the last member name. Click on "OK" when you are finished selecting the desired users.

5. Notice and verify that the users desired are now appearing in the "Group members" list (Figure 5.12). Also, notice that the name is in a *context sensitive* format. This means that it specifies where the user resides in the NDS tree. For example, Glenda's leaf object resides in the Sales Division organizational unit, which resides in the ABC_CO tree. Notice that the context sensitive name does not contain the group name. Recall from our discussion that the group is a leaf object. The context sensitive name shows which container pathway to take to locate the leaf object in question. Notice that the user leaf object name is listed first, followed by a period (pronounced "dot"), followed by the organizational unit that's next highest up in the NDS tree, followed by a period, and finally followed by the tree name itself. This can seem a little overwhelming at first. If you just keep studying it, and practicing, after time it makes more sense and gets easier to understand.

Assigning Security Access

Once a user's NetWare account has been set up, it then becomes important to take a look at security access. The assigning of security access, commonly referred to as trustee rights assignments, falls under the responsibility of Admin, an Admin equivalent, or whoever has been put in charge of the particular directory on the network. A trustee is one that has been entrusted to use property, in this case the property is a file or directory on the network file server's hard drive. Assignment refers to the granting of specific access to a specific direc-

FIGURE 5.12
The users have been added to the
group, and the context sensitive
name appears.
Source: Screen shot from NetWare,
© 1983-1999, Novell, Inc. All rights
reserved. Reprinted and used with
permission.

tory. In short, "trustee" answers the "who" part of security; that is to say, who is being allowed access. "Assignment" answers the "what and where" part; (1) what kind of access or to what extent can the trustee work in the file or directory in question, and (2) where is this file or directory located. A trustee rights assignment grants access to one or more users, or to one or more groups. It is conceivable for a user to have access through association with a group and to have additional access assigned individually.

Viewing Trustee Rights

From the NDS view screen of NWADMIN, select a user or group that needs access to a particular directory. Pressing the "Enter" key or double clicking the mouse button will bring up the user's NetWare account information screen (Figure 5.13) or the group information screen. Use the scroll bar located on the right side of the screen to advance downward and click on the "Rights to Files and Directories" button (Figure 5.14). Clicking on the "Show" button results in the "Select Object" screen to appear. The right side of the browse window allows for moving around in the NDS structure. Once the correct location is visible on the left side, highlight the desired directory or file and press "OK." Think of it this way, the right side of the browse window is for searching; the left side of the window is for selecting. In Figure 5.15 we are checking to see if the user "Amy" has any special trustee rights assigned for SERV1_VOL. Since we are not sure of the exact name of the directory Amy has access to, or suspect that Amy may have access to more than one directory, select the entire volume. If we are only interested in viewing one particular, known directory, then instead of selecting the entire volume, select the directory of interest. After clicking "OK," we observe that Amy has access to her home directory SERV1_VOL1:USERS\AMY. A user directory is a place for Amy to store her data.

Changing Trustee Assignments

To change a trustee assignment, simply follow the same steps listed for viewing, only this time edit the rights currently assigned by clicking on an empty check mark box for the desired right. A right may also be taken away by deselecting it.

FIGURE 5.15

Source: Screen shot from NetWare, © 1983-1999, Novell, Inc. All rights reserved. Reprinted and used with permission.

Adding Trustee Assignments

In order to add a trustee assignment, first follow the directions listed previously for viewing. If the user does not have any rights assigned for a particular directory, then the check mark boxes will show up blank. At this point, click on the check boxes for the appropriate rights needed for the user or group.

Understanding the Rights

Just what are these different rights? The rights available in NetWare 4.1x are listed here for your review:

- File scan: The trustee may view a listing of file and subdirectory names within the assigned directory.
- Read: The trustee may view the contents of the files located in the assigned directory.
- Create: The trustee may create files and subdirectories within the assigned directory.
- Write: The trustee may overwrite and make changes to files and subdirectories within the assigned directory.
- Erase: The trustee may remove files and directories within the assigned directory.
- Modify: The trustee may change the attributes (such as hidden) for files and subdirectories contained in the assigned directory.
- Access control: The trustee may assign other users as trustees for this particular directory and any files or subdirectories contained inside it. The trustees may only assign up to the level of rights that they have been assigned.
- Supervisory: The trustee has all the rights mentioned to the assigned directory and for all subdirectories contained therein. Note that all the other rights can be

blocked or prevented from applying to lower-level directories; once the supervisory right has been assigned, it applies to the NDS tree structure from the point assigned going down into the directory levels below and cannot be blocked.

SUMMARY

NWADMIN (NetWare Administrator) is a powerful tool for creating and managing the NDS tree. In this chapter, we explored the steps involved in creating organizational units, user accounts, and groups. Organizational units provide flexibility by allowing us to add branches to the NDS tree. Organizational units are also referred to as container objects. Each person logging into the network is referred to as a user and must have a user account set up before login is permitted. User accounts are also referred to as user leaf objects and reside inside of container objects. Group objects provide the opportunity to better structure the network. Users are assigned to groups after the group objects have been created. Preplanning allows for the network structure to pattern after the organization's actual physical structure.

EXERCISES

1. Define the following:
   a. NWADMIN
   b. NDS tree
   c. Organizational unit
   d. User leaves
2. What does NWADMIN stand for?
3. List three things that can be created using NWADMIN.
4. In our ABC Company example, what are the names of the organizational unit objects?
5. In our ABC Company example, what are the names of the groups comprising one of the organizational unit objects?
6. Explain the process of creating an organizational unit.
7. Explain the process of creating a user account.
8. Explain the process of assigning a user to a group.
9. Explain the significance of a "context sensitive" object name.
10. Why is it important to preplan the NDS tree structure before actually starting to create one?

LAB #5A

Create a fictitious company. On paper, plan the NDS tree for this company. Include at least one tree, two branches, four groups, and eight users. Explain the process you would go through to implement your plan.

LAB #5B

Refer to the steps mentioned in this chapter and implement your plan developed from Lab 5A.

LAB #5C

Find an existing network. Identify and sketch out on paper the structure for the NDS tree. Include the tree, any branches that you notice, the groups, and at least some of the users.

LAB #5D

Look at your sketches produced in Lab 5C. Now, sketch out the organization's physical structure. You may want to draw a hierarchical organization chart for this purpose. Next, compare the NDS tree structure with the organization chart. Does the NDS tree structure reflect the actual organization's structure? If yes, explain. If not, what could have been done differently?

CHAPTER SIX

SETTING UP ACCOUNTS USING NETADMIN

INSPIRING MOMENT

After successfully working at a company for only a few months, you have been promoted to LAN administrator. It's Monday morning, and you are at your workstation and reading through your routine stack of notes, phone messages, and so forth. Suddenly you come across an urgent message from the Payroll Department. "To: LAN Administrator," it reads. "Our payroll data files have been sabotaged." You rush quickly down the hall to the payroll director's office. The payroll director announces that someone has been making unauthorized changes to personnel salary files. You discover that too many users have the rights to make changes to the Payroll Department's data directory. During your investigation, you discover that many users also have rights to change or even delete the company's customer database files.

QUESTIONS FOR THOUGHT

What would happen if suddenly all the customer files for the entire company got deleted? No longer could invoices go out to the customers. No longer could any correspondence take place. As a LAN administrator, you are responsible for setting up and managing user accounts. What should you do? How could this happen? Could it be a breach of security? Can incidences such as these be prevented? If so, to what extent and how? What would you do if data really did get damaged or changed? Would you hide the evidence? Would you start an investigation? How would you fix the problem? Could backing up the system help alleviate some of the problems?

CHALLENGE

When deciding on the appropriate rights to assign each user, think cautiously. Remember that users may think of how you set up their account or what rights you assign to them only if something goes wrong in this area.

Keep network documentation on what rights you assign to what user. Make notes (history file) of sabotages or other problems on the network. Only assign the necessary rights to each user. Remember that it's easier to give more rights later if needed than to clean up after a misuse of power.

CHAPTER OBJECTIVES

After finishing this chapter, you should be able to:

1. Identify and distinguish between ADMIN and user accounts.
2. Create individual accounts using the NETADMIN utility.
3. Assign trustee directory rights to the user accounts.
4. Explore Novell Directory Services (NDS) and what it means to choose a "context."
5. Identify how to change the context.

THE NETADMIN ACCOUNT

NETADMIN is a user menu utility located in the PUBLIC directory. To have access to LAN and maintain security, accounts are created. Without an account, a user cannot use an organization's LAN. To set up accounts, a person should have access to the ADMIN account or have been assigned ADMIN-equivalent privileges. In a class setting, this may not be possible. Students can view many of the settings to their own accounts, however, which should help the learning process. The only restriction is that students cannot change the settings.

LAN security is an important aspect of assigning trustee directory rights and setting up accounts. With proper training and care in deciding who should gain access to various parts of software and data, setting up and managing accounts can help a company or organization control and share resources on a LAN.

SETTING UP THE ACCOUNT AND VIEWING EXISTING ACCOUNTS

This section describes how administrators set up accounts on a LAN. Administrators are responsible for managing the overall operation of the LAN. Both ADMIN and ADMIN equivalents (another account status) have the power to create accounts. Users may find that this information clarifies how accounts are initially created.

The ADMIN account helps to maintain some source of control in the LAN environment. It is wise not to allow everyone access to this account; the more people with access to the administrator account, the more likely it is that the LAN will become harder to manage and control. The ADMIN account is created automatically when Novell NetWare is first installed. It is intended to allow one or two people the authority to oversee all aspects of the LAN. (If you do not have administrator privileges, log into your user account. Because each location has different procedures for logging in, contact your LAN administrator, manager, or instructor for help.)

First, the administrator would log into his or her account. ADMIN is an account name, but unlike a regular user account, the administrator account has more privileges assigned to it.

After logging into the LAN, the administrator runs a menu utility called NetAdmin, which stands for "network administration." In configuring (or setting up) accounts one at a time, NetAdmin is ideal. Because of its menu-style orientation (see Figure 6.1), it is easy to use.

PLACEMENT OF USER ACCOUNTS

Before creating user accounts, the administrator must first decide where in the Novell Directory Services (NDS) the users should be located. This is considered by Novell as a "must do" first step and is part of the planning of the NDS tree structure. The users on the system

```
NetAdmin  4.55           Thursday  May  18, 1999  1:53pm
Context: CONSULTANTS.abc_co
Login Name: Nancy.CONSULTANTS.abc_co

                    ┌─────────────────────────────────┐
                    │      NetAdmin Options           │
                    ├─────────────────────────────────┤
                    │   Manage Objects                │
                    │   Manage according to search    │
                    │   pattern                       │
                    │   Change context                │
                    │   Search                        │
                    └─────────────────────────────────┘
```

FIGURE 6.1
NetAdmin stands for network administration.

are considered "leaf objects." It is important to decide the context under which the new account will be set up. For example, is the new user a member of a particular organization and department? Rushing through this section too quickly could result in a user who works in one department, say, the development and planning department (.DEV.ABC_CO), getting an account accidentally set up in the operations department (.OPER.ABC_CO). Figure 6.2 shows one company's organizational chart.

MANAGING OBJECTS

The "Managing Objects" option, when selected from NetAdmin's main menu, brings up the "Object, Class" screen and allows a user to take a closer look at the NDS tree. As shown in Figure 6.3, it is common to have the server named after the organization itself. The SYS volume, actually named SERV1_SYS, contains the files and directories that will be used across the network. Notice that the print queue (the waiting line for printing), abcprintq_0, is also located in the root.

The administrator account, ADMIN, is also located in the root. ADMIN is an account created automatically by the system when the Novell NetWare operating system is first installed. The hypothetical company examined in this chapter is organized into departments. Each department (including outside consultants) is listed as an organizational unit in Figure 6.3. The "Object, Class" screen provides an easy way to view the organization's network structure. As the organization's network structure changes, the "Object, Class" screen will also change. Items may be added by pressing Insert and then answering a series of questions. Items may be removed by pressing Delete. Maintaining the "Object, Class" screen is one duty of a network administrator. As disk drives, departments, or users are added physically to the organization, the network administrator needs to provide the proper information to the network operating system (in this case, Novell NetWare).

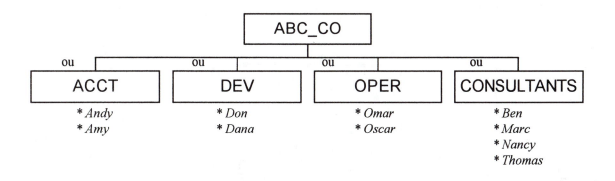

Context: Know the layout of your organization.
Under which Organizational Unit does each user go?

Note: Organizational Units are also known as containers.
       User Objects are also known as leaf objects (that go inside
       containers).

FIGURE 6.2
An organizational chart.

By highlighting the word "parent," located in the top right corner of the screen in Figure 6.3, the organization's network's NDS structure can be viewed level by level. The top left side of the screen indicates that the next level above is the parent or is a level above the current object. The current context is displayed in the upper left corner of the NETADMIN screen. Also displayed is the login name for the user currently logged in. Recall from Chapter 1 that organizational units are used to represent departments. Organizational units are also called containers because the "leaf objects" are placed inside them. In this example, the organization (O=) ABC Company (ABC_CO) has three main departments: accounting, development and planning, and operations (see Figure 6.2). Users are located in each department; that is, they are located in organizational units.

CHANGING THE CONTEXT

Any time a user wants to change the context (for example, to work with a different department), the "Change context" option from the main menu of NETADMIN (see Figure 6.1) should be chosen. Before creating a new user account, let's view an already existing one. In this example, "consultants" is the organizational unit (under the organization called ABC_CO). For the new context, enter CONSULTANTS.ABC_CO. See Figure 6.4.

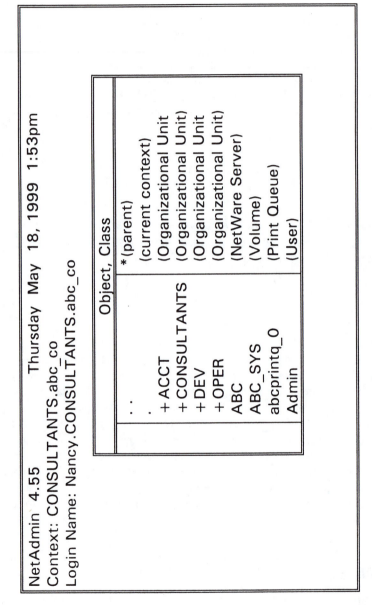

NetAdmin 4.55   Thursday May 18, 1999 1:53pm
Context: CONSULTANTS.abc_co
Login Name: Nancy.CONSULTANTS.abc_co

Object, Class	
. .	* (parent)
.	(current context)
+ ACCT	(Organizational Unit)
+ CONSULTANTS	(Organizational Unit)
+ DEV	(Organizational Unit)
+ OPER	(Organizational Unit)
ABC	(NetWare Server)
ABC_SYS	(Volume)
abcprintq_0	(Print Queue)
Admin	(User)

FIGURE 6.3
The "Object, Class" screen of NetAdmin.

```
NetAdmin 4.55            Thursday  May  18, 1999  1:53pm
Context: CONSULTANTS.abc_co
Login Name: Nancy.CONSULTANTS.abc_co

                ┌─────────────────────────────────────┐
                │        NetAdmin Options              │
                ├─────────────────────────────────────┤
                │    Manage Objects                    │
                │    Manage according to search        │
                │    pattern                           │
                │    Change context                    │
                │    Search                            │
                └─────────────────────────────────────┘

 ┌──────────────────────────────────────────────────────────────┐
 │ Enter context: .consultants.abc_co                             │
 └──────────────────────────────────────────────────────────────┘


Type the context you want or press <Insert> to browse for the context

Enter = Change context    Esc = Exit    Ins = Browse for objects   F1 = Help
```

FIGURE 6.4
Entering the context.

SELECTING THE OBJECT

The next step is to select the actual user object with which to work. From the NETADMIN menu, the administrator or manager selects the "Manage Objects" submenu from the "Available Topics" menu. This submenu allows the administrator to create or make changes to a user account. It also allows users to view information regarding their own personal accounts. When "Manage Objects" is selected, the "Object, Class" screen appears. Pressing Enter while highlighting a container object (in this case, an organizational unit) shows the next level of the network structure. Here the move was from the root to the organization unit for the consultants. Notice that users are normally located inside a container. These user accounts are known as leaf objects.

The "Object, Class" screen appears (Figure 6.5), which shows the contents of the container for consultants. At this point, the object "Nancy" is selected. To select a user, highlight an object name and press Enter. The "Actions for User" menu appears.

"ACTIONS FOR USER" MENU

The "Actions for User" menu, as shown in Figure 6.6, allows users to view how their accounts are set up. This menu gives users some idea about what they can and cannot do. This section explores some of the "Actions for User" options.

```
NetAdmin  4.55              Thursday  May  18, 1999  1:53pm
Context: CONSULTANTS.abc_co
Login Name: Nancy.CONSULTANTS.abc_co

        ┌──────────────────────────────────────────────────┐
        │                  Object, Class                   │
        ├────────────────────┬─────────────────────────────┤
        │   . .              │  (parent)                    │
        │   .                │  (current context)           │
        │   Ben              │  (User)                      │
        │   Marc             │  (User)                      │
        │   Nancy            │  (User)                      │
        │   Thomas           │  (User)                      │
        │                    │                              │
        │                    │                              │
        └────────────────────┴─────────────────────────────┘

Press  <F10>  to select the parent object, <Enter> to change the context.
```

FIGURE 6.5

"Object, Class" screen.

```
NetAdmin  4.55              Thursday  May  18, 1999  1:53pm
Context: CONSULTANTS.abc_co
Login Name: Nancy.CONSULTANTS.abc_co

        ┌──────────────────────────────────────────────────┐
        │               Actions for User: nancy            │
        ├──────────────────────────────────────────────────┤
        │   View or edit properties of this object         │
        │   Rename                                         │
        │   Move                                           │
        │   Delete                                         │
        │   View or edit rights to files and directories   │
        │   View or edit the trustees of this object       │
        └──────────────────────────────────────────────────┘



Press  <Enter>  to edit the properties of this object.

Enter = Select      Esc = Escape                    F1 = Help
```

FIGURE 6.6

Action menu allows for viewing user account details.

Viewing or Editing Rights to Files and Directories

The "View or edit rights to files or directories" selection is used to determine which directories and files a user is allowed to access and to what extent the directory or file may be used. A user who is allowed access to a directory or file is called a *trustee* of that directory or file. The privileges assigned to the user that indicate the extent to which he or she can use the file are called *rights*. When this selection is chosen, the user is prompted for the "Volume object name" (see Figure 6.7). As discussed in Chapter 1, the file server's hard drive has one or more volumes containing NetWare software directories such as PUBLIC, SYSTEM, MAIL, LOGIN, and ETC. The volume also contains software applications and data that users may be sharing. Notice in Figure 6.7 that ABC_SYS is the name of the volume on the file server. Also, notice that a period is keyed in after the volume object name "ABC_SYS." After keying in the volume name and pressing Enter, the "Rights to files and/or directories" screen reappears. Press the F10 function key (display list). The user's "Trustee directory, rights" screen now appears (see Figure 6.7).

Notice that this account does not have any rights assigned. This account does not need any rights assigned to it because it is set up as an ADMIN-equivalent account. ADMIN and ADMIN-equivalent user accounts do not need special permission to access directories and files; they have full reign of the system.

Let's look at another user account to get a better idea of directory and file trustee rights. Go back to "Manage Objects" and choose a user account called "Thomas." Notice that after going through the same steps for the user named "Thomas," the "Trustee directory, rights" screen appears (see Figure 6.8). All the directories or files to which a user has rights are listed on the left side of the screen. In this example, the directory is USERS/THOMAS. On the right side of the screen, [RWCEMFA] indicates that user Thomas has read, write, create, erase, modify, file scan, and access control rights to the directory. (This particular directory, located under USERS, is known as a home directory. It's a private directory containing the user's personal files and directories.) Notice in Figure 6.8 that this user has an entry that appears on the "Trustee, directory rights" screen. Each user is entrusted to use certain files or directories. The administrator or person with supervisory or access control rights can assign trustee rights to users. Refer back to Chapter 5 for a description of available rights.

Viewing or Editing the Trustee of This Object

From the "Trustees of this object" menu, there are three available options: "Inherited rights filters," "Trustees," and "Effective rights" (see Figure 6.9). The following section briefly highlights inherited rights filters. See the RIGHTS command line utility found in Chapter 9 for more information.

Inherited Rights Filters   If a person is given rights at one level of the directory structure, those rights also apply to any subdirectories below that level. Inherited rights filters, however, may block certain rights from trickling down to lower subdirectories. For example, user Henry has been assigned the read, file scan, write, and create (RFWC) rights to a particular directory called REPORTS. Under the REPORTS directory is a subdirectory called YEARLY. If no inherited rights filter (IRF) is applied to the YEARLY directory, user Henry will have the same rights (RFWC) to this directory. If an IRF is applied, Henry will have RFWC rights only if the IRF also has those rights.

```
NetAdmin 4.55          Thursday May 18, 1999  1:53pm
Context: CONSULTANTS.abc_co
Login Name: Nancy.CONSULTANTS.abc_co

              Actions for User: Nancy

              Rights to files and/or directories

    Volume object name        ABC_SYS.:
    Beginning Path:
    Directories/Files:        Directory
    Trustee Search Depth:     All subdirectories

                    Trustee directory, rights

                          (Empty List)



Press <Enter> to view/edit;  <F5> to mark multiple;  <Insert> to add.

Enter = Accept     F5 = Mark     Ins = Add     Del = Delete  Esc = Exit     F1 = Help
```

FIGURE 6.7
"Rights to files and/or directories" screen.

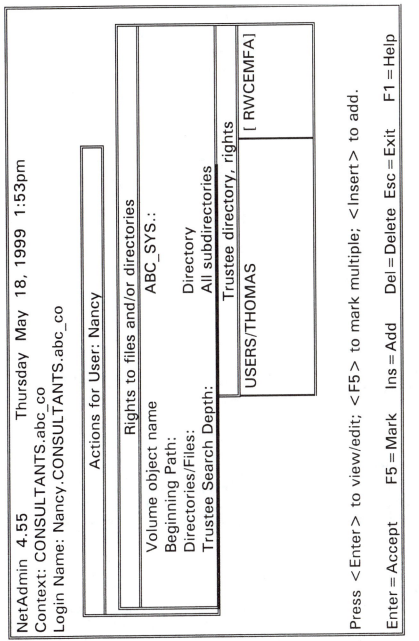

NetAdmin 4.55   Thursday May 18, 1999 1:53pm
Context: CONSULTANTS.abc_co
Login Name: Nancy.CONSULTANTS.abc_co

Actions for User: Nancy

Rights to files and/or directories

Volume object name   ABC_SYS.:
Beginning Path:
Directories/Files: Directory
Trustee Search Depth: All subdirectories

Trustee directory, rights

USERS/THOMAS   [RWCEMFA]

Press <Enter> to view/edit; <F5> to mark multiple; <Insert> to add.

Enter = Accept   F5 = Mark   Ins = Add   Del = Delete   Esc = Exit   F1 = Help

FIGURE 6.8
Trustee directory for Thomas's account.

```
NetAdmin 4.55              Thursday  May  18,  1999  1:53pm
Context: CONSULTANTS.abc_co
Login Name: Nancy.CONSULTANTS.abc_co

    ┌─────────────────────────────────────────────────────┐
    │           Actions for User: Nancy                    │
    │  ┌──────────────────────────┐ this object            │
    │  │  Trustees of this object │                         │        pattern
    │  │  ┌───────────────────────┤                         │
    │  │  │ Inherited rights filter│                        │
    │  │  │ Trustees               │ s and directories      │
    │  │  │ Effective rights       │ f this object          │
    │  └──┴───────────────────────┘                         │
    └─────────────────────────────────────────────────────┘

Press <Enter> to edit the inherited rights filter for this object and its
properties.

Enter = Accept      Esc = Exit                     F1 = Help
```

FIGURE 6.9
"Trustees of this object" screen.

Notes Regarding Rights

See Chapter 8 for the rights available in Novell NetWare.

WORKING WITH HELP

By pressing the F1 function key (help) while on the "Trustee directory, rights" screen, more detail regarding these rights appears (see Figure 6.10). Notice the directions at the bottom of the screen. Use the Page Up and Page Down keys to scroll through the help screens, and press Escape to exit.

MANAGE ACCORDING TO SEARCH PATTERN

If an organization is very large and has many users, printers, or disk volumes, the "Search patterns" screen can help locate information on a particular object. From NETADMIN's main menu (see Figure 6.1), select "Manage according to search pattern." For example, at the search patterns prompt "Enter object name," key in the name of a user, such as Nancy. At the object class prompt, choose user; otherwise, the computer will assume that you do

NetAdmin 4.55   Thursday May 18, 1999 1:52pm
Context: CONSULTANTS.abc_co

                        Trustee Assignments

   This screen lists all trustees of this object and each of its properties.

   You can add or delete trustees, or change the rights of any trustees that
   are listed.

   The list is organized by property, with rights to the object listed first.

   Procedures:

      To add a new trustee, press <Insert>.
      To delete an existing trustee, highlight it with the arrow keys, then
      press <Delete>.
      To see the list of rights that a trustee has to a property, highlight it
      with the arrow keys and press <Enter>.
      To return to the Access Control menu, press <Esc>.

   Property Rights

   To scroll through additional help, use the down and up arrow keys.

   Esc = Exit Help PgDn = Next Screen PgUp = Previous Screen   Alt + F1 = More

FIGURE 6.10
Help with rights.

```
NetAdmin  4.55                Thursday  May  18, 1999  1:53pm
Context: CONSULTANTS.abc_co
Login Name: Nancy.CONSULTANTS.abc_co
```

```
                        Search patterns
Enter object name:            *

Object class:                 /All classes/

Show alias class (Y/N):       No
```

```
 Select a specific object or a wildcard pattern to browse.

Enter = Edit   F10 = Save   Esc = Exit                    F1 = Help
```

FIGURE 6.11
Search patterns.

not know which object type you are interested in and will look through the list of different types of objects before finding the user Nancy's account (see Figures 6.11 and 6.12).

In Figure 6.11, an asterisk signifies "all" possibilities. In Figure 6.12, we are looking for a user on the network by the name of Nancy. Some special keys are noted at the bottom of the screen. To make changes to a particular line, simply position your cursor on that line and press Enter; this will put you in the editing mode. Once the screen is filled in, press the F10 function key to save and process the selections. To change your mind and abort and exit this particular search, press Escape.

The F1 function key provides further information about this screen. Because we specifically requested to find the user Nancy, when the "Object, Class" screen comes again, it will only have Nancy listed on it, even if other users share the same context as Nancy (see Figure 6.13). (Also see Figure 6.5. Notice that there are more consultants than Nancy.) To view account information for user Nancy, simply highlight the name and press Enter. Upon doing so, the "Actions for User" menu should appear on the screen. From this menu, various details regarding the user Nancy can be found. For example, by selecting "Rights to files and/or directories," it's possible to see which files or directories this user is allowed to access.

SUMMARY

This chapter explored how to set up user accounts and manage group assignments using the menu utility called NETADMIN. To set up user accounts, administrator or equivalent authority is needed. A user may view the settings of his or her own account. Chang-

```
┌──────────────────────────────────────────────────────────────┐
│ NetAdmin 4.55            Thursday May 18, 1999 1:53pm          │
│ Context: CONSULTANTS.abc_co                                    │
│ Login Name: Nancy.CONSULTANTS.abc_co                           │
│                                                                │
│              ┌──────────────────────────┐                     │
│         ┌────┴──────────────────────────┴─────────────┐       │
│         │              Search patterns                │       │
│         ├──────────────────────────────────────────────┤      │
│         │  Enter object name:        nancy             │       │
│         │                                              │       │
│         │  Object class:             User              │       │
│         │                                              │       │
│         │  Show alias class (Y/N):   No                │       │
│         └──────────────────────────────────────────────┘      │
│                                                                │
│   Select a specific object or a wildcard pattern to browse.    │
│                                                                │
│  Enter = Edit  F10 = Save  Esc = Exit              F1 = Help   │
│                                                                │
└──────────────────────────────────────────────────────────────┘
```

FIGURE 6.12
Search patterns—object class—Nancy.

ing context allows a user to explore different sections of the NDS tree. The Novell Directory Services (NDS) tree structure is generally based on the company's own hierarchical chart. NETADMIN is also useful for viewing or editing file and directory rights. Trustees are assigned rights at a particular directory level. Effective rights consist of rights that have been assigned or inherited and have not been filtered out by an inherited rights filter (IRF).

EXERCISES

1. Define the following:
   a. network administrator
   b. print queue
   c. SYS volume
   d. container
   e. leaf objects
   f. home directory
   g. rights
   h. trustee
   i. inherited rights filter

NetAdmin 4.55   Thursday   May   18, 1999   1:53pm
Context: CONSULTANTS.abc_co
Login Name: Nancy.CONSULTANTS.abc_co

Object, Class
. .   (parent)
.   (current context)
Nancy (User)

Press <F10> to select the parent object, <Enter> to change the context.

Enter = Change context/Select   F10 = View or edit   F5 = Mark   Ins = Add   Alt + F1 = More

FIGURE 6.13
Object, class—user—Nancy.

2. What do the following stand for?

   a. NDS

   b. O

   c. OU

   d. SRWCEMFA

   e. IRF

   f. *

   g. NetAdmin

3. Briefly explain the difference between being an administrator and being a regular user.
4. What is the purpose of assigning trustee directory rights?
5. List the rights available with Novell NetWare 4.1x and the meaning of each.
6. Explain what a context is and how to change the context.
7. Why is it important to know the structure of the organization when setting up accounts?
8. Explain what is meant by organizations, organizational units, and leaf objects.
9. Under what circumstances might a person use an inherited rights filter?
10. Why is it important to know how to use NetAdmin even if you are not an administrator or manager?
11. If you want to entrust user Abel to the directory SYS:GROWTH, but you do not want him to remove any existing files, make any new files, or change any existing ones, which rights should you give him?
12. In which directory is NetAdmin located?
13. Explain how the help feature is accessed and under what circumstances a user might access it.
14. What is the purpose of the "Search pattern" screen?

LAB #6

In this lab, you will use NetAdmin to view information regarding your user account and also the structure of your network's NDS.

1. Log onto the LAN and bring up the NetAdmin menu by typing the word "*NETADMIN*." Write down the available topics that appear.

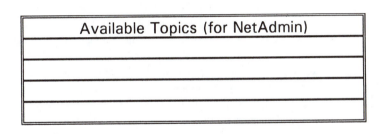

Available Topics (for NetAdmin)

2. Draw a picture of your organization's hierarchical structure. Make sure to identify where you fit into the structure.

3. Choose "Change context." Key in your context (for example, CONSULTANTS. ABC_CO). Write down your context in case you need it later.

4. Select your account name and press Enter.
5. List the options available under "Actions for User."
6. Select "Rights to files and directories" for your account. Which rights does your account have? List the trustee directories and the rights. What can you do in each directory?
7. Press Escape until you arrive back at the "Object, Class" screen. Highlight the line that reads

`. . ¦ (parent)`

and press Enter until you are back as far as possible.
8. Can you find your account information by using the "Object, Class" screen? Walk your way through by pressing Enter on the appropriate context items; do not use "Change context." As you do this, draw a picture of your network's structure.
9. Does your network's structure match your organization's hierarchical chart? Explain any differences.

COMMON TASKS

Part III explores everyday operations such as file management and command utilities.

CHAPTER SEVEN   NETUSER Utility

CHAPTER EIGHT   FILER Utility

CHAPTER NINE   Command Line Utilities

NETUSER UTILITY

INSPIRING MOMENT

Congratulations on your new promotion; you have worked hard for it. In addition to having a new office, you also have a new account on the network. You want to get off to a good start by staying organized. You want to have both the directories for the users for whom you are responsible and your directories well organized in a tree fashion. You also want to communicate and work well with people in a professional manner. How do you accomplish all this?

Some people have briefcases, containers, boxes, and so forth, to organize tools used most often; such organization leads to a day that flows smoothly. Tools are easy to find. Similarly, organized files with labels on them make it easy to access important papers as they are needed. In Chapter 2, you explored directory management and learned how files are grouped into different directories according to their function. You also learned that map drives make finding and working with the files in these directories more manageable. In this chapter, you will build on this foundation. You will learn where to go to create map drives and will explore other options available, such as selecting your printer and sending messages. The goal is to stay organized, and NETUSER makes it easy to do so.

QUESTIONS FOR THOUGHT

Is your daily life organized? Do you have to search everywhere to find a pencil, a pen, paper, or maybe a computer disk? Do you constantly dig through an unorganized file cabinet that contains files with no labels? Could a LAN environment help you? What are some benefits of having an organized LAN environment? Would it be beneficial to have an easy way to find files and directories on the LAN? Would the users at the organization for which you work (or plan to work for) benefit from being able to send messages?

CHALLENGE

In Chapters 2 and 3, directory structures and mapping were explored. Use the skills that you have acquired, plus NETUSER, to organize your home directory. Also, set up your system so that you can go to your subdirectories and run software applications quickly. As you learn how to send messages with the NETUSER utility, respect people's rights and feelings. A LAN should be free of obscenity or profanity. See the common courtesy rules found in the Preface. Keep your working environment clean and professional, and have fun!

CHAPTER OBJECTIVES

After finishing this chapter, you should be able to:

1. Move between file servers if working in a multiserver environment.
2. Create logical drive mappings with NETUSER.
3. Create search drive mappings with NETUSER.
4. View a list of users and groups currently logged in.
5. Send messages to users and groups.
6. Change the default drive.

NETUSER OPTIONS

In the NetWare networking environment, tools used daily are found in a PUBLIC menu utility called NETUSER, which allows a user to access data files quickly, run software application programs, find out who is currently logged in and send messages to those people, and switch between different file servers.

NETUSER provides a menu orientation to several commands normally encountered during a particular work session. Common NETUSER commands include MAP, USERLIST, and SEND. (See also command line utilities in Chapter 9.) The "Available Options" menu (Figure 7.1) appears when NETUSER is keyed in.

PRINTING

Printing and sharing of printers is a major reason companies choose to have a LAN system. After all, not many companies can afford to attach a laser printer to each user's computer, and even if they could afford it, it would not be financially responsible. Users do not normally spend 100 percent of their time printing; more often, they spend time planning, developing, and creating on the computer. Printers are used to print the output or results once everything else is done. It is no wonder that companies choose to have users share printer hardware resources via a LAN.

FIGURE 7.1
NETUSER's "Available Options" menu.

```
Available Options
───────────────────────────────
     |     Printing
     |     Messages
     |     Drives
     |     Attachments
     |
```

Network Printers

Network printers are actually defined and set up using other utilities such as PCONSOLE. (See Chapter 11 for more information on PCONSOLE.) The NETUSER menu utility allows users to share printers once the setup is complete. By selecting "Printing" from NETUSER's "Available Options" screen, a list of the workstation printer ports (available ports) will appear on the screen.

Printer Port

A printer port may be set up as either a local or a network printer port. A local printer port is used when a private printer is attached to a specific workstation solely for one user's individual use. With network port assignments, the local operating system (DOS) is tricked into thinking that the printer is attached to the workstation; actually, the printer may be across the room, far away from the actual workstation making the printing request. From the "Available Ports" screen, users can control whether the printer ports are designated as local or network ports.

Assigning a Port for Network Use

The following steps are used to designate that the port is to point to a network printer:

1. To assign the port as a network port, first highlight the port of interest and press Enter.
2. Next, select "Change Printers."
3. A list of printers and print queues (waiting line for print jobs) appears. Highlight either a printer or a print queue and press Enter. If no printers or print queues appear on the list, then press Insert and choose a different context in which to search for the printer or queue.

Recall from Chapter 5's discussion of context that the NDS is organized in an upside-down treelike design. This upside-down tree is broken up into organization containers ("O="), organizational unit containers ("OU="), and leaves. A print queue, like a user account, is represented as a leaf inside a container. For example, the accounting department may have a container assigned with the user accounts and print queues represented as leaves within that department's container. Print queues are usually placed in an organizational unit. If the goal is to have just the accounting department able to use a particular printer's queue (or waiting line), the printer's queue is placed in that department's container.

Check Jobs Waiting to Print

To check the status of a job waiting to print, such as a report, memo, or program source code, follow these steps:

1. Choose "Printing" from the NETUSER menu.
2. Choose the port to which the job was sent.
3. Select "Print Jobs." A list of print jobs for the chosen port (queues) appears.

MESSAGES

Communication is a prime reason companies opt to use a LAN. Messages may be sent to any user individually or to a group of users, if they are logged in at the time. If they are not logged in, they do not receive the message and the message is not saved for them. Once the "Messages" option has been selected from NETUSER's "Available Options" menu, a submenu appears. This submenu contains three choices, shown in Figure 7.2.

Send Messages to Groups

The "Send Messages to Groups" option allows the user to view a list of the names of groups in which at least one member is logged in. It allows a user to send a message to the entire group. This menu is fairly straightforward and easy to use.

Send Messages to Users

The "Send Messages to Users" option provides a list of current users logged into the system. It allows a user to view more information regarding another user. It also allows a user to send messages. This option is also straightforward and easy to use.

Set Receive Message

The "Set Receive Message" option allows a user to inform the network operating system whether or not messages are to be received and displayed on that user's screen. If "Receive Message" is set to OFF, the user is specifying that messages are to be blocked from appearing on the screen. Any users attempting to send a message to that particular station while the "Receive Message" setting is off would receive an error message informing the sender that the message was not permitted to go through.

Note that the user and group lists are context sensitive. The users to whom someone is trying to send a message may be in a different department; thus their account name may be represented as a leaf inside a different organizational unit container. Unless the organizational unit in which to find them is specified, they will not receive the messages sent. The context, as discussed in Chapter 1, tells the NOS which organizational unit container to search to find the user. To specify a different context than the one currently set as default, press the Insert key. Once Insert has been pressed, NOS will prompt to key in the

FIGURE 7.2
NETUSER's "Available Options" submenu for messages.

Available Options
─────────────────────────

| Send Messages to Users
| Send Messages to Groups
| Set Receive Message: OFF
|

context for the user to whom a message is trying to be sent. If a context is not specified, the NOS will simply search the current context in the NetWare Directory Services™ (NDS). This would result in the NOS not finding users located in other organizational units.

DRIVES

Users frequently find themselves working with drive letter assignments. There are two main types of drives: logical drives and search drives. In both cases, a user takes the file server's hard drive and/or storage media and logically (rather than physically) divides it into smaller sections. The drive is thus more manageable. This section explores logical drives and search drives in more detail.

Drive Mappings

The "Drive Mappings" option displays current map assignments. If additional map assignments are needed, a user may press Insert to add them.

As mentioned earlier, one type of network drive assignment is called a "logical" drive assignment. For example, although the file server's volume is labeled "SERV1_VOL1," the NOS can be instructed to view certain assigned areas of that volume as if the area were a drive by itself. Here the NOS is instructed to view a user's home directory as if it were an H: drive:

```
MAP H:=SERV1_VOL1:USERS\USER01
```

Because there is really no physical drive H:, this drive is commonly referred to as a logical (or pretend) drive.

The Purpose of Logical Drives

Assigning drive letters to long path names allows users to follow a particular path more rapidly. Consider the following examples, and see how fast a user can move to a particular directory once a drive letter has been assigned. In addition, there is less chance of keyboarding errors when drive letters are assigned.

To change to a different directory, the user may key in the change directory (CD) command:

```
F:\>CD \USERS\USER01
F:\USERS\USER01>
```

To change to a different directory that already has a logical drive letter assigned, the user may simply key in the drive name, such as H:, and press Enter. On the screen, it looks like this:

```
F:\>H:
H:\USERS\USER01>
```

Notice that this last example has 15 fewer keystrokes to enter than the first example! Consider the time savings during an eight-hour day in which a user constantly moves between different directories.

Logical drive mappings also cut down the number of keystrokes needed for entering many of the DOS commands and NetWare command line utilities (CLUs). Instead of long path names, users can key in the logical drive name. Consider the following example of NetWare's NCOPY command line utility:

```
NCOPY H:\*.* A:
NCOPY SERV1_VOL1:USERS\USER01\*.* A:
```

Both examples accomplish the same task. All the files in the USER01 directory are copied to the floppy disk in drive A:. The first example, however, requires fewer keystrokes because H: is already mapped to the path SERV1_VOL1:USERS\USER01. NCOPY and other CLUs are discussed in Chapter 9. Commonly used DOS commands are discussed in Chapter 3.

It is advisable to put the map assignment commands used most often in a login script. Map drive assignments are not permanent; they reside in the workstation's RAM. When a user logs out, these assignments are no longer in effect. If the MAP command is placed in a login script, then every time the user logs in, the map assignment is re-created in RAM.

NETUSER and Drive Mapping

NETUSER can be used to view current map assignments and to add new ones. Keep in mind that once a user logs out, any maps not found in the login script will no longer be in effect. If a user wishes to have the new map assignment for every logging-in session, the following way of creating a map assignment is *not* recommended. On the other hand, if a user is working on a special project and only needs the map assignment for this particular project, then using NETUSER in this way is recommended.

To process a map assignment using the temporary approach, follow these steps:

1. Key in the word "netuser" to access the menu utility.
2. From the "Available Options" menu, select "Drives."
3. From the "Drives" menu, select "Drive Mapping." A list of current drive mappings will now appear.
4. Press the Insert key to indicate to the network operating system to add a new drive assignment.
5. When the prompt asks you if you want to map the new drive assignment as a directory root, answer "no." If you answer "yes," your prompt will appear as H:\>, for example, instead of H:\USERS\USER01>. Most users prefer to have the screen prompt display the path in which they are working.
6. When prompted, fill in the directory path.

Logical Drives

Assigning logical drive names allows users to move quickly to different directories. Logical drive names allow users to enter DOS commands and CLUs with fewer keystrokes than otherwise, thus saving valuable time. Logical drive assignments commonly point to directories containing the user's personal data, such as in these examples:

```
MAP H:=SERV1_VOL1:USERS\USER01
MAP I:=SERV1_VOL1:USERS\USER01\PROJECTS
MAP J:=SERV1_VOL1:USERS\USER01\LETTERS
```

A user can easily work with personal data files found in these subdirectories. By the way, the highest directory level for a particular user is called the user's home directory, which in this example is SERV1_VOL1:USERS\USER01. Logical drives, as mentioned, are assigned by using the MAP command line utility or the NETUSER menu utility. Logical drives usually point to the user's home directory and other subdirectories containing data files. A directory that contains files used by more than one user is called a shared data directory. Logical drives may also point to shared data directories, as illustrated here:

```
MAP K:=SERV1_VOL1:USERS\REDTEAM
MAP L:=SERV1_VOL1:SHARED\CLIENTS
```

Logical drive assignments greatly ease the task of managing home directories and other subdirectories assigned to individual users. They also make it easier to manage shared data directories. Logical drive maps normally point to data directories. Search drive maps normally point to application directories. The next section discusses search drive maps and the DOS PATH command, which make it easier and faster to access program or executable files located in application directories.

DOS PATH Command

Because the NetWare search map is similar to the DOS PATH command, reviewing the DOS command will help when learning the LAN counterpart.

The PATH command is often located in a file called AUTOEXEC.BAT. To check, use this command:

```
C:\>EDIT AUTOEXEC.BAT
```

Remember that AUTOEXEC.BAT is like cruise control on a car. This batch file automatically runs every time the computer is cold booted (turned on) or warm booted (reset). Any commands placed in the file will execute at the time of booting. Consider the following PATH statement:

```
PATH C:\;C:\WINDOWS;C:\DOS;C:\WP;C:\DB
```

This command provides the local operating system—in this case, DOS—a list of directory paths through which to search if a program was requested and that program was not immediately found. For example, with

```
C:\>WP
```

the user is attempting to run the word-processing program called WP.EXE. Note that in DOS, if an executable file ends with .EXE, .COM, or .BAT, it is not necessary to key in the file's extension. This command would not immediately result in the execution of the WP.EXE program. The local operating system, DOS, would first need to locate the WP.EXE file before it could run it. In the preceeding example, the computer would do the following:

1. It would look through the root directory of the C: drive for the WP.EXE program, with no success.
2. Next, it would look through the C:\WINDOWS directory with no success.
3. It would then look through the C:\DOS directory, with no success.

4a. Finally, it would look through the C:\WP directory, find the WP.EXE program, and run it.

or

4b. If, after searching all the directories listed in the PATH statement, the program was not found, an error message, "Bad Command or File Name," will appear.

PATH versus Search Mapping

The NetWare search map works in the same way as the DOS PATH statement, with two major exceptions. First, a separate map assignment, or command, is needed for each directory path through which the user wishes the network operating system to search. Second, it's common to use search map assignments to define directory paths for running programs or applications that are stored on the file server's volume. Consider the following example:

```
MAP S1:=SERV1_SYS:PUBLIC
```

Here the search map assignment conveys to the network operating system that the PUBLIC directory, located on volume SERV1_SYS:, is the first place it should look for an executable file if it's not found in the current directory.

The WHOAMI command is actually a program (WHOAMI.EXE) located in the PUBLIC directory. It provides information about who is logged in at the workstation where the command was keyed in.

```
F:\>WHOAMI
```

Note that if the message "Bad Command or File Name" comes up at this point, the user should check to ensure that a search map has been assigned to the PUBLIC directory. Once again, because maps are temporary, any MAP command that a user anticipates using each time he or she logs in should be placed in a login script. NETUSER may be used to make both temporary logical drive map assignments and search map assignments.

To assign a search map using NETUSER, follow these steps:

1. Key in the word "netuser."
2. Select "Drives" from the "Available Options" menu.
3. Select "Search Mapping" from the "Drives" menu. A list of currently assigned search maps appears.
4. Press Insert to indicate to the network operating system that a search map drive is about to be created.
5. When prompted to do so, key in the directory path for the search.

ATTACHMENT

Before a user can log into the network, the workstations must first be attached to a file server. *Attached* means that the file server acknowledges that the computer is not just a stand-alone PC; it's a workstation capable of operating in the LAN environment. Recall from Chapter 2, that key files have to be installed on the PC before it's truly a workstation. The workstation installation process resulted in the NetWare Client being loaded onto the hard drive at the local workstation. Once the LOGIN.EXE screen appears, the workstation is attached to, or recognized by, a file server on the network.

It is possible to have more than one file server on the same network. In a multiserver environment, a user may attach and log into more than one file server during a single work session. The "Attachments" option found in the NETUSER menu utility allows a user to hop over to another file server, so to speak; once recognized by or attached to the other file server, the user is prompted for an account name and password. The "Attachments" option is located on NETUSER's main menu.

Once "Attachments" is selected, another menu appears. This new menu allows users to select the file server to which they wish to attach by selecting the "Server Information" option from the "Attachments" menu. When selected, "Server Information" lists servers to which the user is currently attached and logged in. A user may switch between these servers by simply highlighting the one interested in and pressing Enter. A user is already logged into the servers appearing on this list; therefore, pressing Delete on any of them results in the user being logged out of that particular file server. The Insert key brings up another list of servers, those to which the user has not yet logged in but which are available for use. Highlighting a server sends a signal to the new file server that the workstation would like to be recognized and log in. The new server then prompts the user for an account name and password. The "Attachments" submenu also gives the option of changing your login script and password. The steps are straightforward once the "Attachments" submenu is reached. Follow the directions found on the screen.

Attachment is fairly versatile; it allows a user to hop between file servers already logged into; it allows a user to attach and log into file servers that the user is not yet recognized by, and it also allows the user to change his or her login script and password. Login scripts are discussed more in Chapter 13.

SUMMARY

The NETUSER utility is fairly straightforward. It provides an easy way to create logical and search drive maps, to change between servers, to send messages, and to change a user's login script and password.

EXERCISES

1. Define and/or explain the following:
   a. attachment
   b. port
   c. network printer
   d. logical drive
   e. search mapping
   f. "Bad Command or File Name"
2. Where is the NETUSER utility located, and who can use it?
3. The "Attachments" option is frequently used in what environment?

4. How do you send messages to a user using NETUSER? How else can you send messages?
5. How do you send messages to a group using NETUSER? How else can you send messages?
6. How do you create logical drive maps using NETUSER? How else can you create them?
7. How do you create search drive maps using NETUSER? How else can you create them?
8. How can you change the default drive using NETUSER? How else can you change it?

LAB #7

This lab will give you a chance to practice routine tasks that most users encounter daily. By the end of this lab, you should be able to create both logical and search drive maps assignments. You should also be able to send messages to individual users and to a group of users. You will have the opportunity to put the map assignment into your user login script so that it will automatically execute every time you log in. You will also practice changing your password. You will be managing your LAN environment today using NETUSER. By the end of the lab, you should discover that NETUSER is powerful yet fairly easy to work with.

1. Make a subdirectory inside your home directory. Next, map to that directory.
2. Map a search drive to one of the application directories to which you have rights.
3. Send a message to everyone in your group.
4. Send a message to a friend.
5. Add the maps assignments to your login script. (Test the login script.)
6. Change your password.
7. List the name(s) of the file server(s) available to you.

CHAPTER EIGHT

FILER UTILITY

INSPIRING MOMENT

Congratulations, you are performing well at your new network administration position. Your supervisor and colleagues continually compliment you on your expertise in NetWare 4.1x. Friday marks the end of your 90-day probationary period, and you can hardly wait! This company prides itself in choosing only the very best people to hire permanently. Once you become a permanent staff member, you are then entitled to company benefits such as paid vacations, medical insurance, and a 401K retirement plan. You notice that your supervisor has already begun to complete the temp-to-perm review forms required for all new personnel. As she fills out the review forms, your supervisor watches you more closely than ever before. You know that you have done well up to this point, yet you are nervous. The pressure of the final week as a temporary worker reminds you of preparing for finals at school.

As the week progresses, you continue to do your best. The Marketing Research Department has called on you to organize several of their statistical files on the computer. You recall lessons on directory management and carefully plan which files are going to be copied to which directories. The marketing team has been working all year on these statistical research files, so there are quite a few of them. They have data files from various surveys conducted by the survey teams throughout the community. They also have some custom-built programming applications designed especially for the marketing department for the analysis of the survey data. You are happy that you remember the steps for creating directories and assigning maps to the directories. Everything is going well. Then it happened!

You accidentally copied the statistical marketing programs on top of the survey data files. You accidentally chose "OK" when it asked to "overwrite existing file." The program files had the same name as the data files, so the data files accidentally got overwritten. Now what? The marketing team has invested a lot of time in these files! You inform your supervisor immediately. She walks out of her office without a word and leaves the building. You can tell that she is upset.

QUESTIONS FOR THOUGHT

Could this happen to you? What would you do if it does? Are there some precautions that you can take to prevent something like this from happening? Is there some way to get the lost files back? How do you think this would affect a new employee's review? Do you think that the way that the situation is handled will make a difference in how the supervisor reviews a new employee?

CHALLENGE

Find out as much as you can about managing files and directories. Practice file management operations as much as you can. When you are the person responsible for managing files, have an organized system for backing up your work. Also, acquaint yourself with the salvage options that allow you to bring back files that have been accidentally deleted. In any case, do your best. We all learn from our mistakes. This chapter explores FILER, a menu utility that helps managing files. Read on to learn how you can manage files effectively.

CHAPTER OBJECTIVES

After finishing this chapter, you should be able to:

1. Find the FILER utility and execute it.
2. Identify the options available through the FILER utility.
3. Explore information available on directories.
4. Explore changing drive pointer defaults.
5. View file information under a given directory.
6. Manipulate subdirectories by copying and moving files.
7. List the various FILER options that can be set by the user.
8. View information regarding the file server's volume.
9. Salvage files that have been accidentally deleted.
10. Purge (or permanently delete) files to make more space on the file server's hard drive.

FILER

FILER, which is shorthand for "file maintenance," allows for the management of directories and files. Users can explore different settings and can, if authorized, make changes in settings. Many of the tasks available under FILER can also be accomplished through command line utilities. In addition, the FILER utility of NetWare has a salvage feature that allows files to be brought back if they are accidentally deleted. NetWare also has directory and file attributes that can be placed on the files and directories to prevent accidental erasing.

NetWare's PUBLIC directory houses user menu utilities and command line utilities. The FILER menu utility, located in this PUBLIC directory, has options that appear similar to familiar DOS commands. See Figure 8.1. Although many of these topics are explored in detail in the end-of-chapter lab, brief descriptions are given here.

SELECT CURRENT DIRECTORY

To check information regarding a different directory, the "Select Current Directory" option should be chosen. If users do not remember the name of the directory, then after they choose "Select Current Directory," they may press the Insert key and the system will provide a list of directories from which to choose. After keying in or selecting the directory of interest, the user may choose the selection "Manage Files and Directories" again.

FIGURE 8.1
FILER's "Available Options" menu.

```
Available Options
═══════════════════════════════════════
|Manage Files and Directories
|Manage According to Search Patterns
|Select Current Directory
|View Volume Information
|Salvage Deleted Files
|Purge Deleted Files
|Set Default Filer Options
|
```

MANAGE FILES AND DIRECTORIES

When a user selects "Manage Files and Directories," the "Directory Contents" submenu appears on the screen (see Figure 8.2). This screen lists the files and directories contained under the directory currently chosen. At this point, the user has several options:

1. Change the directory path to a different level.
2. Manage one or more subdirectories.
3. Manage one or more files.
4. View and/or set directory information.

Change the Directory Path to a Different Level

There are three basic ways to move in the NDS tree:

1. To move back one level in the directory tree, a user should highlight ". . (parent)" and press Enter.

FIGURE 8.2
FILER's "Directory Contents" screen.

```
                 Directory Contents
─────────────────────────────────────────────────
    • •              (parent)
    \                (root)
    •                (current)
    ETC              (subdirectory)
    LOGIN            (subdirectory)
    MIGRATE          (subdirectory)
    PUBLIC           (subdirectory)
    SYSTEM           (subdirectory)
    TTS$LOG.ERR      (file)
    VOL$LOG.ERR      (file)
```

2. To move all the way back to the root directory, a user should highlight "\ (root)" and press Enter.

3. To move forward in the directory structure, a user should highlight one of the subdirectories, such as the PUBLIC directory in Figure 8.2. Once the subdirectory is highlighted, press Enter.

Once the subdirectory has been selected, the next step is to manage either the subdirectory or the files contained in the subdirectory.

Manage One or More Subdirectories

To manage a particular subdirectory, a user should highlight the subdirectory of interest from the "Directory Contents" menu (see Figure 8.2). Once the subdirectory has been highlighted, press the Select key, which is the F10 function key. After pressing F10, the "Subdirectory Options" submenu appears, as shown in Figure 8.3. From this menu a user can then copy, move, check rights, or view the directory information for the subdirectory selected.

To work with more than one subdirectory at a time, highlight each subdirectory, one by one, from the "Directory Contents" menu and press the Mark key, which is the F5 function key. After marking each of the subdirectories of interest, press the F10 Select key. A submenu called "Multiple Subdirectory Options" appears on the screen; see Figure 8.4. This submenu offers fewer options than the "Subdirectory Options" menu. The user may copy the subdirectories and set and/or view the owner's name, creation date, and rights. Note that to set—that is, to change—any information, the user must have the rights to do so.

Manage One or More Files

Users may choose to manage files in the same manner as that given for subdirectories. A user should select the files by highlighting the file name and pressing the F10 Select key while at the "Directory Contents" menu. If there are multiple files, the user highlights them one by one and presses the F5 Mark key. Once all the files of interest are selected, the user then presses the F10 Select key.

```
Subdirectory Options
=====================

| Copy Subdirectory's Files
| Copy Subdirectory's Structure
| Move Subdirectory's Structure
| Make This Your Current Dir
| View/Set Directory Information
| Rights List
```

FIGURE 8.3
Subdirectory selected from FILER's directory.

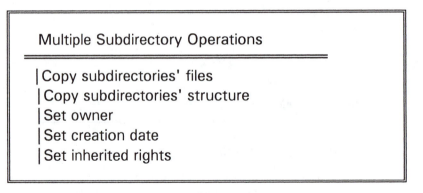

FIGURE 8.4
Multiple subdirectory operations selected from FILER's directory contents.

Next, either the "File Options" or the "Multiple file operations" submenu will appear on the screen. See Figures 8.5 and 8.6. The "File Options" menu allows a user to copy, move, view, check rights, and view and/or set the file's information details for a given file. The "Multiple file operations" screen does not permit the moving of the files, but users may choose to copy them.

View and/or Set Directory Information

Who owns a particular subdirectory? When was it created? Are there any special attributes (such as hide files) applied to this subdirectory? What rights does a particular user have to a particular directory? Which users have been entrusted to use a particular subdirectory? If one is allowed to save files to this subdirectory, is there a space limit? If so, how much?

These questions are all addressed by the "Directory Information" screen. There are two ways to get to this screen:

1. From the "Directory Contents" submenu, select the directory of interest by highlighting the subdirectory's name and pressing Enter. Next, highlight "• |(current)" (see Figure 8.2) and press Enter. "View/Set Directory Information" should appear. Press Enter again to select this option.

FIGURE 8.5
FILER's options screen.

```
File Options
───────────────────────
|Copy File
|Move File
|View File
|Rights List
|View/Set File Information
```

Multiple file operations

| Copy marked files
| Set owner
| Set creation date
| Set last modified date
| Set last accessed date
| Set attributes
| Set inherited rights

FIGURE 8.6
Multiple file operations selected from FILER's directory contents.

2. Another way to get to the "Directory Information" screen is to select "View/Set Directory Information" from the "Subdirectory Options" menu.

The "Directory Information" screen contains the following details regarding the particular subdirectory selected:

- Directory owner
- Date created
- Time created
- Directory attributes
- Inherited rights
- Trustees
- Limit space (yes/no)
- Directory space limit: nnnn kilobytes

Assign Trustees and Their Rights Using the "Directory Information" Screen

Recall from the discussion in Chapter 2 regarding directories that to use a particular directory, users must have permission. Those who have been granted permission to use a particular directory are called *trustees* of that directory; they have been entrusted to use the directory properly. The extent to which they can use the directory is governed by the assignment of rights. Rights dictate to the system what the users can or cannot do inside the directory for which they have been assigned as a trustee. The rights available in NetWare 4.x include the following:

- **File scan:** The trustee may view a listing of file and subdirectory names within the assigned directory.
- **Read:** The trustee may view the contents of the files located in the assigned directory.
- **Create:** The trustee may create files and subdirectories within the assigned directory.
- **Write:** The trustee may overwrite and make changes to files and subdirectories within the assigned directory.

- **Erase:** The trustee may remove files and directories within the assigned directory.
- **Modify:** The trustee may change the attributes (such as hidden) for files and subdirectories contained in the assigned directory.
- **Access control:** The trustee may assign other users as trustees for this particular directory and any files or subdirectories contained inside it. The trustees may only assign up to the level of rights that they have been assigned.
- **Supervisory:** The trustee has all the rights mentioned to the assigned directory and for all subdirectories contained therein. Note that all the other rights can be blocked or prevented from applying to lower-level directories; once the supervisory right has been assigned, it applies to the NDS tree structure from the point assigned going down into the directory levels below and cannot be blocked.

From the "Directory Information" screen, new trustees may be assigned for the current directory. To assign a new trustee for the currently selected directory, highlight "Trustees" and press Enter. A list of current trustees for this directory appears on the screen. Press the Insert key and the system will prompt for the account name of the new trustee. If a user changes his or her mind, a trustee can be removed from the list by highlighting the trustee's account name and pressing the Delete key. Once the trustee's account name has been added to the trustee list, the default rights of read and file scan are assigned. To change this assignment—that is, to add more rights or lessen the number of rights assigned—do the following:

- Once again, go to the trustees list for that directory. Do this by highlighting and pressing Enter where it says "Trustee" on the "Directory Information" screen.
- Highlight the particular trustee of interest and press Enter.
- A list of assigned rights will appear on the screen. To remove one of the rights from the list, simply highlight the right that is to be removed and press the Delete key. To remove more than one right, use the F5 (Mark) key to mark each of the unwanted rights, and then press Delete.
- To add more rights, press the Insert key. A list of rights not yet assigned for this user will appear on the screen. Highlight the right needing to be added and press Enter. To add more than one right, use the F5 Mark key to select them, then press Insert. Press Escape when done to return to the "Directory Information" screen.

The "Directory Information" screen provides a short summary of security and management aspects regarding the directory. It also allows a user to modify the assignment of trustees and their rights to particular directories. Be aware, however, that to make such modifications, the user must have the access control right, which gives permission to give that person's rights away to other users.

MANAGE ACCORDING TO SEARCH PATTERNS

Search patterns are helpful if a user wants to view just a particular set of file or subdirectory names. For example, a user may want to see all the file names that have an extension of .BAT if the file names start with the word PROJECT but not with the word PROJECT1. Setting up a search pattern can accomplish this. When the user selects "Manage According to Search Patterns" from FILER's main menu, the screen called "Set the search pattern and filter" appears, as displayed in Figure 8.7.

```
┌─────────────────────────────────────────────────────────────┐
│                 Set the search pattern and filter            │
├─────────────────────────────────────────────────────────────┤
│                                                               │
│   Pattern:  *.*                                               │
│                                                               │
│   Exclude directory patterns:  ↓ (empty)                      │
│   Include directory patterns:  ↓ *                            │
│                                                               │
│   Exclude file patterns:  ↓ (empty)                           │
│   Include file patterns:  *                                   │
│                                                               │
│   File search attributes:  ↓ (empty)                          │
│   Directory search attributes:  ↓ (empty)                     │
│                                                               │
└─────────────────────────────────────────────────────────────┘
```

FIGURE 8.7
FILER "search pattern and filter" screen.

Exclude Directory Pattern

The "Exclude directory pattern" option tells the computer which subdirectories a particular user does not want to see in the directory listing. This does not delete subdirectories; it just does not show their names in the directory list.

Include Directory Pattern

The "Include directory pattern" option lets a user specify if only certain subdirectories should show in the directory listing.

Exclude and Include File Patterns

The "Exclude and include file patterns" option is similar to the "Exclude" and "Include" options for directories. It allows a user to specify which files to show in a directory list.

File Search Attributes

The "File search attributes" option allows a user to specify if he or she wants to see files in which the attribute flag has been changed. (An attribute is the state or characteristic of the file. One such attribute is "hidden"; see the Chapter 9 discussion on the command line utilities FLAG command for other examples.)

Directory Search Attributes

The "Directory search attributes" option is the same as "File search attributes" except that it deals with subdirectories instead of files. See the Chapter 9 discussion on the FLAG command for a list of directory attributes.

VIEW VOLUME INFORMATION

When chosen from FILER's "Available Options" menu (see Figure 8.1), the "View Volume Information" option provides basic information regarding the file server's volume (hard drive).

WORK WITH DELETED FILES

It's wise to plan for the unexpected, especially when working with networks. Novell did just that by adding the "Salvage" and "Purge" options to their FILER menu utility. The "Salvage" option lets a user rescue deleted files. The "Purge" option lets a user permanently get rid of them.

Salvage Deleted Files

The "Salvage Deleted Files" (see Figure 8.1) option allows a user to retrieve files that have been previously deleted as long as the files have not been purged (*purged* in this sense means "instructed to never come back"). If the directory in which the files were originally located still exists, the files will be returned to that directory. If not, they will be restored to a directory named DELETED.SAV. The DELETED.SAV directory resides right off the SYS volume (SERV1_SYS:DELETED.SAV). DELETED.SAV will not appear in the directory list because it has the directory attributes hidden and system assigned to it.

To salvage a file from the currently chosen directory, choose "Salvage Deleted Files" from FILER's main menu. Three options appear: "View/Recover Deleted Files," "Salvage from Deleted Directories," and "Set Salvage Operations." By selecting "View/Recover Deleted Files," a list of salvageable files will appear. Highlight the file of interest and press Enter. If there is more than one file to bring back, the F5 (Mark) key may be used to select them. Answer "yes" to confirm the operation. Files salvaged using this option are restored to the directories from which they were deleted.

If the directory from which the file was deleted no longer exists, choose "Salvage from Deleted Directories" and proceed as directed above. Files salvaged using this option are restored to the DELETED.SAV directory.

Notice that by selecting "Set Salvage Options," a user may request to see the file names in a particular order. The possibilities are by file name, file size, deletion date, or deletor.

Purge Deleted Files

Sometimes, because of a need for more storage space or for tighter security, it is necessary to delete one or more files permanently. To purge files, select "Purge Deleted Files" from FILER's main menu. Upon doing so, two options appear. "Purge Current Directory Files Only" indicates that a user only wishes to delete files in the current chosen directory, whereas "Purge the Entire Subdirectory Structure" includes not only the currently chosen directory but also any subdirectories found inside (or under) that directory.

When prompted for the file pattern, a user may type in a particular file name. Note that the asterisk (*) indicates that the user wants to purge all files.

SET DEFAULT FILER OPTIONS

Set Default Options

From FILER's main "Available Options" menu, the "Set Default Filer Options" option is available, as shown in Figure 8.1. This option allows a user to structure the computer's response to certain commands or operations.

When the "Set Default Filter" option is selected from FILER's main menu, the "FILER Settings" screen appears, as shown in Figure 8.8. If a user presses the Delete key while highlighting a directory or file name, should the system prompt with a confirmation message, such as, "Are you sure?" or should it simply delete the file? The following section discusses various options for which a user can customize the computer's response.

Confirm Deletions

If set to "Yes," the "Confirm deletions" option instructs the computer to double check with the user after a deletion command has been entered and before actually deleting a file. If set to "No," then when a delete instruction is given, the system will delete files without asking the user, "Are you sure?"

Confirm File Copies

The "Confirm file copies" option, which is similar to the "Confirm deletions" option, will give an "Are you sure?" or similar prompt when a copy command has been entered.

```
+------------------------------------------------------------------+
|                         FILER Settings                           |
+------------------------------------------------------------------+
|                                                                  |
|   Confirm deletions:  No                                         |
|                                                                  |
|   Confirm file copies:  No                                       |
|   Confirm file overwrites:  Yes                                  |
|                                                                  |
|   Preserve file attributes:  Yes                                 |
|   Notify if name space information is lost: No                   |
|                                                                  |
|   Copy files sparse: No                                          |
|   Copy files compressed: No                                      |
|   Force files to be copied compressed:  No                       |
+------------------------------------------------------------------+
```

FIGURE 8.8
FILER settings.

Confirm File Overwrites

If a user attempts to copy a file to another file name and the file name to which the user is copying, the destination file, is already in use, the system will interpret this to mean that the file being copied is supposed to replace this destination file. This replacement process is called overwriting. The "Confirm file overwrites" option asks the computer to double check with the user if the destination file name of a write instruction would result in over-writing a file.

SUMMARY

FILER provides an easy way to check and change file and directory settings as well as a way to see directory listings in a particular manner. Subdirectories can be organized in a way that makes it easy to find needed files. Moving, copying, deleting, salvaging, or purg-ing of files can be accomplished with ease. Once users have mastered working with FILER, they can perform the daily management of files and subdirectories successfully. While FILER is a DOS utility its powerful ability to rescue files leads administrators to continue using it. Trustee rights assignments are quite often administrated using NWADMIN (see Chapter 5). Directory and file copies and Manipulation are commonly accomplished using Windows Explorer as discussed in Chapter 2.

EXERCISES

1. Define the following:
   a. confirm (deletions, file copies, and so forth)
   b. include directory pattern
   c. file search attribute
   d. salvage deleted files
   e. purge deleted files
2. What does FILER stand for, and where is it located? What does it allow you to manage?
3. How does FILER let you look at a different directory than the one you are using?
4. What information about directories can be found through FILER?
5. What information about files can be found through FILER?
6. What information about the file server's volume can be found through FILER?
7. How do you copy a file using FILER?
8. How do you copy all files in a particular subdirectory using FILER?
9. Who or what is a trustee?
10. What rights must you have to assign a trustee?
11. What file attributes are available in NetWare?
12. What FILER option allows you to see hidden files?
13. How do you delete a file using FILER?
14. How can you determine the owner of a particular file through FILER?
15. Why is the "Salvage" option used?
16. Why is the "Purge" option used?

LAB #8

In this lab, you will get firsthand experience working with the FILER menu utility. This lab takes you on a short tour of FILER and lets you take an inside look at your home directory. You will also have the opportunity to give some of your rights to another user. By the end of this lab, you should have a greater appreciation for the power and simplicity of FILER.

Getting Started and Selecting Your Directory

1. Key in the word "FILER" and press Enter to get started.

   ```
   F:\>FILER
   ```

2. In the space provided, write down the available options for FILER.

Available Options

3. Choose "Select Current Directory" from FILER's main menu, and key in the directory path for your personal directory when prompted to do so. Press Enter when you are done. If you do not know your directory path, see your LAN administrator for assistance. Pressing Insert may be helpful if you are stuck; it provides a step-by-step walkthrough approach to arrive at your directory. Here is an example of a current directory path:

   ```
   SERV1_VOL1:USERS\USERXX
   ```

   Here, SERV1_VOL1: is the name of the volume on the file server's hard drive where the home directory is located. USERS is the name of the subdirectory that houses the user home directories. USERXX is one particular user's home directory.

4. Notice that the "current path" found at the top left corner of your screen has changed. Write down your current directory path before proceeding.

Managing Your Directory

1. Now that your home directory has been selected as the current directory, let's take a look at it. Select "Manage Files and Directories" from FILER's main menu. The "Directory Contents" screen now appears. Write down some of the key files and subdirectory names that you notice before proceeding. (If no key files appear, your subdirectory is empty.

Perhaps this is a new home directory, and you have not yet saved any work into it. If this is the case, write the word *empty* in the following chart.)

Directory Contents	
• •	(parent)
\	(root)
•	(current)

2. Next, you will work with the "Directory Information" screen. Highlight "• I(current)" and press Enter twice. Fill in the following chart. It will serve as a nice reference document for your home directory.

Information for directory USERXX
Owner:
Creation date:
Creation time:
Directory attributes:
Current effective rights:
Inherited rights filters: [   ]
Trustees:
Limit space:
Directory space limit: Kilobytes

3. What rights do you have to this directory? Look next to where it says "Current effective rights." Do you see the first letter of each assigned right listed here? Look up these letters in this chapter's text if you have forgotten what they mean. List your rights in the following box. Write out the word, not just the first letter.

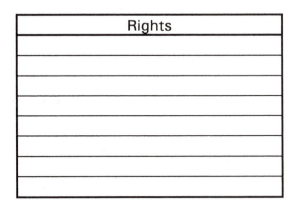

Assigning Trustees and Rights

Would you like to give another user permission to use your home directory? Sometimes this is necessary, especially if you are working on a project with someone. (Before proceeding with this lab, you may want to check with the LAN administrator to make sure that this is OK.)

1. From the "Directory Information" screen, select "Trustees" and press Enter. Next press Insert, select another user's account name from the list that now appears on the screen, and press Enter. If the user for whom you are looking is not on the list, try highlighting "• |(parent)" because that user may be in a different context. "• |(parent)" takes you back a level in the tree; pressing Enter on a container name moves you forward.

2. Next, you will give your new trustee additional rights. Highlight your new trustee from the trustee list now displayed on your screen. Press Enter. A list of assigned rights now appears. (Notice that by default "Read" and "File Scan" have been assigned.) Press the Insert key to add more rights. Give the user create rights by highlighting "Create Directory/File" and pressing Enter. Press Escape when done.

3. Next, you will revoke (deny the use of) the read right for this trustee. Highlight your new trustee and press Enter. Once again, the list of assigned rights now appears on the screen. Highlight "Read from File" and press the Delete key. Answer "yes" when the "Revoke Right" prompt comes up. Press Escape when done. The trustee can no longer read the content of files in your home directory.

4. Finally, you have decided not to entrust this user with your home directory, so you will need to remove that person from the trustee list. Simply highlight the trustee's name and press Delete. Answer "yes" when prompted if you want to delete the trustee. Don't worry: you are not deleting the user's account; you are just taking away the permission to use your directory.

Working with Files

Next, you will explore managing files using the FILER utility.

1. Choose "Manage Files and Directories" from FILER's main menu. You should see a list of files and directories that are located in your home directory. Choose one of your files and press the F10 Select key.

2. The "File Options" menu now appears on your screen. Choose "View/Set File Information." One of the items listed on the "File Information" screen is attributes. You are going to hide the file you have selected by putting an attribute of "hidden" on it. Highlight the word "*attribute*" and press Enter. A list of assigned attributes appears. (The list is most likely empty at this point.) Press Insert to bring up a list of attributes not yet assigned. Make a list of the file attributes. This will serve as a good reference tool.

```
┌─────────────────────────────────────┐
│            File Attributes           │
├─────────────────────────────────────┤
│                                      │
├─────────────────────────────────────┤
│                                      │
├─────────────────────────────────────┤
│                                      │
├─────────────────────────────────────┤
│                                      │
├─────────────────────────────────────┤
│                                      │
├─────────────────────────────────────┤
│                                      │
├─────────────────────────────────────┤
│                                      │
├─────────────────────────────────────┤
│                                      │
├─────────────────────────────────────┤
│                                      │
├─────────────────────────────────────┤
│                                      │
└─────────────────────────────────────┘
```

Highlight "hidden" and press Enter. Your file is now hidden.

3. Verify that the file is indeed hidden. To do so, choose "Managing Files and Directories" again from FILER's main menu. Notice that when the "Directory Contents" screen appears this time, your file no longer exists. You successfully hid the file.

Managing According to Search Pattern

Sometimes it is necessary to look for particular file names. In this case, you would like to view files that are currently hidden. Normally, the "Directory Contents" screen does not display hidden files, but you can instruct the system to search for them.

1. Choose "Manage According to Search Pattern" from FILER's main menu. Select "File Search Attributes" and press Enter. You will see a list of already assigned attribute searches on the screen; it is most likely empty. Press the Insert key to add a new attribute to the "Attribute Search" screen. A list of attributes not yet chosen appears on the screen. Highlight "hidden" and press Enter. You have now added the hidden attribute to the file search attributes. To see the results of this request, press the F10 (Continue) key.

A listing for the currently chosen directory appears. Even though your file is flagged as being hidden, it now appears on the screen in the directory list. Press Alt F10 (Quick Exit) to get out of FILER quickly.

2. Be aware that even though you just saw your file, it is still hidden. To prove this point, exit FILER all the way by pressing Alt F10 (Fast Exit). Use the DOS DIR command to view the directory listing. You should be at your home directory for this step:

```
F:\USERS\USERXX>DIR/W
```

Notice that the file you hid does not appear in the directory listing.

3. Since you may need to work on this file at a later date, you need to practice unhiding files. Go back to FILER to unhide your file:

```
F:\USERS\USERXX>FILER
```

Select "Managing Files and Directories" from FILER's main menu. Once again, notice that your hidden file is not listed. When you left FILER and went to the DOS prompt, the system reset the search pattern back to normal.

4. Press the Escape key to return to FILER's main menu. You need to set the file search pattern again. Choose "Manage According to Search Pattern." Next, select "File Search Attributes." Now press Insert and choose "hidden." Press the F10 (Continue) key. Notice that you have successfully requested the system to search your directory and to include files that have the hidden attribute in the resulting directory listing.

5. Next, you want to unhide your file. To do so, first, highlight your file and press the F10 (Select) key. You should now see the "File Options" submenu on your screen. Details regarding attributes are located on the "File Information" screen. Select "View/Set File Information" at this time. Highlight "attributes" and press Enter. This file's current attributes are now displayed on the screen. Highlight the "hidden files" attribute and press Delete. Confirm the deletion by choosing "yes." You have now completed the steps for unhiding your file.

6. To verify that the file is indeed unhidden, first, exit FILER by pressing Alt F10 (Quick Exit). You should be at your home directory for this next step. Display a directory listing for your home directory.

```
F:\USERS\USERXX>DIR/W
```

Notice that your file now appears in the directory listing. You were successful in unhiding your file. You should practice hiding and unhiding files until you feel competent doing so. Repeat steps 1 through 6 here until you are comfortable with the process.

Copying Files Using FILER

Copying files is a very common task that users perform routinely. In this portion of the lab, you will practice the copy procedure.

1. Make sure that you have already selected your home directory, and go back into FILER.

```
F:\USERS\USERXX>FILER
```

2. Choose "Managing Files and Directories" from FILER's main menu. Next, highlight the file you would like to copy. We will call this particular file the source file. In computer terms, *source* consists of the directory path of the file you are copying from. Press F10 (Select) to proceed. The "File Options" menu now appears on your screen. Select "Copy File" and press Enter.

3. The system now prompts you for your destination directory. *Destination* means where you are going to put the newly copied file. In this case, make sure your home directory is entered as the destination: ABC_SYS:USERS\USERXX, for example. Press Enter after putting in your destination directory's name.

4. The computer will now prompt you for the destination file name. Enter the name that you wish to call the new file. For this example, call your file NEWFILE.TXT. If you were copying to a different directory and you wanted to keep the same name, you could have simply pressed Enter. But because you are copying to the same directory, you cannot use the same file name, so you must provide a different file name.

5. Press Escape to return to the "Directory Contents" screen. You should now see the new file in the directory listing. You have successfully completed the procedure for copying the file. Review and practice steps 1 through 5, copying files, until you feel competent.

Deleting Files Using FILER

It is advisable to go through your directories periodically and delete any files no longer needed. By doing so, you will free up disk space and make your directories and files more manageable.

1. Once again, go into FILER (if you are not already there). Select your home directory (if it's not already chosen). Select "Managing Files and Directories" from FILER's main menu.

2. Highlight the file you wish to remove. For this example, highlight NEWFILE.TXT, which was created as the result of the file copying procedure. Once the file name is highlighted, press the Delete key. Confirm the deletion by choosing "yes." You have now successfully deleted the file.

Viewing Volume Information

It is particularly helpful to know where your files are being saved. "Volume Information" gives details about the file server's volume. Remember that a volume is located on the file server's hard drive or on a disk subsystem that is attached to the file server. A disk subsystem is a unit that contains multiple storage devices such as hard drives. A disk subsystem can also contain a CD-ROM drive.

1. You would like to get information about the volume that contains your home directory. Go into FILER and select "View Volume Information" from FILER's main menu.

2. Fill in the details that you discover about the volume.

```
┌─────────────────────────────────────────────────┐
│              Volume Information                   │
├─────────────────────────────────────────────────┤
│  Server Name                                      │
│  Volume Name                                      │
│  Volume Type                                      │
│  Total Bytes                                      │
│  Bytes Available                                  │
│  Maximum Directory Entries                        │
│  Directory Entries Available                      │
└─────────────────────────────────────────────────┘
```

Lab Summary

You have now successfully completed the FILER lab. FILER is fairly easy to use; it's powerful, and it can do quite a few things. Go through the steps found in this lab several times until you are familiar with them.

CHAPTER NINE

COMMAND LINE UTILITIES

INSPIRING MOMENT

You are working at your new position in the Data Processing Department. Networking is new to you, and you hear other people in the department discussing commands for the network. When you get stuck with a problem, they often ask you if you have tried a particular command. You don't want to sound like a novice, yet there are so many commands that you have been running into daily that you wonder if you will ever learn them all. You may even think to yourself, "I wonder how long I can survive in this company before they find out that I don't know what I'm doing." You feel that all the prior training you have had with computers is useless and was perhaps a waste of time. That prior experience listed on your resume doesn't seem to make you an asset to this company. Your confidence level may not be very high at the moment.

QUESTIONS FOR THOUGHT

Could exploring and practicing the most commonly used command line utilities (CLUs) help you perform better? Could you benefit by having a reference list of commonly used CLUs to refer to as needed? Could you benefit by sharing notes and questions with your colleagues who are also trying to improve their ability in using CLUs? Could you benefit by saying the commands and how they are used into a tape recorder, and then playing back the tape during the day? Could you benefit by implementing another system of learning that you know of or have used in the past? Do you think it would be beneficial to review the CLUs periodically, even before you have to really use them in a work environment? Would this periodic review of CLUs improve your retention and help you feel more confident in using them? Do you think that negative self-talk is beneficial for improving your performance in a LAN environment? Do you think most LAN administrators know everything there is to know about networking? What kinds of self-talk are beneficial for improving your performance?

CHALLENGE

Do not be afraid to experiment with a new way of learning something. Decide which system of learning works best for you, and write it down in your own words. Keep your written notes in a file, and make a copy of them so that they are available to you. Share with others. If you are able to explain something to someone else, not only do you help others, but you reinforce your own understanding and knowledge of that subject. Don't be hard on yourself. If CLUs seem a little overwhelming at first, give yourself time and keep practicing. Start with the commonly used CLUs, and add to your learning every day. Many CLUs work similarly to local operating system commands (such as DOS), so do not tell yourself that the time you spent learning the local operating system and other commands was useless. You will be an even greater asset to your current or future organization if you are comfortable working in both the local operating system and network operating system environments.

CHAPTER OBJECTIVES

After finishing this chapter, you should be able to:

1. Identify the location of command line utilities.
2. Explain the importance of mapping to the PUBLIC directory.
3. Explore the most commonly used command line utilities.
4. Distinguish the command line utilities from menu utilities.

COMMAND LINE UTILITIES BASIC COMMANDS

As the name implies, command line utilities (CLUs) are entered on the command line, which is commonly referred to as the prompt. If a user has worked in the DOS environment, he or she will find many similarities between NetWare commands and DOS commands.

CLUs are located in the PUBLIC directory and have an .EXE extension. Users have access to these commands. CLUs differ from menu utilities in that the instructions are not in a menu format; instead, the instructions are simply keyed in. There are many CLUs, but in this chapter, the discussion is limited to those commands used most often.

Caution: Because these commands are located in the PUBLIC directory, users must always have a search map drive pointing to the PUBLIC directory. Most organizations will have this set up in the system login script.

ROUTINE SYSTEM COMMAND LINE UTILITIES

Routine system CLUs include logging in and out of the network, finding the file server's current time, changing the user's password, and finding what version of NOS is loaded on the file server.

LOGIN

LOGIN allows a user to sign onto the LAN.

LOGIN /NS

LOGIN /NS allows a user access to the network without executing the login scripts. This is particularly useful if the login script contains an error that is causing problems while logging in. It's also useful if the login script is lengthy and the user just needs to log in briefly to do a simple task, such as send a message to another user.

LOGIN SERV2/USERXX

LOGIN SERV2/USERXX allows a user to log into a different file server than the one set as default. A user may be logged into more than one file server simultaneously. Simply put the file server's name, followed by a slash (/), and then key in the user's account name for that particular file server.

LOGOUT

LOGOUT allows a user to sign off the LAN.

LOGOUT SERV2

LOGOUT SERV2 allows a user to log out of a particular file server (in this case, SERV2). If no file server name is specified, the user is logged out of the entire network.

SYSTIME SERV2

The SYSTIME command allows a user to see the date and time on a particular file server to which he or she is attached. This function is particularly useful if the server is out of the state or the country and is handy in a wide area network (WAN) environment.

To view the time on the current server, use the same command without specifying the file server name:

```
F:\PUBLIC>systime
Current system time: Thursday 5-18-99 2:03:58 pm
```

SETPASS

The SETPASS command allows a user to change his or her password.

SETPASS SERV2/

SETPASS SERV2/ allows a user to change the current password assigned for a particular file server (in this case, SERV2).

NVER

The NVER command displays the version of NetWare currently in use.

NPATH

The NPATH command allows a user to view the path currently assigned in memory (see Figure 9.1).

```
F:\PUBLIC>npath
Based on the following workstation information:
    Current working directory: F: = CN=ABC_SYS: \PUBLIC
    Utility load directory: F: = CN=ABC_SYS: \PUBLIC
    NWLANGUAGE=ENGLISH
    PATH=Y:.;C:\NWCLIENT\;C:\WINDOWS;C:\;C:\DOS;C:\WPWIN;C:\DB;C:\WP

The search sequence for message and help files is:
    F: = CN=ABC_SYS: \PUBLIC
    F: = CN=ABC_SYS: \PUBLIC\NLS\ENGLISH
    F: = CN=ABC_SYS: \PUBLIC
    Y: = CN=ABC_SYS: \PUBLIC
    C:\NWCLIENT
    C:\WINDOWS
    C:\
    C:\DOS
    C:\WPWIN
    C:\DB
    C:\WP
    F: = CN=ABC_SYS: \PUBLIC\NLS\ENGLISH
```

FIGURE 9.1
NPATH command.

COMMUNICATING ON THE NETWORK

As discussed in Chapter 1, a key benefit of having a network is the ability to communicate with others. The following CLUs help users find out who is currently logged into the network, to specify if messages should be received or blocked, and then to send messages to other users or groups of users.

NLIST USER

The NLIST command displays a list of all the users currently logged in (see Figure 9.2). Key in NLIST /? for a listing of other available options.

WHOAMI

WHOAMI displays the name under which a user is logged in. Various options can be applied to this command. To see a listing of the options, add /? to the end of the command.

WHOAMI/ALL

The WHOAMI/ALL command displays information about the user currently logged onto the station (see Figure 9.3). The /ALL option gives all the details.

```
┌─────────────────────────────────────────────────────────────────────┐
│ NLIST              General Help Screen                    4.19        │
├─────────────────────────────────────────────────────────────────────┤
│ Purpose: View information about users, groups and other objects.      │
│ Syntax: NLIST class type [property search option]                     │
│                          [display option] [basic option]              │
├─────────────────────────────────────────────────────────────────────┤
│ For details on:                          Type:                        │
│  Property search options                 NLIST /? R                   │
│  Properties                              NLIST /? P                   │
│  Display options                         NLIST /? D                   │
│  Basic options                           NLIST /? B                   │
│  All Help Screens                        NLIST /? ALL                 │
│ Class types:                                                          │
│  * (all class types)      User                Print Queue             │
│  Server                   Group               Printer                 │
│  Computer                 Volume              Print Server            │
│  Directory Map            Profile             Organization            │
│  Organizational Unit      Alias               AFP Server              │
│ Enclose in double quotes all class types or properties containing spaces. │
└─────────────────────────────────────────────────────────────────────┘
```

FIGURE 9.2
NLIST command.

```
┌─────────────────────────────────────────────────────────────────┐
│ F:\PUBLIC > whoami                                                │
│                                                                   │
│ Current tree:  ABC_CO                                             │
│ Other names: Nancy Blackmon Velasco                               │
│ Title:         LAN Instructor                                     │
│ Description:   for CBS/Operations Courses                         │
│                                                                   │
│                                                                   │
│ User ID:       Nancy.CONSULTANTS.abc_co                           │
│ Server:        ABC  NetWare 4.10                                  │
│ Connection: 3 (Directory Services)                                │
│                                                                   │
└─────────────────────────────────────────────────────────────────┘
```

FIGURE 9.3
WHOAMI command.

SEND "How about lunch?" TO USER11
SEND "Can someone help me?" TO LANCLASS

The SEND commands allow a user to send messages to another user or to an entire group.

SEND/A=C

The SEND/A=C command allows a user to block messages from being received by his or her station. All messages except console messages are blocked. Console messages are sent by the console operator who monitors activity on the network.

SEND/A=N

The SEND/A=N command allows a user to block all messages from being received by his or her station. All messages, including console messages, are blocked.

SEND/A

The SEND/A command removes the message blocks.

MANAGING DIRECTORIES WITH COMMAND LINE UTILITIES

CLUs for managing directories allow users to assign drive maps, rename directories, manage directory rights, copy an entire directory, and manage directory attributes.

MAP G:=SERV1_VOL1:USERS\USER05; MAP S4:=SERV1_SYS:APPS\WP

The MAP commands allow a user to create a logical or search drive mapping to point to a particular directory. See Figures 9.4 and 9.5. Chapter 2 provides more details on the MAP command.

MAP INS S4:=SERV1_SYS:APPS\WP

The INS S4 option instructs the system to create a new search drive map and make it the fourth directory path searched. If another directory path is already set as the fourth search path, the one that is already set will move down and become the fifth search path.

MAP DEL G:

MAP DEL G: instructs the system to remove the drive mapping for drive letter G:.

MAP N SERV2/SYS:APPS\PROJECTS

The N (next) option instructs the system to create a new logical drive map and assign it the next available drive letter.

```
F:\PUBLIC > map

Drives A,B,C,D,E map to a local disk.
Drive F: = ABC_SYS: \PUBLIC
Drive H: = ABC_SYS: \USERS\NANCY
Drive Z: = ABC_SYS: \PUBLIC
       -----     Search Drives    -----
S1: = Y:. [ABC_SYS: \PUBLIC]
S2: = C:\NWCLIENT\
S3: = C:\WINDOWS
S4: = C:\
S5: = C:\DOS
S6: = C:\WPWIN
S7: = C:\DB
S8: = C:\WP
```

FIGURE 9.4
MAP command.

MAP	General Help	4.12
Purpose: To assign a drive to a directory path.		
Syntax: MAP [option	/VER] [search: = [drive: =]]	[drive: =] [path] [/W]		

To:		Use:
Insert a search drive.		INS
Delete a drive mapping.		DEL
Map the next available drive.		N
Make the drive a root directory.		R
Map a drive to a physical volume on a server.		P
Change a regular drive to a search drive or a search drive to a regular drive.		C
Display version information		/VER
Do not change master environment.		/W

For example, to:	Type:
Map the next available drive to the login directory on server FS1	MAP N FS1/SYS:LOGIN
Map drive W: as a search drive to the WP directory	MAP S16: = W: = APPS:WP

FIGURE 9.5
MAP command help.

MAP S16:=ABC_SYS:APPS\DB

The S16: option instructs the system to assign the next available search sequence to the given directory path. Remember that the system does not assign search numbers out of order. Thus, even though S16: may be requested, if S4: was the last number assigned, S5: would automatically be used next.

RENDIR USER\USER05\PRACTICE USER\USER05\KEEPIT

The RENDIR command allows a user to rename a directory.

RIGHTS ABC_SYS:USERS\USER05

The RIGHTS command displays a user's rights to a particular directory (see Figure 9.6). If the directory path is not specified, the default directory will be used.

RIGHTS SERV1_SYS:APPS\WP /T

The /T option instructs the system to display a list of trustees who have been assigned rights to a particular directory. If the directory already has a drive letter mapped to it, the shortcut for this command can be used:

```
RIGHTS G: /T
```

In this example, the trustees for the directory path to which the drive letter G: points would be displayed on the screen.

```
F:\PUBLIC > rights
ABC_SYS:\PUBLIC
Your rights for this directory:  [SRWCEMFA]
    Supervisor rights to directory.        (S)
    Read from a file in a directory.       (R)
    Write to a file in a directory.        (W)
    Create subdirectories and files.       (C)
    Erase directory and files.             (E)
    Modify directory and files.            (M)
    Scan for files and directories.        (F)
    Change access control.                 (A)
```

FIGURE 9.6
RIGHTS command.

RIGHTS SERV1_SYS:APPS\WP /I

The /I option instructs the computer to display a list of users who have inherited rights to this directory. When a trustee is assigned rights to a particular directory, the user being assigned the rights automatically inherits the same rights for any subdirectories contained within the directory to which the rights were originally assigned. Therefore, the user has what is called *inherited rights* to the subdirectories. The inherited rights are assigned automatically, unless the person who has supervisory rights to the subdirectory has placed an inherited rights filter on the subdirectory. An inherited rights filter (IRF) specifies which rights are allowed to trickle down. If there is an IRF on the subdirectory, any rights not listed in the IRF, even though they may have been initially assigned as trustee rights in the upper directory, do not go into effect. Even though the user initially inherited rights to the subdirectory, the rights may have been filtered out. Effective rights refer to the actual rights to a given directory that apply once the IRF has been taken into consideration. Trustee rights are not filtered out by IRF at the level they were assigned, because trustee rights are direct assignments at that particular directory level. Consider the following example.

In the directory SERV1_VOL1:APPS\WP, user INSTRUCTA has been assigned RFCEW rights. This is a direct assignment. If any IRFs are assigned to this same directory level, it would not affect INSTRUCTA's assignment. INSTRUCTA's trustee rights are RFCEW and they are not blockable; therefore, INSTRUCTA's effective rights (usable ones) are the same (RFCEW).

In the directory SERV1_VOL1:APPS\WP\TUTORS, user INSTRUCTA does not have any assigned rights, but because SERV1_VOL1:APPS\WP is at a directory level above this one, the RFCEW rights assigned for SERV1_VOL1:APPS\WP trickle down. Since there were no IRFs assigned for the TUTORS directory, then RFCEW trickles down. Instead of being assigned RFCEW rights, INSTRUCTA inherits RFCEW access to the TUTORS directory. Thus, INSTRUCTA's effective rights become RFCEW for the TUTORS directory.

Suppose there is a subdirectory under TUTORS called SPECIAL (SERV1_VOL1: APPS\WP\TUTORS\SPECIAL). Suppose that ADMIN, ADMIN equivalent, or a person with access control authorization has decided to place a filter (IRF) on the SPECIAL directory. Suppose the IRF is equal to RFM (read, file scan, and modify). Normally RFCEW would trickle down from SERV1_VOL1:APPS\WP, get passed on to the SERV1_VOL1: APPS\WP\TUTORS directory as an inheritance, and then get subsequently passed on down the chain to the SERV1_VOL1:APPS\WP\TUTORS\SPECIAL directory. However, if an inherited rights filter of RFM has been assigned to the SPECIAL directory, then only the corresponding RFM rights can be passed down. So the formula for determining the effective rights active for the user INSTRUCTA in regards to the SPECIAL directory would be RFCEW (rights assigned at the WP directory level) minus anything **not found** in the inherited rights filter. Therefore, RFCEW minus CEW (those rights not contained in the filter), leaves INSTRUCTA with RF (read and file scan). INSTRUCTA was permitted to inherit read and file scan without them being filtered out. Therefore, INSTRUCTA's effective rights for the SPECIAL directory is read and file scan (RF). Notice that even though M is shown in the IRF example, it does not go into effect because INSTRUCTA does not have an initial trustee assignment of M (modify).

RIGHTS ABC_SYS:APPS\WP\TUTORS\SPECIAL RFCEW /NAME=INSTRUCTA,USERXX

The /NAME option allows a user to assign trustee rights to other users or groups. Notice that the list of rights to be assigned goes immediately prior to /NAME, followed by the users' account names. Note that if a drive map has already been assigned to the particular path, the RIGHTS command can be shortened as follows:

```
RIGHTS G: RFCEW /NAME=INSTRUCTA,USERXX
```

FLAG H:*.* RO /S /DO

The FLAG command with the /DO option allows a user to set directory attributes. In the command, *.* means that all the files in this directory are to be flagged. The attribute RO stands for "read-only." The /S option instructs the system to flag files located in subdirectories. In NetWare, the directory attributes include the following:

N	Normal
H	Hidden
P	Purge
Dc	Don't compress
Dm	Don't migrate
Sy	System
Di	Delete-inhibit
Ri	Rename inhibit
Ic	Immediate compress

MANAGING FILES WITH COMMAND LINE UTILITIES

NDIR

The NDIR command allows a user to view the names of files in a particular directory. It is similar to the DOS DIR command but more detailed.

NMENU MYMENU

The NMENU command allows a user to run a particular menu that has already been created.

NCOPY G:MYTEST.TXT A:MYTEST.BAK

NCOPY is the NetWare copy command for copying files. See Figures 9.7 through 9.9. NCOPY is very similar to the DOS COPY command. Wild cards can be used with this command. A number of special options can be applied to NCOPY. For a listing of them, key in NCOPY /?.

NCOPY	General Help	4.13
Purpose: To copy files and directories.		
Syntax: NCOPY source path [target path] [options]		

To:	Use:
Copy subdirectories	/S
Copy subdirectories including empty directories	/S/E
Copy files with archive bit set	/A
Copy files with archive bit set, then clear the bit	/M
Copy sparse files	/F
Inform when non-DOS file information will be lost	/I
Copy only DOS information	/C
Read after write verify on local drives (DOS only)	/V
Retain compression on supported media	/R
Retain compression on unsupported media	/R/U
Display version information	/VER

For example:	Type:
To copy all files and subdirectories from volume SYS to drive G:	NCOPY SYS:*.* G:*.* /S

FIGURE 9.7
Examples of NCOPY.

```
Example without map shortcuts:

H:\USERS\NANCY > ncopy h:\users\nancy\one\hi.txt h:\users\nancy\two\hi.txt

  From H:\USERS\NANCY\ONE\
  To   H:\USERS\NANCY\TWO\
  HI.TXT      (13)

  1 file was copied.
```

FIGURE 9.8
NCOPY help.

NCOPY H:*.* I:*.* /S

One popular option is to include subdirectories, and the /S option allows users to accomplish this. With this command, all files and subdirectories located in the directory path assigned to drive H: are copied into the directory path assigned to drive I:. (Recall from the DOS review in Chapter 3 that *.* means all files.)

```
Example with map shortcuts:

H:\USERS\NANCY > map i: = sys:users\nancy\one

Drive I:  =  ABC_SYS: \USERS\NANCY\ONE

H:\USERS\NANCY > map j: = sys:users\nancy\two

Drive J:  =  ABC_SYS:\USERS\NANCY\TWO

H:\USERS\NANCY > ncopy i:hi.txt j:hi.txt

  From I:\USERS\NANCY\ONE\
  To   J:\USERS\NANCY\TWO\
  HI.TXT        (13)

  1 file was copied.
```

FIGURE 9.9
MAP and NCOPY examples.

PURGE H:*.*

The PURGE command instructs the computer to remove any deleted files permanently. Recall from the Chapter 8 discussion of FILER that if a file is deleted, it can be salvaged as long as it has not been purged. Purging files clears out any files that have been deleted from the disk. Once they have been purged, they can no longer be salvaged. It's a good idea to execute the PURGE command once a month to free up space on the hard drive. Depending on the amount the LAN is used at a facility, this command may be executed more or less often than once a month. Purging is also useful for maintaining security of highly sensitive files. Once the files are no longer needed, it is a good idea to delete and then purge them. In the command PURGE H:*.*, all deleted files found in drive H: directory are permanently removed.

PURGE H:*.* /S

The /S option of the PURGE command instructs the system to purge deleted files from subdirectories contained inside the directory to which the drive letter H: is pointing.

FLAG ABC_SYS:USERS\USER01\MYTEST.TXT RO /FO

The FLAG command allows a user to change file attributes. When no attributes are specified, the current attribute settings for that particular file are displayed. Wild cards are

The following is an example of using the flag command:

H:\USERS\NANCY > flag

Files	= The name of the files found
Directories	= The name of the directories found
DOS Attr	= The DOS attributes for the specified file
NetWare Attr	= The NetWare attributes for the specified file or directory
Status	= The current status of migration and compression for a file or directory
Owner	= The current owner of the file or directory
Mode	= The search mode set for the current file

Files	DOS Attr	NetWare Attr	Status Owner	Mode
41SCREEN	[Rw---A]	[----------------]	.Nancy.CONS...	N/A
41MAP	[Rw---A]	[----------------]	.Nancy.CONS...	N/A
41SCRNS.95A	[Rw---A]	[----------------]	.Nancy.CONS...	N/A
PUBDIR41.595	[Rw---A]	[----------------]	.Nancy.CONS...	N/A
SCRN41B.595	[Rw---A]	[----------------]	.Nancy.CONS...	N/A
SCRN41C.595	[Rw---A]	[----------------]	.Nancy.CONS...	N/A
SCRN41D.595	[Rw---A]	[----------------]	.Nancy.CONS...	N/A
SCRN41E	[Rw---A]	[----------------]	.Nancy.CONS...	N/A

FIGURE 9.10
FLAG command.

allowed. Recall from the DOS review in Chapter 3 that * is a wild card, which stands for all files. Consider the following:

```
FLAG G:*.* RO /FO
```

All files in the drive G: directory would be flagged as read-only. See Figure 9.10.

The /FO option stands for "file attribute." In the above example, RO stands for "read-only." The following attributes can be applied to files.

Ro	Read-only
H	Hidden
P	Purge
Di	Delete-inhibit
Sh	Shareable

Ci	Copy-inhibit
Dm	Don't migrate
Dc	Don't compress
ALL	All
Rw	Read-write
Sy	System
A	Archive-needed
Ri	Rename-inhibit
T	Transactional
X	eXecute-only
Ic	Immediate compress
Ds	Don't suballocate
N	Normal

Commonly used options and their descriptions are as follows.

Ro   Read-only means that the users cannot make changes to the file; they can only read it. Note, however, that if users have been assigned modify rights, the Ro flag can be removed. Recall that the modify right gives users the authorization to change file attributes.

H   Hidden means that the file is really there, but it is hidden so that it does not appear in the regular directory listing. Recall from the FILER discussion in Chapter 8 that the user can still see the hidden files in the directory listing by going to FILER, for example, and viewing them through the "Search Pattern" option.

P   Purge means that after this attribute is set on a particular file, if it is ever deleted for whatever reason, it is to purge immediately, with no chance of salvaging it.

Sh   Shareable means that more than one user can access the file at a time. This very common attribute is used for files that are located in application directories where programs are located. It gives permission, for example, for user A to run it at the same time as user B.

Rw   Read-write means that the contents of a file may be viewed and changed. Note that for this attribute to be advantageous, the user must also have RFW trustee rights.

A   Archive-needed is a flag that the system puts on a file when the file is either new or has been modified in some way since the last backup was done.

X   The execute-only attribute does not allow users to view, copy, or change the contents of the file. The user is only allowed to run the file. Once the execute-only attribute has been applied, it cannot be removed. If a change is needed, the original software disks have to be reloaded onto the system.

CONTROLLING PRINTING WITH COMMAND LINE UTILITIES

As mentioned in Chapter 1, one benefit of having a LAN is the ability to share hardware resources. To print on a network, several extra steps are needed than when printing on a stand-alone PC. Printing is discussed further in Chapters 10 and 11. This section acquaints you with some commonly used CLUs associated with printing.

CAPTURE B=SINGERS C=2 FF L=1 Q=PRINTQ_1 S=SERV1 TI=15 AU NOTI

The CAPTURE command allows a user to specify how future print jobs in this session will be set up. This is particularly useful when printing from within an application. The abbreviations used are as follows:

B	Banner name
C	Number of copies
FF	Form feed
L	Printer port number
Q	Name of print queue
S	Name of server
AU	Automatically end the capture request for each print job.
TI	The length of time the network should wait once the print command has been given to make sure that additional printing is not coming.
NOTI	Notify user when the job has printed.

Figures 9.11 through 9.13 display the various options that a user can incorporate with the CAPTURE command.

CAPTURE	General Help	4.10

Purpose: CAPTURE allows you to redirect DOS and OS/2 print
  jobs to a network printer (or file) from an application
  designed to print to a parallel (LPT) port. It also
  allows you to print screen text to a network printer.

Syntax: CAPTURE [options]
Options:
 Create (CR = <path>) - Create a file to store printed data in.
 Server (S = <NetWare bindery server>) - Specify the NetWare
        server containing the bindery queue you
        want to send the print job to.
 Job (J = <configuration>) - Specify the print job
        configuration name to be used.
        You can also specify the context in which to look
        for a configuration if it is outside the current
        search path by identifying the container or user
        owning the configuration:
            J = <configuration> : <context>
 Hold (HOLD) - Send a print job to a queue without having it print.

FIGURE 9.11
CAPTURE options, page 1.

```
┌─────────────────────────────────────────────────────────────────────┐
│ CAPTURE              General Help Page              4.10              │
├─────────────────────────────────────────────────────────────────────┤
│ Job configuration overrides:                                         │
│   LPT port (L = < 1-9 > )                                            │
│   Keep (K)                                                            │
│   Banner (B = <banner name>)  Name (NAM = <name>)  No Banner NB)     │
│   Form (F = <form or number>)                                        │
│   Queue (Q = <queue name>) Printer (P = <printer name>)              │
│   Copies (C = < 1-65000 > )                                          │
│   Tabs (T = < 1-18 > )  No Tabs (NT) (default)                       │
│   Timeout (TI = < 0-1000 > )                                         │
│   Form Feed (FF)  No Form Feed (NFF)                                 │
│   Autoendcap (AU)  No Autoendcap (NA)                                │
│   Notify (NOTI)  No Notify (NNOTI)                                   │
│                                                                       │
└─────────────────────────────────────────────────────────────────────┘
```

FIGURE 9.12
CAPTURE options, page 2.

```
┌─────────────────────────────────────────────────────────────────────┐
│ CAPTURE              General Help Page              4.10              │
├─────────────────────────────────────────────────────────────────────┤
│                                                                       │
│ Job configuration overrides:                                         │
│   LPT port (L = < 1-9 > )                                            │
│   Keep (K)                                                            │
│   Banner (B = <banner name>)  Name (NAM = <name>)  No Banner (NB)    │
│   Form (F = <form or number>)                                        │
│   Queue (Q = <queue name>) Printer (P = <printer name>)              │
│   Copies (C = < 1-65000 > )                                          │
│   Tabs (T = < 1-18 > )  No Tabs (NT) (default)                       │
│   Timeout (TI = < 0-1000 > )                                         │
│   Form Feed (FF)  No Form Feed (NFF)                                 │
│   Autoendcap (AU)  No Autoendcap (NA)                                │
│   Notify (NOTI)  No Notify (NNOTI)                                   │
│                                                                       │
└─────────────────────────────────────────────────────────────────────┘
```

FIGURE 9.13
CAPTURE options, page 3

PSC PS=PS0 STAT

The PSC (print server control) command allows users to display the status of the printers and print servers. In the command PSC PS=PS0 STAT, the print server's name is PS0 and STAT stands for "status." Other options available may be discovered by keying in PSC /?.

NPRINT H:MYTEST.TXT Q=PRINTQ_0 B=NANCY FF

NPRINT (see Figure 9.14) is very similar to CAPTURE, with the exceptions that a user also needs to specify the file name being printed and that the settings apply only to this particular print job. (See CAPTURE for comparison.) A description of available options is available by keying in NPRINT /?. Here, the file H:MYTEST.TXT is being sent to the print queue called PRINTQ_0, and the banner name to appear on the cover sheet of the output is NANCY. After the job is printed, the printer will eject to the top of the next page in accord with the FF (form feed) setting.

```
NPRINT                  General Help Screen                 4.10
Purpose: Send files to a network printer.
Syntax: NPRINT <path/filename> [options]
Options:
 Delete (DEL)
 Job (J=<configuration>). You can also specify the
            context in which to look for a print
            job configuration if it is outside the
            current search path by identifying
            the container or user owning
            the configuration:
                J=<configuration>:<context>
 Queue (Q=<queue name>)   Printer (P=<printer name>)
 Server (S=<NetWare bindery server>)
 Details (D)
 Version (/VER) - Display program version information
 Hold (HOLD)   - Send a print job to a queue without having it print.
Other help: Type /? or /? ALL.
>>>Enter = More  C = Continuous Esc = Cancel
```

FIGURE 9.14
NPRINT features.

SUMMARY

Command line utilities are different than menu utilities: CLUs are keyed in and have no menus. These commands can be entered at the prompt or can be put in a login script or a menu. Several CLU commands are similar to DOS commands. The commands are useful for daily operation of a LAN.

EXERCISES

1. Define the following:
   - **a.** inherited rights filter
   - **b.** attach
   - **c.** file attributes
   - **d.** directory attributes
   - **e.** granting rights
   - **f.** trustee rights versus inherited rights
2. What do the following stand for?
   - **a.** CLU
   - **b.** CAPTURE parameters: B; C; FF; Q; S; TI; and NOTI.
   - **c.** FLAG file options: A; EO; H; I; N; NS; RO; RW; S; and T.
   - **d.** FLAG directory options: DI; H; N; P; RI; and SY.
3. Which CLU commands are similar to DOS commands?
4. Which CLU commands allow you to work with or view directory information?
5. Which CLU commands allow you to work with or view printer information?
6. Where are command line utilities located and who may use them?
7. What is the difference between command line utilities and menu utilities?
8. Which commands are used when communicating on a network?

LAB #9

The following lab will give you practice with using command line utilities. You are presented with different problems that are answerable using the CLUs learned in this chapter. Practice this lab periodically to increase your confidence in using CLUs.

1. Hide one of your files that is located in your home directory.
2. Set your entire directory to private.
3. Grant a friend read and file scan rights to your directory.
4. Find out how much space the volume SYS: has allocated. How much space is in use? How much space is still available?
5. Use the NPRINT command to print one of your files.

6. Find out the version of NetWare currently in use.
7. Write down the first two account names that appear on the list of users currently logged onto the system.
8. What is your station number?
9. What servers can you log onto?
10. Unhide any files that you have previously hidden in your directory.
11. Display the rights to your directory.
12. Send a message to a friend.
13. Take away the rights that you had previously assigned to a friend in step 3.

PRINTING

The management of printers takes planning, insight, practice, and patience to master. This section seeks to break down the printer management process into manageable steps.

CHAPTER TEN   Managing Printers Using NWADMIN

CHAPTER ELEVEN   Print Utilities

MANAGING PRINTERS USING NWADMIN

INSPIRING MOMENT

The end users whom you serve every day care about the basics. Do their reports print? You look around and notice quite a few printers at your new place of employment. Employees are sharing the printers. It's not just one printer per staff member! You have been called upon to understand where the printers are located throughout the organization. Also, if someone reports difficulty printing, you are to assist in locating and printing to the correct printer. As new printers are purchased, you will be assisting with adding them to the network.

QUESTIONS FOR THOUGHT

How are all these printers tied to the network? How are the end users assigned to the printers? How does the network know where to send the output?

CHALLENGE

Get familiar with the location of each printer. Know each printer's name and overall configuration, know where the user manuals are located for each printer, and become very comfortable with using NWADMIN to manage the printers. Also, it is highly possible that your organization uses a separate printer administration utility provided by the printer manufacturer. Explore the administration software applicable to your organization's particular printers. Read the associated instruction booklets where applicable. When printers go down, you will want to get them back up as quickly as possible; therefore, it is recommended to do some research, practice, and training *before* this happens.

Printer setups vary greatly depending on the size of the organization, the printer manufacturer, and the number of users sharing the same printer. The variety makes it difficult to clearly present the "best" way for setting up printers at your organization. However, after reading through and exploring Chapters 10 and 11, you should be able to stand back and look at the big picture.

CHAPTER OBJECTIVES

After finishing this chapter, you should be able to:

1. Distinguish between local and network printers.
2. Explore the relationship between the relevant NDS objects necessary for establishing print operations.
3. Discuss setting up and managing printers.
4. Describe the purpose of a print queue.

UNDERSTANDING PRINTING CONCEPTS

Molding and shaping the printer setup steps, to best fit the needs of your organization, requires a great deal of insight, planning, and patience. Printer management takes time and practice to master. First, study the concepts associated with printer management. Then, seek to understand the steps involved in setting up and managing the printing environment.

Local versus Network Printers

A printer attached to a workstation is considered a *local printer* if the only person printing to it is the user sitting at that particular computer. If, however, other users also print to it, then it becomes a *network printer.* The printer becomes a shared resource and is referenced on the network.

It's also possible to have a printer attach to the network without connecting to the workstation at all. There are a variety of ways to make this type of connection. In any case, a printer connecting to the network without having to physically connect to a workstation is also called a network printer.

Check to see if multiple workstations can print to a particular printer. This will help you distinguish the local printers from the network printers most of the time. (A printer switch box may be an exception to this, depending on whether or not the switch box attaches to the network.)

Four Special Objects Required for Printing

In NetWare Directory Services™ (NDS), printers are represented as leaf objects. They reside inside of container objects or off the root of the tree itself. In our example, the Accounting printer, along with other objects, resides inside of the Sales Division organizational unit container (Figure 10.1). Four leaf objects work together to accomplish the task of printing: a print server, a print queue, a printer, and a user. In Figure 10.1, APrintQ is the queue assigned for Accounting's printer. Print requests are sent to this queue, where they stand in line waiting to ride on the printer. APrinter is the printer name assigned for Accounting's printer. APrtServer is the name assigned to Accounting's print server. The print server manages the print request.

Submitting a Print Request

Imagine it this way: The user selects "File," "Print" from a Windows-based software application. This action results in the creation of a print job. In effect, the user's workstation is raising its hand and politely asking permission to print. The request to print a particular report, letter, graph, or other item is referred to in networking terms as a *print job.*

FIGURE 10.1
Accounting's printer is located inside of the Sales Division organizational unit container.
Source: Screen shot from NetWare, © 1983-1999, Novell, Inc. All rights reserved. Reprinted and used with permission.

Waiting in the Print Queue Line

The print job must compete for a shared resource—the printer. The print job is one of many submitted by the network users. It waits its turn in line according to the priority rules set up by the network administrator. Typically in a network environment, multiple waiting lines, or queues, exist. Recall from Chapter 5 that users are assigned to groups such as the group for the Accounting Department or the group for Marketing. Similarly, users are also assigned print queues. In networking terms, the end user is considered a *print queue user* of a particular print queue when the network administrator has made this assignment. If the end users are print queue users for a particular print queue, they may submit print jobs to the associated printer.

Note: Although end users are associated with particular print queues, in Windows they select printers, not queues per se. End users are not expected to know the names of the print queues; they just need to know the name of the printer.

The Printer

The printer leaf object represents the actual physical printer device on the network. Depending on the printer manufacturer, the printer leaf object may actually be created through the use of special printer administration software specific to that line of printers. Hewlett

Packard and Lexmark, among others, are famous for this approach. Once the printer object has been created, the network administrator or the special vendor-dependent administration software may assign (or link) the appropriate print queue object to the printer object.

The Print Server

So far we have mentioned the user object needing to be assigned to the print queue object, and the print queue object needing to be assigned to the printer object. Yet there is one key association missing. How does the network operating system tie into the printer object? Keep in mind that the network operating system stays fairly busy handling other tasks such as *authenticating* users (in other words, verifying login requests). In addition to authenticating users, the file server responds to requests from workstations to run applications and share data. Think about it. How many print requests take place every day in a network environment? If the file server had to manage each request, the network would operate very slowly. Instead the print server handles this load. The print server has the responsibility of managing the printers. Once the print server object is created, the network administrator or vendor-dependent administration software needs to assign the printer to the print server.

Completing the Circle

Now we have completed the circle! The user leaf object is assigned to a print queue object. A print queue object is assigned to a printer object. A printer object is assigned to a print server object.

Important Documentation

When setting up the print environment, the challenge is to keep track of the assignments between the four leaf object types mentioned in this discussion. Make sure not to skip one of the linkages during the setup process, or the print process will not occur. Also, it's advantageous to document the assignments in a manner that makes sense to the technical staff that will be responding to service requests. Discuss with your organization's technical staff the best way to accomplish the feat of documentation. The goal is to lessen the amount of downtime, keep the printers printing, and keep the end users happy with the results—output!

PRINTER SETUPS AND MANAGEMENT

In this section, we will explore the steps involved in setting up the print environment. If you are new to the networking field, you may want to reread the prior section to gain a thorough understanding of printing concepts and the relationship of the leaf objects involved before you continue on through this section.

Creating Print Queue Leaf Objects

It's actually easier to create the objects starting with the print queue leaf object if working primarily with NWADMIN. However, please refer carefully to the booklet that came with your organization's particular printer. The printer manufacturer may have provided special instructions and may have specified a different order. Remember, the print queue is the waiting line for the print job. Ideally you will want to create the print queue, the printer, and the print server leaf objects in the same NDS context that your user leaf objects are in.

For our example, we are setting up a new printer in the Client Sales Department as follows:

Create the Print Queue

1. First, go to NWADMIN and double click on the "Sales Division" organizational unit to expand it (Figure 10.2).
2. With "Sales Division" still highlighted, click on "Object," then click on "Create" from the NWADMIN menu, select "Print Queue," and click "OK" (Figure 10.3).
3. Next, provide a name for the new print queue. Also, click on the NDS button to select the disk volume location for saving the print requests for this queue. When done, click on the "Create" button (Figure 10.4).

Assign Users to the Print Queue

1. To assign users to a particular queue, double click on the print queue leaf object. In our case, we double click on "CSprintq" (Figure 10.5).
2. From the "Print Queue" screen, click on the "Assignments" button (Figure 10.6).
3. Next, click the "Users" button, then the "Add" button, and select the users that you would like to have permission to use this print queue (Figure 10.7). In our example, we

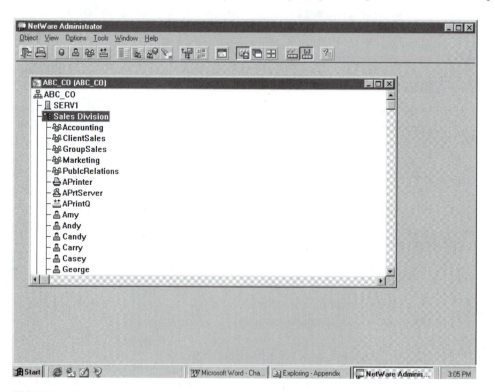

FIGURE 10.2

Find the container that you want to put the new print queue object inside.

Source: Screen shot from NetWare, © 1983-1999, Novell, Inc. All rights reserved. Reprinted and used with permission.

FIGURE 10.3
Click on "Object," then "Create" from the NWADMIN menu, and select "Print Queue."
Source: Screen shot from NetWare, © 1983-1999, Novell, Inc. All rights reserved. Reprinted and used with permission.

FIGURE 10.4
Name the print queue and select the volume for storing the print jobs.
Source: Screen shot from NetWare, © 1983-1999, Novell, Inc. All rights reserved. Reprinted and used with permission.

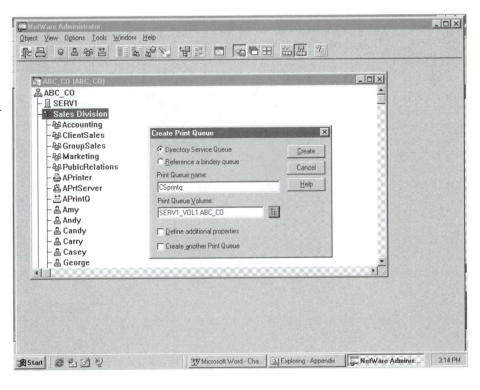

FIGURE 10.5
Assign users to the print queue.
Source: Screen shot from NetWare, © 1983-1999, Novell, Inc. All rights reserved. Reprinted and used with permission.

FIGURE 10.6
Click on the "Assignments" button to assign users to the print queue.
Source: Screen shot from NetWare, © 1983-1999, Novell, Inc. All rights reserved. Reprinted and used with permission.

FIGURE 10.7
Specify the users you want to assign for this particular print queue.
Source: Screen shot from NetWare, © 1983-1999, Novell, Inc. All rights reserved. Reprinted and used with permission.

will select "Client Sales" and click on "OK." This will allow all of the Client Sales staff to print to this printer.

4. By default, the entire Sales Division has been assigned as users for the print queue. Click on the "Sales Division.ABC_CO" assignment in the user list, and then click on the "Delete" button to remove this assignment (Figure 10.8). Click on "OK" to commit the changes.

Create the Printer Leaf Object and Assign the Print Queue

1. Indicate the context by clicking on the "Sales Division" container. We want the printer leaf object to reside in the same context as the print queue leaf object.
2. Next, click on "Object," then click "Create" from the NWADMIN menu, and select "Printer" as the type of object you want to create (Figure 10.9). Click on "OK."
3. Next, type in a name for the new printer. Also, click on the check box for "Define additional properties." Click on the "Create" button (Figure 10.10).
4. From the "Printer" screen, click on the "Assignments" button. Now, click on the "Add" button to select the print queue. In our example, we are selecting "CSprintq" (Figure 10.11). Click on "OK" twice to commit the changes.

Create the Print Server Leaf Object and Assign the Printer

1. Specify the context for this print server by once again clicking on the "Sales Division" organizational unit container object located in the NDS. Click on "Object," then click

FIGURE 10.8
Delete "Sales Division.ABC_CO"
from the user assignment list.
Source: Screen shot from NetWare,
© 1983-1999, Novell, Inc. All rights
reserved. Reprinted and used with
permission.

FIGURE 10.9
Create a printer leaf object.
Source: Screen shot from NetWare,
© 1983-1999, Novell, Inc. All rights
reserved. Reprinted and used with
permission.

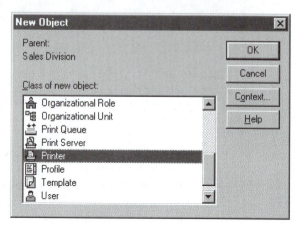

on "Create" from the NWADMIN menu, and select "Print Server" as the type of object
(Figure 10.12). Click on "OK."

2. Next, type in the name for the new print server. Click on the check box for "Define additional properties" (Figure 10.13). Click on the "Create" button.

3. Just as you assigned the print queue to the printer, you will now assign the printer to the
print server by clicking the "Assignments" button. In our example, after clicking on the
"Assignments" button, we click on the "Add" button and select the "CSprinter" (Figure
10.14). Click on "OK" to commit the changes.

FIGURE 10.10
Give the printer a name.
Source: Screen shot from NetWare, © 1983-1999, Novell, Inc. All rights reserved. Reprinted and used with permission.

FIGURE 10.11
Assign the print queue to the printer.
Source: Screen shot from NetWare, © 1983-1999, Novell, Inc. All rights reserved. Reprinted and used with permission.

FIGURE 10.12
Create a print server leaf object.
Source: Screen shot from NetWare, © 1983-1999, Novell, Inc. All rights reserved. Reprinted and used with permission.

FIGURE 10.13
Name the print server.
Source: Screen shot from NetWare, © 1983-1999, Novell, Inc. All rights reserved. Reprinted and used with permission.

SUMMARY

Four leaf objects work together to carry out the print process. The user leaf object is assigned to a print queue leaf object. A print queue leaf object is assigned to a printer leaf object. A printer leaf object is assigned to a print server leaf object. A print server manages the printer. A printer references the actual physical device on the network. A print queue holds print jobs in a prior-

FIGURE 10.14
Assign the printer to the print server.
Source: Screen shot from NetWare, © 1983-1999, Novell, Inc. All rights reserved. Reprinted and used with permission.

ity fashion. A print job is created when the user clicks on "File," "Print" at the workstation. Becoming comfortable with printer management takes practice, planning, insight, and patience.

EXERCISES

1. Define the following:
   a. local printer
   b. network printer
   c. print queue object
   d. printer object
   e. print server object
   f. authenticating
2. Distinguish between a local and network printer.
3. List the four types of leaf objects that work together to complete the print process.
4. Explain how the four special leaf object types work together to complete the print process.
5. Explain how to create the four types of leaf objects.
6. Why is it important to document the printer setups?

LAB #10A

Explore the configuration of your organization's printer setups. Identify the names and relationships of the key objects involved.

LAB #10B

Draw a diagram of the relationships noted in Lab 10A. Now look at the diagram. Would you make any changes to it? Do the printer setups fit this organization's actual physical structure?

LAB #10C

Create a fictitious company. Plan out how you would set up the printers for each of the departments in your fictitious company. Make sure to indicate the names and context of the various objects involved.

LAB #10D

Following the steps given in this text, implement your plan developed in Lab 10C.

LAB #10E

Explore the booklets associated with at least one printer. Particularly find one where the manufacturer has its own printer administrative software.

CHAPTER ELEVEN

PRINT UTILITIES

INSPIRING MOMENT

You are busy in your new position as a network administrator. You enjoy your job, but there is one problem. Users from various departments continue to come to you complaining about the printers or their printouts. Some common questions and concerns are:

"Where's my printout? I've been waiting a long time for it."

"Did my print job go to the printer on the first floor or the tenth floor?"

"How can I make sure my reports come out in sets of two and in condensed print?"

They all look to you for answers. Sometimes, they are very demanding and get upset when their printouts do not come out right. As a network administrator, you are responsible for maintaining the printers and coordinating the sharing of them. You want to keep the users content as much as possible. How do you make sure they get their reports and other printouts *and* ensure they are printed the way each user wants?

QUESTIONS FOR THOUGHT

If you were in charge of printing and output distribution, how would you set up your system to lessen the error rate? How would you inform the users of the procedures?

CHALLENGE

Once you understand which forms go to which printers, make a chart. Your chart should show the printer, print queue name, type of form, and other relevant information. File this chart for safekeeping; use a copy for reference. If you are in charge of users, share this chart with them. If you are in a situation where the printers are not working correctly and your coworkers are upset, remain calm and try to rectify the problem. If necessary, call your supervisor for assistance.

CHAPTER OBJECTIVES

After finishing this chapter, you should be able to:

1. Discover the main purpose of PCONSOLE, PRINTCON, and PRINTDEF.
2. Walk through steps normally taken to set up and print a job using the print menu utilities PCONSOLE, PRINTCON, and PRINTDEF.

3. Explain how Novell NetWare makes use of print queues to print jobs.

4. Explore the options available for print configurations.

5. Explore the options available for printer definitions.

6. Define printer device modes and functions.

7. Explain how to specify different print forms.

EXPLORING PRINT UTILITIES

Three NetWare menu utilities—PRINTDEF, PRINTCON, and PCONSOLE—function together to allow a user to print documents.

PRINTDEF

The PRINTDEF utility requires administrative or equivalent status. It allows an administrator to identify forms and printer font capabilities. Normal end users cannot make changes to PRINTDEF settings. The top user on the system is known as ADMIN, which is short for "administrator." The administrator can increase the power of an end-user account to be the same as ADMIN; this is called ADMIN equivalent. See Figure 11.1. PRINTDEF stands for "printer definition."

Print Devices

To choose a printer, first select "Print Devices" from the "PRINTDEF Options" menu. Upon doing so, the "Print Device Options" menu will appear. See Figure 11.2. Select the "Import Print Devices" option.

FIGURE 11.1
PRINTDEF's "Options" menu.

```
PrintDef Options

 | Print Devices
 | Print Forms
 | Change Current Context
```

FIGURE 11.2
The menu used to set up printers.

```
Print Device Options

 | Edit Print Devices
 | Import Print Devices
 | Export Print Devices
```

At this point, the computer will ask for the directory location of the print device files (.PDF). The administrator may specify a local drive's directory or a network drive. SYS:PUBLIC is the usual response to this prompt. Several .PDF files reside in the SYS:PUBLIC directory. The import print device steps are repeated for each print device file you wish to import. For example, HPJ4.PDF and HP3.PDF could both be imported; the files are selected separately, however. A list of all .PDF files found in the specified directory will appear next. The supervisor should choose the one appropriate for the network's printer.

If for some reason the supervisor wants to change the .PDF file, he or she may do so using "Edit Print Devices" from the "Print Device Options" menu.

Edit Print Devices   Upon choosing "Edit Print Device" from the "Print Device Options" menu, a list of imported print device definition files (PDF) appears. A user can then select the desired one, such as HP Laserjet 4, and press Enter. Then the "Edit Device Options" menu appears. See Figure 11.3.

Choosing "Device Modes" brings up a list of fonts and corresponding pitches. Upon selecting a particular font/pitch combination, that particular selection's functions appear. Functions are coded lines that instruct the computer to carry out the font/pitch as requested. At this point, the administrator may make corrections or changes to the coded lines and press Escape when done. This option is useful if the network's printer does not appear on the list.

New printers usually come with instructional guides, which usually contain a listing of escape codes for that particular printer. If a user does not find a .PDF file for a particular printer, it is possible to select a similar printer and modify the escape codes found in the selected printer's .PDF file. A user can change the escape codes to those listed in the printer guide for the printer in which no .PDF file exists. Make some modifications to an existing mode and function. This can come in handy if a printer manufacturer comes up with a new model. When a new printer is manufactured, quite commonly the .PDF file has not yet been released or for some reason is not available to the user. These files are printer dependent, which means that each file contains instructions for a particular printer's operation.

Print Forms

To bring up the "Print Forms" utility, choose "Print Forms" from the PRINTDEF menu. A list of currently defined forms appears. Press Insert to add a new form definition. The system will prompt the user for a name for the new form. After keying in a name, press Enter. Then the "Form Definition" screen appears. See Figure 11.4. Enter the width in number of characters fitting across the page. The default is 80. Enter the length in number of lines of characters fitting vertically on the page. The default is 66. Press Escape to save the form.

FIGURE 11.3
Supervisors may make customized changes to a printer's mode or function by using the "Edit Device Options" menu.

```
Edit Device Options
═══════════════════════════════
 | Device Modes
 | Device Functions
```

FIGURE 11.4
The form definition function helps administrators identify forms by name and by number.

```
Form Definition
═══════════════

 |
 |Name
 |
 |Number   0
 |
 |Length   66
 |
 |Width    80
 |
```

Change Current Context

If a user is trying to work with customized print device files rather than the predefined ones located in the PUBLIC directory, it may be necessary to change context to locate the files. To do this, choose this option and key in the context where the customized print devices are stored.

PRINTCON

With so many users on a LAN, PRINTCON setups, which is shorthand for "print job configurations," vary depending on the needs of the particular user. Some users may prefer documents with tiny print; other users prefer large print. This utility allows a user to specify how he or she wishes to set up print configurations. Once into PRINTCON, the "Available Options" menu appears. See Figure 11.5.

Edit Print Job Configuration

To create a print configuration, choose "Edit Print Job configuration." Press Insert to let the computer know that this is a new configuration. The system will prompt the user for a name for the new print job configuration. The user would then key in a name and press Enter.

FIGURE 11.5
Customizing print configurations through PRINTCON.

```
Available Options
═════════════════

 |Edit Print Job Configuration
 |Select Default Print Job Configuration
 |Change Current Object
 |
 |
```

Next, fill in the details for the particular configuration. The details required are fairly straightforward, such as "number of copies" and "form name." Form name, device, and mode require the same names used under PRINTDEF; pressing Enter on these entries will bring up names from which to choose. To add names to the list, the administrator must use the PRINTDEF utility.

Select Default Print Job Configuration

It's common to have several print job configurations defined. For example, for some reports, a user may select a configuration that instructs the printer to print two copies of each report. Other reports require only one copy. Suppose a user sets up two separate print job configurations. Once the print job configurations have been added through the edit option, the "Select Default" option specifies the configuration that will be used most of the time. A user simply highlights the print job configuration name that he or she would like to set as the default and presses Enter. A small asterisk appears by the name denoting which configuration is the default.

Change Current Object

If the administrator would like to create a print job configuration for one or more users, the "Change Current Object" option allows the administrator to specify which user or container (if for a group) to set as current. When "Change Current Object" is selected, the system asks the administrator to enter a new object name. In this case, users and containers are considered as objects. Pressing Insert brings up a list of users and containers from which to choose.

Using the Print Job Configuration

To invoke the print job configuration, use the CAPTURE command and specify the name that was assigned to the configuration:

```
CAPTURE J=MYPRINT
```

Note in this example that if the J=MYPRINT was left off, the system would use the print job configuration marked as default. If no configurations are marked as default, an error message would appear on the screen. The DOS TYPE command may be used to print once the CAPTURE command has been invoked:

```
TYPE MYFILE.TXT>PRN
```

Another way to print is through a word-processing application software. Anything that would normally go to a printer attached to the user's workstation would be redirected to the printer specified in the print job configuration.

PCONSOLE

PCONSOLE stands for "print console." The PCONSOLE utility allows users to see the print jobs currently in the queues and to add others. It is also used to add queues and print servers. When a user brings up PCONSOLE, the "Available Options" menu appears. See Figure 11.6.

FIGURE 11.6
PCONSOLE options.

```
┌─────────────────────────────────────────────────────────┐
│                                                           │
│        Available Options                                  │
│        ─────────────────────────                          │
│        |    Print Queues                                  │
│        |    Printers                                      │
│        |    Print Servers                                 │
│        |    Quick Setup                                   │
│        |    Change Context                                │
│        |                                                  │
│                                                           │
└─────────────────────────────────────────────────────────┘
```

```
┌──────────────────────────────────────────────────────────────────┐
│ NetWare Print Console  4.10    May  18, 1999 1:58pm                │
│  Context: abc_co                                                   │
│                                                                    │
│  ┌────────────────────────┐                                       │
│  │ Print Queues           │                                       │
│  │ abcprintq_0            │ vailable Option │ Print Queue Information │
│  │                        ├─────────────────┼──────────────────────┤
│  │                        │ Print Queues    │ Print Jobs           │
│  │                        │ Printers        │ Status               │
│  │                        │ Print Servers   │ Attached Print Servers │
│  │                        │ Quick Setup     │ Information           │
│  │                        │ Change Context  │ Users                │
│  │                        │                 │ Operators            │
│  │                        │                 │ Print Servers        │
│  │                        │                                       │
│  └────────────────────────┘                                       │
│                                                                    │
│  Press < Enter > to view a list of print jobs in the print queue.  │
│                                                                    │
│ Enter = Select   Esc = Exit                          F1 = Help     │
└──────────────────────────────────────────────────────────────────┘
```

FIGURE 11.7
The information screen for a particular print queue that has already been selected.

Print Queues

When the "Print Queues" option is selected, a list of defined print queues displays on the screen. A print queue is a waiting line for print jobs (requests) waiting to print. If a user highlights the print queue of interest and presses Enter, the "Print Queue Information" menu appears. If the queue doesn't exist yet and the user is authorized to create a new print queue, the system will prompt the user for the name of the new queue after Insert is pressed.

Print Queue Information

After a user presses Enter on the particular queue of interest, the "Print Queue Information" menu appears on the screen, as shown in Figure 11.7.

By choosing "Print Jobs," a user can see a list of print jobs currently printing or waiting to print. See Figure 11.8. When a user sends something to the print queue for

```
┌─────────────────────────────────────────────────────────────────────┐
│                                                                       │
│ NetWare Print Console  4.10          Thursday  May  18, 1999  1:58pm  │
│  Context: abc_co                                                      │
│   ┌───────────────────────────────────────────────────────────────┐  │
│   │ Seq Name      Description          Status     Form   Job ID     │  │
│   │                                                                 │  │
│   │                                                                 │  │
│   │                                                                 │  │
│   │                                                                 │  │
│   │                                                                 │  │
│   │                                                                 │  │
│   │                                                                 │  │
│   │                                                                 │  │
│   │                                                                 │  │
│   │                                                                 │  │
│   │                                                                 │  │
│   └───────────────────────────────────────────────────────────────┘  │
│ Select a job to view its configuration. Press <Insert> to create new jobs. A │
│ job can be changed or deleted by its owner or a queue operator.       │
│                                                                       │
│ Enter = Select   Ins = Ins   Del = Del   F5 = Mark   Esc = Escape     F1 = Help │
└─────────────────────────────────────────────────────────────────────┘
```

FIGURE 11.8
The "Print Job" menu shows jobs waiting to print.

printing, the information sent, including the instructions noting how it should be printed, is called the print job.

Specifying File to Print

If a user wants to submit a file to print, by pressing the Insert key the menu shown in Figure 11.9 will appear. If the user is not sure of the exact file name and its path, pressing the Insert key again will inform the network operating system that he or she wants to be prompted. The first prompting screen is for the volume name; see Figure 11.10.

After the user highlights the desired volume and presses Enter, the second prompting screen appears asking the user to select a directory name. See Figure 11.11. Notice that if the chosen directory has subdirectories under it, the user may be prompted to se-

```
NetWare Print Console  4.10          Thursday  May  18, 1999  1:58pm
  Context: abc_co

 ┌─────────────────────────────────────────────────────────────────┐
 │ Seq Name        Description           Status      Form   Job ID   │
 │┌─────────────────────────────────────────────────────────────────┐│
 ││           Select Directory From Which to Print                   ││
 ││                                                                  ││
 │└─────────────────────────────────────────────────────────────────┘│
 │                                                                   │
 │                                                                   │
 │                                                                   │
 │                                                                   │
 │                                                                   │
 │                                                                   │
 └───────────────────────────────────────────────────────────────────┘

Enter a directory, or press <Insert> to browse
Enter = Select  Ins = Ins  Del = Del   F5 = Mark   Esc = Escape      F1 = Help
```

FIGURE 11.9
In the "Specifying File to Print" menu, the system is prompting for the name of the file to print.

```
NetWare Print Console 4.10          Thursday May 18, 1999 1:58pm
Context: abc_co

┌─────────────────────────────────────────────────────────────────┐
│ Seq Name          Description              Status      Form  Job ID│
├─────────────────────────────────────────────────────────────────┤
│              Select Directory From Which to Print                  │
│                                                                     │
│                                                                     │
│ ┌───────────────────────────────────────────────────────────────┐ │
│ │                          Volumes                               │ │
│ ├───────────────────────────────────────────────────────────────┤ │
│ │ [Additional Volume Objects]                                    │ │
│ │ [Additional Servers]                                           │ │
│ │ ABC_SYS                      (DS Volume Object)                │ │
│ │ A:                           (Local Drive)                     │ │
│ │ B:                           (Local Drive)                     │ │
│ │ C:                           (Local Drive)                     │ │
│ │                                                                │ │
│ └───────────────────────────────────────────────────────────────┘ │
│                                                                     │
│ Press <Enter> to view the next level.  Press <Esc> to select the current path. │
│                                                                     │
│ Enter = Next Level   Esc = Select Current Path   Del = Log out   Alt + F1 = More │
└─────────────────────────────────────────────────────────────────┘
```

FIGURE 11.10
Prompting for volume name.

lect a subdirectory name, as shown in Figure 11.12. Once finished with selecting names at the directory level, the user may press Escape and be prompted for the file name. See Figure 11.13.

CHANGING PRINT PARAMETERS

Both the owner of a particular print job and the queue operator can change some of the printing parameters. To view and/or change the parameters, highlight the print job of interest and press Enter. The parameter screen appears; see Figure 11.14. The user can now make the needed changes and save them by pressing Enter. Changing the status of a print job is common. For example, the queue operator or user may change the status parameter to hold.

```
NetWare Print Console  4.10           Thursday  May  18, 1999  1:58pm
  Context: abc_co

    Seq Name         Description            Status      Form   Job ID

    ┌──────────────────────────────────────────────────┐
    │      Select Directory From Which to Print         │
    │ ABC_SYS:USERS                                      │
    └──────────────────────────────────────────────────┘

    ┌──────────────────────────────────────────────────┐
    │ Network Directories                                │
    │                                                    │
    │ ..                                                 │
    │ ALAN                                               │
    │ ASHLEY                                             │
    │ BEN                                                │
    │ DONNA                                              │
    │ DOUG                                               │
    │ MARC                                               │
    │ NANCY                                              │
    └──────────────────────────────────────────────────┘

  Press <Enter> to view the next level.  Press <Esc> to select the current path.

  Enter = Next Level   Esc = Select Current Path    F1 = Help
```

FIGURE 11.11
The "Select Directory From Which to Print" screen.

See Figures 11.15 and 11.16. The user or queue operator may also choose to wait until a certain time before the job can print. This is done by answering "Yes" to "Defer printing" and specifying a date and time to print. See Figure 11.17.

If a print job is placed on hold, it will not print. When the hold is removed, by selecting "No" for this option, the print job would then wait its turn in line for printing. It may already be at the top of the line, depending on how long it's been on hold.

Status

Choose the "Status" option of the "Print Parameters" screen to view the current status of a particular printer. The "Status" screen will let a user know if the printer is "active" or "stopped." Sometimes the print queue operator has stopped the printer for maintenance or to change forms.

```
NetWare Print Console  4.10          Thursday  May  18, 1999  1:58pm
 Context: abc_co

┌─────────────────────────────────────────────────────────────────┐
│ Seq Name        Description              Status      Form   Job ID │
├───────────────────────────────────────┬───────────────────────────┤
│   Select Directory From Which to Print │                           │
│ ABC_SYS:USERS\NANCY                    │                           │
│ ┌───────────────────────────────────┐ │                           │
│ │ Network Directories               │ │                           │
│ ├───────────────────────────────────┤ │                           │
│ │ ..                                 │ │                           │
│ │                                    │ │                           │
│ │                                    │ │                           │
│ │                                    │ │                           │
│ │                                    │ │                           │
│ │                                    │ │                           │
│ │                                    │ │                           │
│ └───────────────────────────────────┘ │                           │
└───────────────────────────────────────┴───────────────────────────┘

 Press  <Enter>  to view the next level.  Press  <Esc>  to select the current path.

 Enter = Next Level   Esc = Select Current Path    F1 = Help
```

FIGURE 11.12
The specifying subdirectory.

Print Queue ID

The "Print Queue ID" option presents a list of the print queue names currently assigned.

Queue Users

The "Queue Users" option provides a list of users allowed to use the currently selected queue. By pressing Insert, the administrator can add more users to the list. See Figure 11.18.

Operators

The "Queue Operators" option provides a list of users who have been designated by the administrator as queue operators. By pressing Insert, the administrator can add more users or an entire group to this list. See Figure 11.19.

```
NetWare Print Console  4.10          Thursday  May  18, 1999  1:58pm
Context: abc_co
┌──────────────────────────────────────────────────────────────────┐
│ Seq Name        Description              Status   Form     Job ID  │
├──────────────────────────────────────────────────────────────────┤
│        ┌───────────────────────────────────────────────┐          │
│        │        Select Directory From Which to Print    │          │
│        ├───────────────────────────────────────────────┤          │
│        │  ABC_SYS:USERS\NANCY                            │          │
│        │            ┌───────────────────────┐           │          │
│        │            │     Available Files    │           │          │
│        │         .. │ 41MAP                  │           │          │
│        │            │ 41SCREEN               │           │          │
│        │            │ 41SCRNS.95A            │           │          │
│        │            │ PUBDIR4.595            │           │          │
│        │            │ SCRN41B.595            │           │          │
│        │            │ SCRN41C.595            │           │          │
│        │            │ SCRN41D.595            │           │          │
│        │            │                        │           │          │
│        └────────────┴────────────────────────┴──────────┘          │
│  Choose the file (or files) to be printed.                         │
│                                                                     │
│  Enter = Select    F5 = Mark                    F1 = Help           │
└──────────────────────────────────────────────────────────────────┘
```

FIGURE 11.13
Selecting the file name.

Print Servers

The "Print Servers" option provides a list of print servers that the administrator has set up. Print servers, used in companies with many printers to manage, lessen the load of the file server by managing the printing resources. By pressing Insert, the supervisor can add more print servers to the list. See Figure 11.20. If a user highlights the desired print server and presses Enter, the screen that lists the printers for that particular print server appears.

The "Printers" Screen

The "Printers" screen lists the printers that are assigned to a particular print server. See Figure 11.21. Upon highlighting a particular printer and pressing Enter, the "Printer Configuration" screen appears. See Figure 11.22. On this screen, notice that the most common type of printer is the parallel printer; see Figure 11.23. Parallel printers receive data for printing at a faster rate than serial printers. Parallel printers receive data byte by byte, whereas se-

```
NetWare Print Console  4.10          Thursday  May  18, 1999  1:58pm
Context: abc_co

┌──────────────────────────────────────────────────────────────────┐
│                   New Print Job to be Submitted                     │
├──────────────────────────────────────────────────────────────────┤
│  Print job:                          File Size:                     │
│  Client:                Nancy[3]                                    │
│  Description:           41MAP                                       │
│  Status:                                                            │
│                                                                     │
│  User hold:             No           Entry date:                    │
│  Operator hold:         No           Entry time:                    │
│  Service sequence:                   Form:            0             │
│                                      Print banner:    Yes           │
│  Number of copies:      1            Name:            Nancy         │
│                                      Banner name:     41MAP         │
│                                                                     │
│  File contents:         Byte stream                                 │
│  Tab size:                                                          │
│                                      Defer printing:  No            │
│  Form feed:             Yes          Target date:                   │
│  Notify when done:      No           Target time:                   │
└──────────────────────────────────────────────────────────────────┘

  Enter up to 49 characters to describe the print job.

  Esc = Escape    F10 = Save                      F1 = Help
```

FIGURE 11.14
The "Print Parameters" screen.

rial printers receive data bit by bit. (Eight bits make up one byte.) Other types of printers are also available.

Service Modes for Forms

There are four options under "Service Modes" for forms: "Change forms as needed," "Minimize form changes within print queues," "Service only currently mounted form," and "Minimize form changes across print queues." See Figure 11.24.

Change Forms as Needed The "Change forms as needed" option takes print requests on a first come, first served basis. With this particular option, form changes would occur each time a print job requesting a form that is not currently loaded arrives to the top of the queue.

```
NetWare Print Console  4.10           Thursday  May  18, 1999  1:58pm
   Context: abc_co

   ┌─────────────────────────────────────────────────────────────────┐
   │               New Print Job to be Submitted                       │
   ├─────────────────────────────────────────────────────────────────┤
   │ Print job:                          File Size:                    │
   │ Client:               Nancy[3]                                    │
   │ Description:          41MAP                                        │
   │ Status:                                                           │
   │                                                                   │
   │ User hold:            Yes           Entry date:                   │
   │ Operator hold:        No            Entry time:                   │
   │ Service sequence:                   Form:          0              │
   │                                     Print banner:  Yes            │
   │ Number of copies:     1             Name:          Nancy          │
   │                                     Banner name:   41MAP          │
   │ File contents:        Byte stream                                 │
   │ Tab size:                                                         │
   │                                     Defer printing: No            │
   │ Form feed:            Yes           Target date:                  │
   │ Notify when done:     No            Target time:                  │
   └─────────────────────────────────────────────────────────────────┘

   Choose yes to put the print job on hold.

   Esc = Escape   F10 = Save                        F1 = Help
```

FIGURE 11.15
When a user places a hold on a print job, this screen appears.

Minimize Form Changes Within Print Queues   The option to minimize form changes within print queues seeks to have the printer process all the jobs requesting the same form before printing other jobs in the print queue.

Service Only Currently Mounted Forms   The option to service only currently mounted forms allows only the jobs requesting the form that is currently mounted on the printer to go through. All other jobs are left waiting indefinitely.

Minimize Changes Across Print Queues   It is conceivable to have more than one print queue assigned to a printer. By choosing the option to minimize changes across print queues, the system prints all jobs requesting the currently mounted form from all the queues assigned to the printer before handling any form change requests.

```
NetWare Print Console  4.10         Thursday  May  18, 1999  1:58pm
Context: abc_co
┌──────────────────────────────────────────────────────────────────┐
│                    New Print Job to be Submitted                   │
├──────────────────────────────────────────────────────────────────┤
│ Print job:                         File Size:                      │
│ Client:                 Nancy[3]                                   │
│ Description:            41MAP                                       │
│ Status:                                                            │
│                                                                    │
│ User hold:              No          Entry date:                    │
│ Operator hold:          Yes         Entry time:                    │
│ Service sequence:                   Form:         0                │
│                                     Print banner: Yes              │
│ Number of copies:       1           Name:         Nancy            │
│                                     Banner name:  41MAP            │
│ File contents:          Byte stream                                │
│ Tab size:                                                          │
│                                     Defer printing: No             │
│ Form feed:              Yes         Target date:                   │
│ Notify when done:       No          Target time:                   │
└──────────────────────────────────────────────────────────────────┘
  Choose yes to put the print job on hold.

  Esc = Escape    F10 = Save                       F1 = Help
```

FIGURE 11.16
When an operator places a hold on a print job, this screen appears.

SPECIAL NOTES REGARDING PRINTERS

There are many categories and types of printers currently on the market:

Laser printers provide clear output and can be used for heavy volume usage and fast printing.

Ink-jet printers provide clear output but less volume usage than laser printers.

Dot matrix printers, which print letters made by forming small tiny dots together, are slower than laser and ink-jet printers and are not suited for high-volume printing.

To choose a printer, the volume of printing anticipated and the number of users that will be sharing the same printer must be determined.

NetWare Print Console 4.10   Thursday May 18, 1999 1:58pm
Context: abc_co

───
          New Print Job to be Submitted

Print job: File Size:
Client: Nancy[3]
Description: 41MAP
Status:

User hold: No   Entry date:
Operator hold: No   Entry time:
Service sequence: Form: 0
                                     Print banner: Yes
Number of copies: 1   Name: Nancy
                                     Banner name: 41MAP
File contents: Byte stream
Tab size:

Form feed: Yes   Defer printing: Yes
Notify when done: No   Target date: 5-19-1999
                                     Target time: 11:59:59 pm

Enter the date when the print job will be printed. For example, "6 30 99"
specifies June 30, 1999 (6-30-99)
Esc = Escape   F10 = Save   F1 = Help

FIGURE 11.17
The "Time Deferment Requested" screen for changing print parameters.

```
NetWare Print Console 4.10          Thursday  May  18, 1999 2:01pm
Context: abc_co

 ┌─Print Queues───────────┐          ┌─Print Queue Users──────────┐
 │ abcprintq_0            │          │ ABC_CO.          (Group)   │
 │                        │          │ ACCT             (Group)   │
 │                        │          │ Admin            (User)    │
 │                        │          │ CONSULTANTS      (Group)   │
 │                        │          │ DEV              (Group)   │
 │                        │          │ OPER             (Group)   │
 │                        │          │ [Root]           (Group)   │
 └────────────────────────┘          └────────────────────────────┘
```

These are the objects which can submit jobs to this print queue.

Ins = Insert   Del = Delete   F5 = Mark   Esc = Exit   F1 = Help

FIGURE 11.18
The "Queue Users" option.

NetWare Print Console 4.10   Thursday May 18, 1999 2:01pm
Context: abc_co

```
┌─ Print Queues ──────┐          ┌─ Print Queue Operators ──────┐
│ abcprintq_0         │          │ Admin                 (User)  │
│                     │          │ Ben.CONSULTANTS       (User)  │
│                     │          │ Marc.CONSULTANTS      (User)  │
│                     │          │ Nancy.CONSULTANTS     (user)  │
│                     │          │ Thomas.CONSULTANTS    (user)  │
│                     │          │ (Root)                        │
└─────────────────────┘          └───────────────────────────────┘
```

These are the objects which can manage the status of this print queue and its
print job entries.

Ins = Insert   Del = Delete   F5 = Mark   Esc = Exit   F1 = Help

FIGURE 11.19
The "Queue Operators" option.

FIGURE 11.20
Print servers.

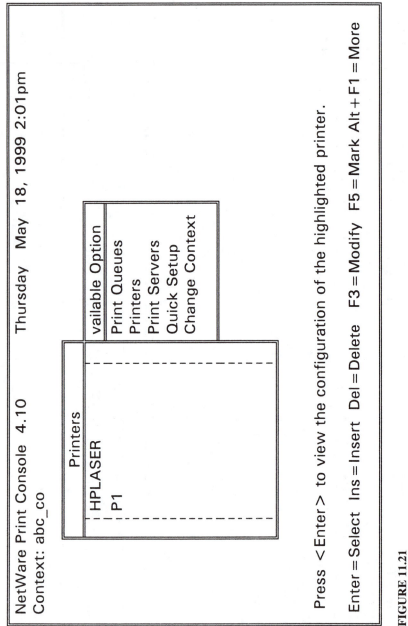

FIGURE 11.21
"Printers" screen.

NetWare Print Console 4.10   Thursday May 18, 1999 2:01pm
Context: abc_co

Printer HPLASER Configuration

Print server: PS_CLC
Printer number: 0
Printer status: (unavailable)
Printer type: Parallel
Configuration: (See form)
Starting form: 0
Buffer size in KB: 3
Buffer type: Text
Service mode for forms: Minimize form changes within print queue
Sampling interval: 5
Print queues assigned   (See list)
Notification   (See list)

Specify the logical number (0-254, inclusive) assigned to this printer.

Enter = Select   F10 = Save   F8 = Port Driver Name   Esc = Exit   F1 = Help

FIGURE 11.22
"Printer Configuration" screen.

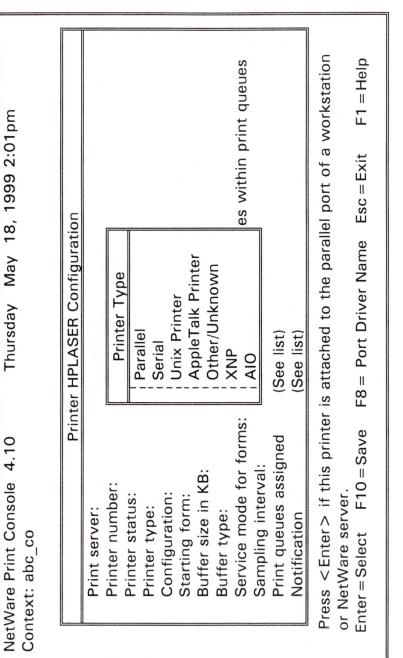

NetWare Print Console 4.10   Thursday May 18, 1999 2:01pm
Context: abc_co

Printer HPLASER Configuration

Print server:
Printer number:
Printer status:
Printer type:
Configuration:
Starting form:
Buffer size in KB:
Buffer type:
Service mode for forms:
Sampling interval:
Print queues assigned: (See list)
Notification   (See list)

Printer Type
Parallel
Serial
Unix Printer
AppleTalk Printer
Other/Unknown
XNP
AIO

es within print queues

Press <Enter> if this printer is attached to the parallel port of a workstation
or NetWare server.
Enter = Select   F10 = Save   F8 = Port Driver Name   Esc = Exit   F1 = Help

FIGURE 11.23
Printer types.

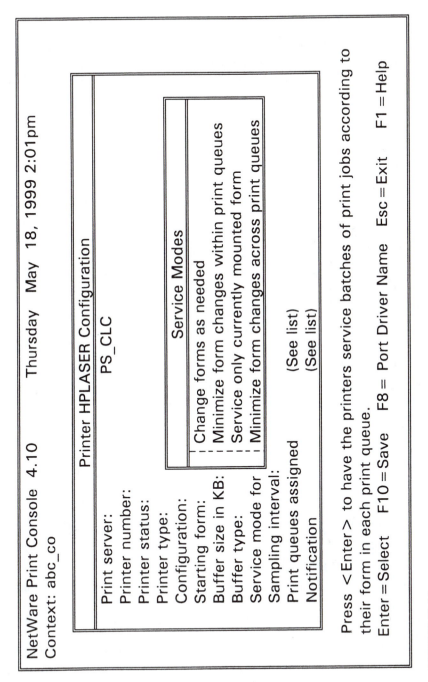

NetWare Print Console 4.10   Thursday May 18, 1999 2:01pm
Context: abc_co

Printer HPLASER Configuration

Print server: PS_CLC
Printer number:
Printer status:
Printer type:
Configuration:
Starting form:
Buffer size in KB:
Buffer type:
Service mode for
Sampling interval:
Print queues assigned   (See list)
Notification   (See list)

Service Modes

Change forms as needed
Minimize form changes within print queues
Service only currently mounted form
Minimize form changes across print queues

Press <Enter> to have the printers service batches of print jobs according to
their form in each print queue.
Enter = Select   F10 = Save   F8 = Port Driver Name   Esc = Exit   F1 = Help

FIGURE 11.24
Service mode for handling form change requests.

SUMMARY

Three print utilities work together to end up with the final result: a printed document. PRINTDEF allows the supervisor to define printers and forms and make changes to fonts and pitches if needed. PRINTCON allows users to use the forms and printers defined by specifying job configurations. PCONSOLE allows users to monitor their jobs in the print queues and to add other jobs. It also allows the administrator to add more printing queues and queue operators and specify which users can use the queues.

EXERCISES

1. Define the following:
   a. print forms
   b. print device
   c. form number
   d. print job configuration
   e. CAPTURE
   f. print queue
   g. print job
   h. sequence
   i. print parameters
   j. operator hold
   k. user hold
   l. queue operator
   m. print server
   n. printer configuration
   o. service mode

2. What do the following stand for?
   a. PDF
   b. PRINTCON
   c. PRINTDEF
   d. PCONSOLE

3. Explain and walk through what you as a user would do to add a print job to the print queue.

4. What is meant by *mode* and *function*? Under what circumstances might the supervisor make changes to the modes and functions?

5. What are the differences among PCONSOLE, PRINTCON, and PRINTDEF?

6. Explain what a print queue is used for.

7. A company wants to allow users to use three different forms: GREENBAR, WHITE, and INVOICE. Which menu utility allows the administrator to enter the form definition?

What information would the administrator need for adding each form? How should the administrator add these forms?

8. You would like to have two copies print every time. You also would like to print regular ASCII text files. How would you do this?

LAB #11

The following lab will allow you to gain experience with PRINTCON and PCONSOLE. After going through this lab, you may want to experiment by creating other print job configurations and using them.

1. Use PRINTCON to create a print job configuration. You would like two copies of your output. You also want condensed printing. For the form name, use your first name. Name the print job configuration GONOW.
2. At the F:\> prompt, invoke the CAPTURE command to let the computer know that it should use the print job configuration.
3. Use the DOS editor to key in the following text and save it as HELLO.TXT.:

```
Hello. This is a test of printing using a print job
configuration. This is only a simple test.
```

4. Print HELLO.TXT using the DOS TYPE command.
5. Print HELLO.TXT using PCONSOLE. (See print queue information.)
6. Go to the PUBLIC directory and locate PRINTCON, PRINTDEF, and PCONSOLE.

SAFEGUARDING THE LAN

This section discusses the importance of LAN security, troubleshooting, and data protection.

CHAPTER TWELVE   LAN Security, Safeguards, and Troubleshooting

LAN SECURITY, SAFEGUARDS, AND TROUBLESHOOTING

INSPIRING MOMENT

As part of your new position in the Data Center, you are responsible for responding to users. Users come to you when they have problems. All the users who work at this location have workstations that are connected to a NetWare 4.1x LAN. Recently, there have been several reports of breaches in security. In addition, users frequently ask you to help them with logging onto the network because they forgot their password. You have decided to educate the users on the importance of LAN security. For example, unsuspecting users may not realize that using their pet's name as their password may leave their account open to intruders. You now need to explore and learn more about LAN security.

QUESTIONS FOR THOUGHT

Why are passwords needed? What damages could occur if someone broke into the LAN? Could files become damaged or get erased? Why is it important to control how much access a user has to a particular directory? How can you minimize the chances of someone breaking into your account? How do viruses invade computer systems, and what can be done about them?

CHALLENGE

Even as you study and practice networking, get in the habit of learning about and practicing security. Never leave your workstation unattended when you are logged in. Be careful selecting your password. Notify the administrator if you see indications that someone has been in your account. Remember that your organization or company may count on you to ensure the confidentiality of files or directories.

CHAPTER OBJECTIVES

After finishing this chapter, you should be able to:

1. Identify restrictions that can be set through NETADMIN or NWADMIN to limit user accounts.
2. Explain the importance of password protection.
3. Explain what intruder lockout means and how to use it.

4. Explain why it is important to monitor directory trustee assignments.

5. Explain the use of the password restrictions and time restrictions.

6. Explain why viruses are a threat to a LAN and identify some measures that can help prevent them from invading a system.

LAN SECURITY

LAN security can save a company or organization in terms of both time and money. Each year, companies lose money through corruption of software and data. Whether intentional or not, many of these losses could have been prevented by following the simple guidelines discussed in this chapter.

ACCOUNT RESTRICTIONS

While in NWADMIN, double click on a user object to manage the particular user's account (Figure 12.1). Recall from Chapter 4 that NWADMIN is used to set up user accounts and groups. NWADMIN is also a great tool for tightening network security. NETADMIN could

FIGURE 12.1
Inside of NWADMIN, double click on a user object to manage the user's account.
Source: Screen shot from NetWare, © 1983-1999, Novell, Inc. All rights reserved. Reprinted and used with permission.

also be used for managing accounts. NWADMIN is the Windows version and NETADMIN is more for DOS users. If using NETADMIN, go to the "Account Restrictions" screen by following these steps:

1. Access NETADMIN by keying in "netadmin" at any prompt.
2. Select "Manage Objects."
3. Select the user for whom you wish to restrict the account.
4. Select "View or Edit Properties."
5. Select "Account Restrictions."

There are five types of account restrictions: login restrictions, password restrictions, network address restrictions, login time restrictions, and volume/space restrictions.

Login Restrictions

Login restrictions such as "Account disabled," "Account has expiration date," and "Limit concurrent connections" govern the logging-in process (Figure 12.2).

Account Disabled   The "Account disabled" restriction prevents a user or anybody else from logging in. It's either set to yes or no. If set to yes, no logins are allowed. The account would become disabled under these circumstances:
1. If an intruder unsuccessfully tries to break into the account.
2. If an administrator chooses to disable it. For example, if a user was going on vacation, the administrator may want to disable that account for the period that the user is away from the office.

In any case, an administrator or manager can enable the account again by entering "no" at the "Account disabled" prompt through NETADMIN.

FIGURE 12.2
Login restrictions can help in limiting the possibility that a user might forget to sign out and sign in somewhere else.
Source: Screen shot from NetWare, © 1983-1999, Novell, Inc. All rights reserved. Reprinted and used with permission.

Account Has Expiration Date If needed, an administrator could answer yes to the "Account has expiration date" line. In this case, the administrator would be prompted for the date on which the account will expire. After that date, the user could not log in.

Limit Concurrent Connections To prevent users from working at more than one station at a time, an account can be limited to only one sign-on per account at any given time. If this option is set to yes, the administrator is prompted about the number of concurrent sign-ons to allow. This option is especially helpful if new users are on the system. Users sometimes forget to log out and may be logged in to a number of workstations before the day is over; thus those accounts would not be very secure.

Password Restrictions

Administrators can use many options to control password security (Figure 12.3).

Allow User to Change Password When set to yes, the "Allow user to change password" selection gives users the ability to change their passwords. In departments where several people share an account, an administrator may want to set this option to no.

Require Password If the "Require a password" selection is set to yes, a user is required to have a password to access a system. If set to no, a user may have a password, but it is not required. Also if this option is set to no, a statement will appear on the administrator's SECURITY.EXE report stating that a password is not required for that account.

Minimum Password Length Short passwords are easier to guess than long passwords. To make it difficult for intruders to access accounts, an administrator can require a

FIGURE 12.3
Password restrictions allow administrators to control password security.
Source: Screen shot from NetWare, © 1983-1999, Novell, Inc. All rights reserved. Reprinted and used with permission.

minimum password length. In working with computers, it is recommended that passwords have at least eight characters; the default is five characters.

Force Periodic Password Change   If the "Force periodic password changes" selection is set to yes, an administrator or manager would be prompted about the number of days to allow before prompting the user to change his or her password.

Limit Grace Logins   If the "Limit grace logins" selection is set to yes, an administrator is prompted to enter a number. This number specifies how many times the user can log in once his or her password has expired. Once the number of grace logins has been exceeded, the user can no longer log in.

Require Unique Password   If the "Require unique passwords" selection is set to yes, a user will not be allowed to change his or her password to one used before. A new password would be required.

Network Address Restrictions

Network address restrictions allow an administrator to specify particular workstations at which a particular user may sit. Before using this option, the administrator must know the workstation's network interface card (NIC) address. The following user command line utility (CLU) indicates whether someone is already logged in at that particular workstation:

```
G:\>NLIST USER /A
```

This will provide the address and node number. The address number corresponds to the network number. A node number is assigned to each NIC by the manufacturer. It's advisable for the administrator to sit down and log in at the particular workstation of interest (that is, the one that the user is going to be assigned).

To implement the restriction using NETADMIN, select "Network Address Restriction." Press Insert. The computer then prompts for the address. If you are using NWADMIN, go to the user's account, click on "Network Address Restrictions," and click "Add." You will be prompted to enter the network and node number (Figure 12.4).

Login Time Restrictions

User accounts can also be restricted by the amount of time or the particular hours that a user is logged in. That is, an administrator can require that a user not log in during a certain period. To do so, "Time Restrictions" are entered and viewed under the "User Information" menu of the NETADMIN utility. Note, however, that this login time restriction only applies to the login process. If, for example, the administrator restricts the user to logging in between 9:00 A.M. and 5:00 P.M., Monday through Friday, the user may log in at 4:59 P.M. and stay as long as desired, unless, of course, the administrator issues a clear connection instruction. Thus, the restriction only applies to logging in, and it doesn't kick the users off when they go over their allotted time.

Volume/Space Restrictions

Volume/space restrictions allow for limiting the amount of disk space a user can have on the file server. This option is available with NETADMIN.

FIGURE 12.4
Network address restrictions specify where a user may sit.
Source: Screen shot from NetWare, © 1983-1999, Novell, Inc. All rights reserved. Reprinted and used with permission.

DIRECTORY TRUSTEE ASSIGNMENTS AND LAN SECURITY

The process of assigning trustee directory rights was explored in Chapter 5. The number of directories assigned to a user should be limited to those that he or she will actually need. The number of rights to those directories should also be limited. These steps help prevent accidental (or nonaccidental) deletion or modification of files and information leaks.

TRUSTEE DIRECTORY RIGHTS

To work with a given directory, the user must first have been entrusted to use that directory by the administrator or the owner of that directory. In other words, the user must have certain *trustee directory rights*. Depending on the user's needs, the administrator may give all or some of the following rights:

R	Read	Allows a user to read the contents of files
FS	File Scan	Allows a user to search through file names (DIR)
W	Write	Allows a user to write to or make changes to a file
C	Create	Allows a user to create a new subdirectory or file
E	Erase	Allows a user to delete a subdirectory or file

M	Modify	Allows a user to change file attributes and file names
AC	Access Control	Allows a user to entrust others to a directory
S	Supervisor	Allows a user all rights to the directory

PASSWORDS AND LAN SECURITY

In Chapter 9, the SETPASS command line utility (CLU) that allows users to change their passwords was discussed. Review the list presented in Figure 12.5 for some helpful rules regarding selecting passwords. Wisely selecting and implementing password-protected accounts helps keep a LAN secure.

VIRUS THREAT

What is a computer virus? Some programmers write programs that are undetectable by normal means such as the DIR command. Virus programs are called viruses because just as people can pass a biological virus to another person, these destructive programs can be

---

Using Passwords—Rules to Keep in Mind

1. Memorize your password immediately. Do not write it down; it may fall into the wrong hands.

2. Do not use a password that can be found in the dictionary. Sometimes people use special programs that search through passwords in a dictionary fashion to try to break into accounts.

3. Do not use the name of people, places, or pets that are familiar to you. If they are familiar to you, they could be familiar to others also.

4. Longer passwords are harder to guess or figure out than shorter passwords. Pick a password that is at least eight characters long.

5. Mix letters and numbers together in your password. Such passwords are difficult to guess.

6. Always log out of your account when you leave your workstation. Never leave your computer on and unattended.

7. Change your password periodically. Avoid changing it so often that you have difficulty remembering your new password, however.

8. Users can change their passwords unless an administrator specifically sets up those accounts to disallow password changes. Once the password has been changed by the user, only that user knows the password. Although administrators may still change the password to something else, there is no option to show even an administrator what password the user chose. An administrator's screen prompts are a little different. When requesting a change of password, he or she is not prompted to enter the old password first, just the new one.

9. Check with your company, school, or organization and follow the procedures in place.

FIGURE 12.5
Rules for selecting passwords.

passed to different computers. The most common sources for virus spreading are floppy disks and modem transmittals, especially while accessing the Internet.

A virus detection program should be run daily. LAN floppy disks should be protected to ensure that they do not become infected. (Make sure that the floppy disks are virus-free before write-protecting them.) A $3\frac{1}{2}$-inch floppy disk may be protected by leaving the notch found at the top of the disk open. This form of protection is called *write protect* because the computer cannot change the contents by writing new data to it or removing data from it. Note that work disks containing files that the user deliberately wants to work with and change should not be write-protected. If the disk is write-protected when the user attempts to save to it, then an error message occurs.

SAFEGUARDS AND TROUBLESHOOTING

A LAN administrator wants a LAN that operates efficiently and that does not crash. Although nothing can guarantee those results, the following tips may help.

Troubleshooting

Many problems involving efficient operation of a LAN in terms of hardware are associated with cables and connections. The following list is certainly not conclusive, yet it provides a starting ground for troubleshooting problems associated with users not getting onto the network:

1. Do the shortcuts look OK on the desktop? Shortcuts pointing unsuccessfully to the network will usually appear as a small white box with a blue border. If the shortcuts do not look OK, then either the user's drive mappings are not correct or the workstation is not connecting the network.
2. If you are still not sure if the user is connected properly to the network, go to Windows Explorer. Do you see any network drives listed? Can you view the directory structures for these particular drives?
3. If the user is not connecting to the network, try rebooting the workstation. Check again for network connectivity as mentioned in steps 1 and 2.
4. Next, go to the back of the workstation central processing unit (CPU) case and double check that the cables are not all bent and crinkled, particularly if using coaxial cabling.
5. Also, leading into the back of the workstation's CPU case, check the connection of the cable where it plugs into the NIC. Make sure it's in securely. You may try disconnecting and connecting it back again. Keep a flashlight handy for this purpose. If you are using RJ45 connectors or the like, make sure when you connect it back in that you hear a click sound.
6. While looking at the back of the workstation, notice whether or not the NIC has any lights flickering. If no lights are visible, then it's possible that the NIC is not seated all the way down on the motherboard. Seek assistance if needed. You may need to pop open the case, discharge the static from your hands by touching the power supply (unplugged of course), and then make sure the NIC is all the way plugged into the slot. If you still do not see any lights, then it's possible that the NIC is bad and needs to be replaced.

7. If using hubs or switches, check to make sure the connection and cables are both good leading into the hub or switch unit. You should see a light on the hub or switch indicating that the hub and workstation are both talking together. If that light is on, then chances are high it's not the cables, connections, or the NIC.

8. If the cables, connections, and NIC have been ruled out as the source of the problem, you may try reinstalling the NetWare Client 32 software.

Uninterruptible Power Supply (UPS)

Because a file server has several workstations relying on it at any given time, losing power to it also impacts those stations. The files currently open on the file server's drive may become corrupted or may not get updated properly. To make sure that this problem does not occur, an uninterruptible power supply (UPS) should be connected to the file server. A UPS provides battery power to the file server for a few minutes so that the console operator can bring the server down more smoothly. If economically possible, UPSs should be connected to workstations that are processing sensitive data.

Backups

All volumes on the LAN should be backed up periodically. Although backing up takes time, it safeguards the software and data for future use if an emergency occurs. Every company should have a policy of keeping one backup on site and one off site. Some companies have a policy that forbids taking sensitive data off site, and some companies forbid leaving them on site when not in use; therefore, it is wise for the person responsible for making backups to check company policy regarding this issue.

It is also important to recognize that installing the NetWare software onto the file server from scratch usually takes longer than restoring the setup from a tape. A high-speed tape drive capable of backing up a large storage capacity is highly recommended for networks today.

SYSTEM FAULT TOLERANCE

Directories and files located in the file server's volumes are usually used by many people. Therefore, preventing damage to the files and directories is necessary. *System fault tolerance* seeks to do just that. It compensates for hardware problems encountered during saving (or writing) operations.

Novell NetWare uses SFT I as a built-in safeguard. Some networks go even further and have SFT II or SFT III.

SFT I

SFT I involves the use of a *hot fix*. If the file server receives an instruction to write something on the disk and does so, it will read it to confirm that the write operation was successful. If it was not successful (that is, if that area of the disk is damaged), the material that the server was trying to write to the disk is relocated to a different area of the disk. This is a hot fix.

SFT II: Disk Mirroring and Duplexing

In a network that has SFT II, two hard drives exist. The server writes to both drives identically. With *disk mirroring,* one controller card connects both drives to the main motherboard. With *disk duplexing,* each drive has its own controller card.

SFT III: Two Servers and Server Mirroring

In a network that has SFT III and two servers, if the file server goes down, the second server takes over automatically. This is *server mirroring.*

SUMMARY

Maintaining security, keeping the LAN up and running, and taking precautions not only help ensure a better system of operation but also help a company work more profitably. Administrators and managers have a duty to enforce security measures. Installing or upgrading safeguard measures such as SFT II and SFT III and adding a UPS may be a responsibility of the administrator or possibly the equipment support person of a particular organization. In any case, each user should be aware of the importance of security, should always operate under security guidelines, and should offer suggestions for improvement when called upon.

EXERCISES

1. Define the following:

   a. account restrictions

   b. login restrictions

   c. password restrictions

   d. login time restrictions

   e. volume/space restrictions

   f. concurrent connections

   g. grace logins

   h. network address

   i. system fault tolerance

   j. hot fix

   k. disk mirroring

   l. disk duplexing

   m. server mirroring

2. Why are passwords important? List several tips on their use.
3. What kinds of restrictions can be placed on user accounts?
4. List some rules for selecting a password.
5. Why is it important to limit directories assigned and their rights?
6. What can you do to help prevent the spread of viruses?
7. What is intruder lockout?
8. Under what two conditions could an account become disabled?
9. What is the minimum number of characters recommended for a password?

LAB #12

In this lab, you will get firsthand experience at LAN security. You will explore the security of your particular account on the LAN. After completing this lab, you will understand what security measures have been implemented for your account. You will be comfortable with changing your password. You will also be comfortable controlling whether a disk is write-protected or not.

1. Practice changing your password. First, log into the system. Key in "setpass." (If you get an error message, check with your LAN administrator.) You should be prompted for your current password. Key it in correctly and press Enter.

    Next, you should be prompted for a new password. Key it in and press Enter. After doing so, you will be prompted to enter the new password again to verify that you did not make an error when typing it in the first time. Notice that as you type, passwords do not appear on the screen.
2. Attempt to log in using an incorrect login name. Type "login superuser." Write down the error message that is displayed.
3. Attempt to log into your user account, but use the wrong password. What error message is displayed? Do not do this step repeatedly; doing so could result in your account having an "intruder detection" lock placed on it.
4. Following the steps mentioned in this chapter, find out if your particular user account has any account restrictions placed on it. Write a brief description of the restrictions you notice.
5. Following the steps mentioned in this chapter, find out if your particular user account has any login restrictions placed on it. Write a brief description of the restrictions you notice.
6. Following the steps mentioned in this chapter, find out if your particular user account has any password restrictions. Write a brief description of the restrictions you notice.
7. Following the steps mentioned in this chapter, find out if your particular user account has any login time restrictions placed on it. Write a brief description of the restrictions you notice.
8. Following the steps mentioned in this chapter, find out if your particular user account has any volume/space restrictions placed on it. Write a brief description of the account restrictions you notice.

9. To demonstrate the use of write-protecting your disk to protect programs, get out a floppy disk, preferably a $3\frac{1}{2}$-inch floppy disk. Slide the write-protect notch, located at the top of the disk, into the open position. Your disk is now write-protected.

10. To demonstrate that the disk is truly write-protected, place the write-protected disk into the disk drive. Next, use the DOS editor to create a small text file and try to save it onto this disk. Since you are trying to write (save) to a disk that has been write-protected, an error message should appear on your screen. Write down the error message that appears.

    If the network or computer at which you are sitting had a virus, write-protecting your disk will keep the virus from writing to the disk as well.

11. Take out your disk and change it to be not protected. Now attempt to create a file on it using the DOS editor. Notice that this time you can successfully save your work.

AUTOMATION

Once user accounts have been created, automation tools provide an added customization for the user. This part explores the creation of login scripts and menus as part of the automation process.

CHAPTER THIRTEEN   Login Scripts
CHAPTER FOURTEEN   Menus

CHAPTER THIRTEEN

LOGIN SCRIPTS

INSPIRING MOMENT

Suddenly you find yourself faced with controlling part of the logging-in process for the users in your department. Some users need to be reminded of various meetings that they are to attend. Some users require the setting of special drive mappings when they first log in. Some users are new and would like a menu to come up to prompt them about their selections.

In addition to helping these users, you want to provide a motivational thought for the day on the screens of all users as they log in. And, as they start their session, you would like the date and time to display on each user's screen.

QUESTIONS FOR THOUGHT

How would you accomplish this? How can a LAN administrator interact with the users and others most effectively to contribute to a smooth operating environment? How can new users learn to feel more comfortable in a short time working in a network? How can LAN administrators customize the login process to fit the needs of individual departments? Could setting up menus for each department and making them run upon logging in help standardize the way users access and use information on the LAN? Could greeting messages make the workplace more pleasant for users? Could opening messages keep users informed?

CHALLENGE

Login scripts provide a way to have an environment already set up each time a user logs in. Determine what tasks you do daily and ask other users about their routines. See if login scripts may provide a way to automate the tasks.

CHAPTER OBJECTIVES

After finishing this chapter, you should be able to:

1. Distinguish among the four login scripts available with NetWare and identify when they execute.
2. Create a login script using NWADMIN or NETADMIN.

3. Explore the use of the WRITE command to display messages on a user's screen.
4. Define variable replacement and make use of it in a login script.
5. Explore the use of the INCLUDE command for incorporating text files into a login script.
6. Explore the use of the DRIVE command for specifying the default drive.
7. Discuss the use of IF . . . THEN commands for conditional operations.
8. Explain the use of the EXIT command and how to execute menus upon exiting a login script.
9. Discuss how to execute internal DOS commands within a login script.
10. Discuss the importance of mapping to the PUBLIC directory in at least one login script.

LOGIN SCRIPT FILES

Login script files, as the name implies, execute upon logging onto a LAN. They consist of commands placed in sequential order, similarly to an actor reading a script for a play line by line. Login scripts bear some resemblance to the AUTOEXEC.BAT file found in the DOS environment. AUTOEXEC.BAT executes after booting up a PC automatically (provided that it exists on the disk) and also contains commands that are executed in a sequential order.

Four kinds of login scripts exist in Novell NetWare: container, profile, user/personal, and default. Figures 13.1 through 13.4 summarize the properties of NetWare's login scripts.

Container Login Script

After logging on, the container login script executes first. An administrator creates the container login script. When executed, the system date and time are usually flashed on the screen, along with a greeting and any special announcements from the administrator. Then

Container Login Script	
Who can create it?	ADMIN, ADMIN equivalent, user with administrative rights (read and write) to the organizational container.
Where is it stored?	NDS
Where to go to create it	NETADMIN Right click on the container object of interest. Click on "Details." Click on "Login Script."
	NETADMIN Select "Manage Object." Choose a container object. Press F10 for the "Object, Action" screen to appear. Select "View or Edit Properties." Select "Login Script."

FIGURE 13.1
Container login scripts may be created using NWADMIN or NETADMIN.

Profile Login Script	
Who can create it?	ADMIN, ADMIN equivalent, user with administrative rights (read and write) to the users' container that the profile login script is for.
Where is it stored?	NDS
Where to go to create it	NWADMIN 1. Create a profile. Select "Object" from the main NWADMIN menu. Click on the "Create" button. Select "Profile" and click on "OK." Enter a name for the profile when prompted. 2. Key in the login script. Double click on the newly created profile in the NDS tree in NWADMIN. Click on "Login Script." 3. Assign the user to the profile. Double click on the particular user object. Click on "Login Script." Click on the "Select Object" button located to the right of the profile line. Select the profile by double clicking on it.
	NETADMIN 1. Create a profile. Select "Manage Objects," press Insert, highlight "Profile" for the object type, name the new profile 2. Key in the login script From the "Object, Action" screen, select "View or Edit Properties," press F10, choose "Login Script." 3. Assign the user to the profile Select "Manage Objects," select the user from the "Actions for User" menu Select "View or Edit Properties," select "Login Script."

FIGURE 13.2
Profile login scripts may be created either through NWADMIN or NETADMIN.

drive mapping will take place. Most institutions have search drive mappings set up, at least for the PUBLIC directory. The container login script runs if a user in that particular container logs in.

Profile Login Script

The profile login script executes after the container login script. In effect, it is a login script for a group of users. The system executes the profile login script if a member of a particular profile logs onto the system.

User/Personal Login Script	
Who can create it?	ADMIN, ADMIN equivalent, users with administrative rights (read and write) to the container in which the user/personal account is located, or the individual user.
Where is it stored?	NDS
Where to go to create it	NWADMIN Double click on the user object of interest. Click on "Login Script."
	NETADMIN Select "Manage Object." Choose the container object that the user account is found in, choose the user account, press F10 for the "Object, Action" screen to appear. Select "View or Edit Properties." Select "Login Script."

FIGURE 13.3
User/personal login script may be created using NWADMIN or NETADMIN.

FIGURE 13.4
The default login script is created by Novell.

Default Login Script	
Who can create it?	Software manufacturer Novell
Where is it stored?	Directory: LOGIN File name: LOGIN.EXE
Where to go to create it	Not applicable to users

User/Personal Login Script

The user/personal login script executes after the profile login script finishes. The user login script is customized for a particular user. This user can create and maintain his or her own login script using the NWADMIN or NETADMIN utility by following the steps given in Figure 13.3.

Default Login Script

The default login script executes if the user did not create a login script. If there is no user login script, the network executes the default login script provided by Novell. See Figure 13.5.

```
MAP DISPLAY OFF
MAP ERRORS OFF
MAP *1:=SYS:
MAP *1:=SYS:%LOGIN_NAME
IF"%1"="ADMIN" OR "%1"="SUPERVISOR" THEN MAP *1:=SYS:SYSTEM
MAP INS S1:=SYS:PUBLIC
MAP INS S2:=SYS:%MACHINE/%OS/%OS_VERSION
MAP DISPLAY ON
MAP
```

FIGURE 13.5
Default login script.

CREATING AND LOCATING THE LOGIN SCRIPT

Figures 13.1 through 13.4 show the steps involved to get to the actual screens for keying in login scripts. Notice that the container login script runs for the user logging into that specific container; thus it is advantageous to separate departments of an organization into different containers. Having a different login script for each department saves the administrator time in the long run, especially if everyone in one department uses the same software daily. Having the same login script also helps the administrator set up the same working environment for the users in a particular department (container).

Profile login scripts are handy when handling cases where a group of people not necessarily in the same department need to share the same software or have the same environment settings. For example, the president of an organization may decide that all managers in the company need access to some sensitive data files. Because the managers are in different departments, a profile login script is needed.

User/personal login scripts allow customizing individual user environments. Any special features needed by certain people and not the whole department can possibly be handled in the user's login script. The container, profile, and user/personal login scripts are all created using the NWADMIN or NETADMIN user menu utility, which are located in the PUBLIC directory. The actual login scripts created are physically stored in the network's NDS (Novell Directory Services).

The default login script may not be modified by any user. The default login script, unlike the other types of login scripts, is not located in the NDS; rather, it is located in the LOGIN directory and is built into the LOGIN.EXE program. Recall from Chapter 2 that LOGIN.EXE is the program that controls the login process. When a user keys in the words "LOGIN USER01," for example, he or she is instructing the network operating system to execute the LOGIN.EXE program. (Recall that if a program's file name ends with the extension .EXE, .COM, or .BAT, the user does not need to key in the extension name.)

COMMON LOGIN SCRIPT COMMANDS

Several login script commands and examples of how to use them are presented in this section. These commands can be placed in the container, profile, or user/personal login script. As noted earlier, the default login script also contains a number of commands.

WRITE Command

The WRITE command allows messages to be displayed on the screen, as shown in this example:

```
WRITE "Hello There"
```

Sometimes a user may wish for a different message, depending on when he or she logs in. To accomplish this, NetWare has a number of variable replacements, which all start with a percent sign (%). Some common variable replacements are shown in Figure 13.6. The following list represents a few variable replacements; others are included in the documentation that comes with the NetWare software.

WRITE "Today is %DAY_OF_WEEK" to display the current weekday.

WRITE "The month is %MONTH_NAME" to display the current month.

WRITE "Are you a graduate of %SHORT_YEAR" to display the last two numbers of the year.

WRITE "%YEAR is a good year" to display the complete year.

WRITE "Today is the %DAY" to display the current date.

WRITE "Today is %MONTH_NAME %DAY %YEAR" to complete the date. Note that more than one variable replacement may be used on the same line.

WRITE "The time now is %HOUR: %MINUTE %AM_PM" to display the current time followed by A.M. or P.M.

WRITE "The time is %HOUR24:%MINUTE:%SECOND" to display the time in a 24-hour format.

WRITE "Good %GREETING_TIME" to display a greeting as morning, afternoon, or evening, depending on the current time.

WRITE "Hello %FULL_NAME" to display the user's full name. This is the same as that found under "user information" through NETADMIN.

WRITE "Your account name is %LOGIN_NAME" to display the account name, such as USER01.

WRITE "You are at station number %STATION" to display the station number.

WRITE "The local operating system is %OS_VERSION" to display the version of the local operating system, such as DOS, currently running.

WRITE "You are logged in as %CN" to display the user's common name.

WRITE "Your computer is a %MACHINE" to display the type of computer at which a user is sitting.

Sounding Alerts Command

The command FIRE PHASERS 4 causes the computer to make an alert sound four times. This is a good way to detect someone logging into a particular account. The administrator may put FIRE PHASERS 4 in the container login script for the Marketing Department and FIRE PHASERS 5 in the one for the Accounting Department. From across the room, the administrator can tell if users are logging into a marketing account or an accounting account simply by the number of beeps.

Variable Replacement	Meaning Assigned to Variable Replacement
%ACCOUNT_BALANCE	Amount of funds remaining in the user's account.
%CN	Common name. This is normally referred to as the user's login name.
%FILE_SERVER	Name of the file server currently active for this user's session.
%FULL_NAME	Full name of the user. This is entered when the account is set up in NETADMIN.
%LAST_NAME	Last name of the user. This is entered when the account is set up in NETADMIN.
%LOGIN_CONTEXT	Login context to which the system is currently pointing in the NDS.
%LOGIN_NAME	User's login name.
%MACHINE	Type of computer, IBM-PC, for example.
%OS	Local operating system, for example, MS-DOS.
%OS_VERSION	Version of the local operating system in use by the workstation.
%PASSWORD_EXPIRES	Number of days before password expires.
%PROFILE	Profile name, if the user belongs to a profile.
%STATION	Displays the workstation's address.
%SURNAME	Displays the last name of the user as keyed in under NETADMIN when the account was set up.
%TELEPHONE_NUMBER	Displays the user's telephone number as entered under NETADMIN when the account was set up.
%TITLE	Displays the user's title as keyed in using NETADMIN when the account was set up.
%AM_PM	Displays either "AM" or "PM," depending on the time of day at which the user logs in.
%GREETING_TIME	Displays "morning," "afternoon," or "evening," depending on the time of day at which the user logs in.
%HOUR	Displays the hour that the user logs in.
%HOUR24	Dispalys the hour that the user logs in based on a 24-hour clock; for example, 1 P.M. is equal to 13.
%MINUTE	Displays the number of minutes past the hour when the user logs in.
%SECOND	Displays the number of seconds past the minute when the user logs in.
%DAY	Displays the date when the user logs in.
%DAY_OF_WEEK	Displays the day of the week when the user logs in; for example, Monday.
%MONTH	Displays the number of the current month.
%MONTH_NAME	Displays the name of the current month.
%YEAR	Displays the current year in four digits.
%SHORT_YEAR	Displays the current year in two digits.

FIGURE 13.6
Commonly used variable replacements.

DISPLAY Command

The DISPLAY filename command displays text files. For example, by typing

```
DISPLAY SERV1_SYS:PUBLIC\ANNOUNCE.TXT
```
daily announcements that the administrator has placed in the ANNOUNCE.TXT file located in the PUBLIC directory will be displayed. Users may wish to place reminders or project notes in a text file and then have the file displayed during the login process.

INCLUDE Command

The INCLUDE command pieces together login script files. For example, by typing

```
INCLUDE H:LOGSCRIP.LOG
```
the computer will process the script commands located in the specified file when the IN-CLUDE statement is reached in the login script. After that, control of execution will return to the line immediately below the INCLUDE statement.

Executing .EXE, .COM, and .BAT Commands

The #filename command is used to run a file that ends with .EXE, .COM, or .BAT from within a login script.

Changing Default Drives

By using the DRIVE G: command, the computer is instructed to change the default drive to the previously mapped drive G:. (Remember that maps are also permitted in login scripts.)

Conditional Instructions

By typing a conditional instruction such as

```
IF DAY_OF_WEEK = "Monday" THEN WRITE "Hello again"
```

the computer will check to see if the condition is true before performing the WRITE command. These conditional instructions are also known as IF . . . THEN commands. Notice that even though DAY_OF_WEEK is a variable replacement, the % sign is not used in the above example. When a variable replacement is used in an IF . . . THEN statement, the % sign is left off.

Running Programs upon Exiting

The EXIT "NMENU MYTRY" command instructs the computer to perform the command that is in quotes upon exiting the login script. In this example, the menu MYTRY is executed. This command should be placed last in the login script. It is advisable to keep menu names short, no more than five characters instead of the standard eight, because no more than 11 characters are permitted between the quotes on the EXIT command. A menu called CUSTOMER would not run if requested within the EXIT command. If problems are encountered while attempting to run a menu using the EXIT command, the user may want to have the EXIT command execute a batch file and have the batch file run the menu. See Chapter 14 for more details regarding running menus.

Executing Internal DOS Commands

The commands #COMMAND/C TIME and #COMMAND/C DATE demonstrate how to run the internal DOS DATE and TIME commands. The command COMMAND/C work with any internal DOS command.

Mapping

Mapping, as mentioned earlier, can also be done in the login script (see Chapters 2 and 3). Remember that maps are not permanent, however, so by placing the MAP command in the login script, the mapped drive gets re-created each session (Figure 13.7).

SUMMARY

Login scripts, which execute immediately after the user logs on, make it easy to automate the execution of various commands. Four types of login scripts can exist on the network: container, profile, user/personal, and default. A container login script is useful for customizing the work environments for users in the same department. Profile login scripts allow for customizing by other factors, such as job title. User/personal login scripts allow users to customize their work environments. The default login script, created by Novell, runs only if there is no user login script for the particular user logging in. Variable replacements help set up commands when missing information is not known ahead of time. Login scripts are flexible to allow for the running of DOS internal commands, NetWare menus, and other programs.

EXERCISES

1. Define the following:

    a. login scripts

    b. container login script

    c. profile login script

    d. user/personal login script

    e. default login script

    f. variable replacement

    g. conditional instruction

2. What do the following mean in NetWare?

    a. %

    b. #

    c. %AM_PM

    d. %HOUR24

    e. %OS_VERSION

    f. %CN

    g. %MACHINE

3. What are the four kinds of login scripts available in Novell NetWare, and who creates them?

4. When are login scripts executed?

5. Login scripts are similar to what file in DOS?

6. Where are login scripts created?

7. Where on the file server's drive are login scripts stored?

8. A map drive should be created in the container login script on which directory?

9. In what order are login scripts processed?

10. True or false: An administrator's login script is called a container login script.

11. What is the purpose of the WRITE command?

12. Explain what variable replacement is used for and what symbol precedes it.

13. What is the purpose of the INCLUDE and DISPLAY commands?

14. What is the purpose of the EXIT command?

15. How would you put the DOS directory command in a login script?

LAB #13

In this lab, you will create your own user/personal login script and will incorporate the commands discussed in this chapter. After completing this lab, you should be able to find the "User Login Script" screen and create a login script. You will also demonstrate your understanding of the commands presented in the chapter.

1. Go to the "Login Script" screen using the steps provided in this chapter (Figure 13.3). If you are not sure of your container name, ask the person who set up the account. Find

your user name and press F10 to bring up the "Object, Action" screen. Select "View or Edit Properties" of this object. Finally, select "Login Script."

2. Key in the WRITE commands found earlier in this chapter. Each command should start on a new line and line up with the left margin.

3. Sound an alert using the FIRE PHASERS 4 command. Avoid putting a very high number on the FIRE PHASERS command; you do not want to alarm other users that much.

4. Use the DISPLAY command to display one of your text files on the screen. (If you do not have a text file yet, save and exit your login script by pressing Escape. Keep pressing Escape or press Alt F10 to get out of NETADMIN. You may use the DOS editor to create a text file; refer to Chapter 3 for details regarding the DOS editor. After creating a text file, return to your login script screen following the instructions given in step 1.)

5. Ask your administrator or instructor if there is a login script file on the network that you may practice accessing using the INCLUDE command.

6. When you log into the network, you would like the system to send a message to a friend automatically to announce your arrival. Remember that SEND is actually a program found in the PUBLIC directory; its extension is .EXE. Therefore, to run it from a login script, you must start with the # (pound) sign. For example,

```
#SEND "Good morning, I just arrived." TO USER02
```

7. Create a logical drive map assignment to point to your home directory. Notice that even though MAP.EXE is a program located in PUBLIC, it's an exception to the rule regarding the # sign. The # sign is not needed with the MAP command. For example,

```
MAP H:=SERV1_VOL1:USERS\USER01
```

8. Add some daily motivational messages to your login script. Here are some examples:

```
IF DAY_OF_WEEK = "Monday" THEN WRITE "This is a great
week!"
IF DAY_OF_WEEK = "Tuesday" THEN WRITE "Reach new heights!"
IF DAY_OF_WEEK = "Wednesday" THEN WRITE "Go Go Go Go!"
IF DAY_OF_WEEK = "Thursday" THEN WRITE "I am confident!"
IF DAY_OF_WEEK = "Friday" THEN WRITE "Get to work!!!"
IF DAY_OF_WEEK = "Saturday" THEN WRITE "Take a rest!"
IF DAY_OF_WEEK = "Sunday" THEN WRITE "Visit friends!"
```

Remember not to include the % (percent) sign in the IF . . . THEN statements. DAY_OF_WEEK should be in ALL CAPS to work properly.

9. Set up your login script to display the listing for your home directory using the DOS DIR command. An example of this is:

```
#COMMAND/C DIR H:
```

Make sure that this command does not come before the MAP statement you have already entered for drive H:, otherwise, the system will not know to what H: is pointing.

10. You are now ready to save and test your login script.

11. When you log into the network, notice any errors that occur during the execution of your login script. Return to your login script screen and correct any problems you noticed.

CHAPTER FOURTEEN

MENUS

INSPIRING MOMENT

Time seems to pass so quickly at your new position. You really enjoy working with Net-Ware 4.1x networks, but you are exhausted. The particular company for which you are working uses quite a few temporary helpers for administrative tasks such as keying in customer names and addresses for mailings, entering inventory control data, and processing mail correspondence. Your supervisor has asked you to be in charge of the temporary workers. They are quite skilled at using the keyboard, but most of them do not know anything about networks. You are constantly having to show them where to find various software applications and how to run commonly used routine commands. There has got to be an easier way.

QUESTIONS FOR THOUGHT

Could an automated menu system help in this situation? What kinds of things would you put in an automated menu system for new users to select? What kinds of tasks do users perform on the network every day? Could an automated menu system help new users find their way around the network even if they do not know how the directories are laid out? Could an automated menu system lessen the amount of user errors that normally occur on a network? Could an automated menu system help existing users? If so, in what ways? Could you benefit from an automated menu system?

CHALLENGE

Menus save time and also lessen the stress normally associated with training users how to use the network. Explore the steps needed for creating menus and practice them as much as you can. Make a list of things you do on the LAN routinely and experiment with creating menus that will allow you to do these tasks more efficiently. Check with your LAN administrator to see if there are some already-created menus for practice. Reviewing other users' menus is also an effective way to develop the art of creating menus. Creating menus is an art, not a science, so be creative and design some menus.

CHAPTER OBJECTIVES

After finishing this chapter, you should be able to:

1. Explore how menus are constructed and create a menu.

2. List the rights necessary to create a menu.

3. List the rights necessary to use a menu.

4. Explain menu syntax.

NETWARE MENUS

Menus provide a powerful way to automate command and program selections. This chapter is particularly helpful in showing users how to speed up daily work, especially if particular programs or commands are used frequently. Menus are also handy when training people who do not have NetWare experience to get to needed programs or run needed commands. Unlike many programming languages today, users can construct menus in very little time with very little training. This ease of creating and using menus makes NetWare menus unique.

RIGHTS REQUIRED TO CREATE MENUS

To create a menu, a user must have trustee directory rights to the directory on which he or she wishes to place a menu. The rights required for the directory into which a user wishes to place the menu are

Read (R)

File scan (F)

Write (W)

Create (C)

Erase (E)

In addition to the directory required for creating the menu, a user needs to have access to a directory in which the system will place temporary controlling files. This directory itself is not temporary, but the controlling files that the system creates during the running of the menu are. The user must have the following rights to the directory that will be used for the temporary controlling files:

Read (R)

File scan (F)

Create (C)

Modify (M)

Erase (E)

REQUIREMENTS FOR RUNNING A MENU

The network operating system (NOS) creates and uses temporary files while running a menu. The SET command,

```
SET S_ FILEDIR = F:\MENUAREA\
```

is used to specify into which directory the NOS should place these files. This command may be keyed in at any prompt, such as the F:\> prompt. The administrator of an organization's LAN should create a common directory for all users on the system. To ensure that the NOS is accessing the same directory for each user, the following SET command should be added to the container login scripts:

```
SET S_ FILEDIR = "F:\MENUAREA\"
```

Notice that if the command is placed in a login script, quotation marks must be placed around the directory path. If the SET command is manually keyed in at a prompt, the quotation marks are excluded. (Menus and accompanying SET commands can be either processed manually at the prompt or automated in a login script.) The administrator should ensure that trustee directory rights RWCEMF (read, write, create, erase, modify, and file scan) were assigned.

In addition to specifying the directory name for temporary menu use, the administrator may also want to specify the temporary file name. This is done by placing the following SET command in the container login script:

```
SET S_ FILE = "%STATION"
```

This command helps avoid problems encountered when two users log in at the same time with the same login name. For example, if everyone in the Accounting Department logs in the same way, such as "LOGIN ACCT," a problem with the menus would most likely occur. By default, the system would take the user's login name as the temporary file name to use. In the above SET command, "%STATION" indicates that the station connection number should be used as the temporary file name. Because no two users can log into the same connection number on the same network, each user's temporary file would have a unique name.

ADVANTAGES TO USING MENUS

Menus provide a user a way to automate the selection process. Selections can range from running a DOS or NetWare command to running a software application.

Menus are particularly useful when working on a LAN. Because a user can have mapped drives up to the letter Z: and because many directories can be set up, menus provide a convenient way to access software easily without having to think every time about where the files are located. By providing selections in an organized manner, menus also provide a way to train new users.

SAMPLE MENU

Figure 14.1 shows the order for menu construction. The menu title goes first, and it is usually lined up on the left margin. The second line begins with the word "*item*," and it contains a choice or selection option that is usually indented one tab stop from the left margin. Whatever is keyed on the second line becomes an option on the menu. The lines indented, usually two tab stops, that follow the choice line are made up of commands. The computer executes these commands whenever that choice is selected. Notice that lower-level menus can be called from the main menu, as shown in Figure 14.2.

Figure 14.3 shows a sample menu based on Figure 14.2. NetWare automatically puts the choices in alphabetical order. Figure 14.4 shows the sample's lower menu when "Artist Menu" of Figure 14.3 is chosen.

FIGURE 14.1
Order for menu construction.

```
MENU 01, Title{}
     ITEM  Choice or Option{}
          commands
     ITEM  Choice or Option{}
          commands
     ITEM  Choice or Option{}
          SHOW 02
MENU 02, lower menu title{}
          ITEM  Choice or Option{}
               commands
```

FIGURE 14.2
Menu script file.

```
MENU 01, Music Man{}
     ITEM  Records and Hits{}
          EXEC MUSIC.EXE
     ITEM  Sheet Music{}
          EXEC SOLOS.EXE
     ITEM  Music Books{}
          EXEC BOOKS.EXE
     ITEM  Menu{}
          SHOW 02
MENU 02, Performers{}
     ITEM  Lookup by Name{}
          EXEC NAME.EXE
     ITEM  Lookup by Song{}
          EXEC SONG.EXE
```

FIGURE 14.3
Sample menu when executed.

```
Music Man

| Artist Menu
| Music Books
| Records and Hits
| Sheet Music
```

FIGURE 14.4
The lower menu of Figure 14.3, if "Artist Menu" is chosen.

```
Performers

| Lookup by Name
| Lookup by Song
```

Executing a Menu

To execute a menu, "NMENU" followed by the name of the menu should be keyed in. For example, to run a menu located in the user's home directory, key in as follows:

```
H:\USERS\USER01>NMENU MUSIC
```

If this particular menu should appear automatically each time the user logs in, add the following lines to the end of the user's login script:

```
MAP H:=SERV1_VOL1:USERS/USERS01
DRIVE H:
EXIT "NOW.BAT"
```

Use the DOS editor or Notepad to create the batch file NOW.BAT. The batch file contains the command for executing the menu:

```
H:\USERS\USER01>EDIT NOW.BAT
NMENU H:MUSIC
```

See Chapter 2 for more information about Notepad. See Chapter 3 for more information about the DOS editor.

EXEC Command

When writing menus, the EXEC command should be used to execute .EXE and .COM files from within a menu.

The steps for developing a menu system are shown in Figure 14.5. Each step is necessary to plan, create, and implement a menu system.

Planning, Creating, and Implementing a Menu System

1. Planning

Design on paper what the menu should look like. What should happen when each selection is chosen?

2. Create a Common Directory to Hold Temporary Files

This common directory allows the network operating system access to creating temporary files while processing menus.

3. Assign Users RWCEMF Rights to the Common Directory

READ, WRITE, CREATE, ERASE, MODIFY, and FILE SCAN rights to the common directory created in step 2 need to be assigned.

4. Decide the Placement of the Menu

Decide where the actual menu will be created and stored. Create a directory for the menu(s) that are shared among users.

5. Assign RFWCE Rights to the User Creating the Menu

READ, FILE SCAN, WRITE, CREATE, and ERASE rights need to be assigned to the user creating the menu. The rights should be assigned for the directory mentioned in step 4.

6. The Creator of the Menu Will Now Change to the Directory

To make sure that the menu will get stored in the proper directory, the creator of the menu will change to the directory mentioned in step 4 (for example: F:\MENUS\ACCT>).

7. Assign R and F Rights to the Users Executing the Menu

Grant users READ and FILE SCAN rights to the directory mentioned in step 4 so that users can run the menu(s).

8. Create the Menu Script File

To create the menu, use an ASCII editor such as Windows Notepad or the DOS EDIT command (F:\MENUS\ACCT>EDIT TOOLS.SRC). When the edit screen comes up, key in the menu.

FIGURE 14.5
Setting up a menu system (part 1 of 2).

AUTOMATING A MENU

The following lines may help automate a menu further:

1. In the container login script, include these lines

```
MAP INS S3: = SERV1_VOL1:MENUS\ACCT
EXIT "GOMENU"
```

9. **Compile the Menu Script File**

Use F:\MENUS\ACCT>MENUMAKE TOOLS.
Note: If the menu script file's extension is SRC, the extension does not have to be keyed in after the file name when using the MENUMAKE command line utility (CLU). The compiling process produces a file with the extension DAT.

10. **Update the User's Login Script**

Include the two SET commands in the user's login script:
SET S_FILEDIR = "F:\MENUAREA\" and SET S_FILE = "%STATION".

11. **Log In**

Log in to test the user's account.

12. **Test Run the Menu**

Use F:\>NMENU TOOLS. It is not necessary to include the DAT extension.

13. **Troubleshooting**

If the menu does not work properly, go back through the steps and debug each step that did not work correctly. *Special reminder:* If any changes are made to the ASCII file, don't forget to recompile the menu.

14. **Automate a Menu (Optional)**

The following lines may help automate a menu further by instructing the system to execute a menu automatically when the user logs in.

a. In the login script, include the lines:
MAP INS S3: = ABC_ SYS:MENUS\ACCT
EXIT "GOMENU"
b. Change the directory to the location of the menu and create a small batch file.
F:\>CD \MENUS\ACCT
F:\MENUS\ACCT>EDIT GOMENU.BAT
NMENU H:TOOLS
c. Log out, then log back in to test if the menu will now appear automatically when the login script is executed.

2. Change the directory to the location of the menu and create a small batch file:

```
F:\>CD \MENUS\ACCT
F:\MENUS\ACCT>EDIT GOMENU.BAT
NMENU H:TOOLS
```

Save the batch file.

3. Log out, then log in again to test if the menu will now appear automatically when the login script is executed. *Note:* You must log into the account for which the menu was created to see the results. You must log in again because the login script changes that were made do not take effect until the next login session.

SUMMARY

Extensive programming is not required to construct NetWare menus. By following the simple guidelines presented in this chapter regarding required rights and the placement of the menu titles, choices, and commands, users can easily construct their own menus.

The following rules help when creating menus:

1. The word "menu nn" (where nn is a number) appears on the first line to indicate the menu title. Titles line up with the left margin.
2. Options/selections start with the word "item." These choices are like a description. Although options lines are normally indented, they do not have to be.
3. After each option, the commands needed for that option are listed. Commands are normally indented from the left margin two tab stops.

EXERCISES

1. Define the following:
   a. menu
   b. menu script file
   c. menu title
   d. menu item
   e. directory containing temporary system-created files
   f. temporary file
2. What do the following mean in NetWare?
   a. S_ FILEDIR
   b. S_ FILE
   c. %STATION
   d. EXEC
   e. ITEM
3. What rights are required to create a menu?
4. What rights are required to run a menu?
5. What are the benefits of setting up menus?
6. What goes on the first line of a menu?
7. What goes on the second line of a menu?
8. What goes on the third line of a menu?
9. What type of files can be executed by the EXEC command?

LAB #14

In this lab, you will explore an already-existing menu. Then you will create a menu on your own. By the end of this lab, you should feel comfortable with menus and be able to create menus and explain the instructions found in them.

1. Use the NetWare COPY command to copy the menu called MAIN.SRC to your home directory. (MAIN.SRC comes with the NetWare software.) Give it a new name.
   `F:\PUBLIC>`**`NCOPY MAIN.SRC \USERS\USERxx\TRYIT.SRC`**

2. Next, go to your home directory. Follow the steps for compiling and executing the menu TRYIT.SRC.

3. You should now see different selections on the menu. Try each selection, one at a time. Make notes on what each selection is doing.

4. Now create a menu of your own. Automate the selection of commonly used NetWare commands, or whatever else you deem appropriate. You may want to assign a map to software application directories that contain word processing or spreadsheets. After you assign the maps, set up a menu to run these applications.

EXPLORING SOFTWARE

This part explores common questions and terminology encountered when selecting software for a LAN. Suggestions for finding information on software applications are also discussed.

CHAPTER FIFTEEN   Selecting Software

SELECTING SOFTWARE

INSPIRING MOMENT

As part of your job as a LAN administrator, you are responsible for keeping the directories and files on the file server's volumes organized and manageable. Many users share the file server's hard drive. You are now in the midst of a storage crisis. The hard drives on the file server are full, and many applications are no longer in use. Users have dumped hundreds of miscellaneous files onto the drives, ranging from games to obscene files to important business-related files. Your supervisor wants you to ensure that directory structures are organized and maintained.

QUESTIONS FOR THOUGHT

How would you decide which software to put and/or keep on your network? How would you decide which software to put and/or keep on your workstations? How would you monitor piracy on your network and workstations? What would you do if your users were bringing in their own software and putting it on the network or on their workstation? How would you educate users about your company's policy on piracy and copying software?

CHALLENGE

Keep the network clean. The network administrator should have written guidelines in place regarding what is and is not allowed on the network. An organization is a professional place for conducting business, and obscenity should not be tolerated. To determine whether or not games and other personal software should be permitted on the network or workstations, ask yourself the following question: Is your organization licensed to do so?

CHAPTER OBJECTIVES

After finishing this chapter, you should be able to:

1. Identify different categories of software and the major purpose of each category.
2. Know how to choose the source or vendor from which to buy software.
3. Know how to decide among software alternatives.

4. Identify where to go for further information on software.

5. Determine how many workstations can use a particular software package.

6. Know what software metering is and why it is important.

7. Identify different uses for software today.

SELECTING AND BUYING SOFTWARE

Once accounts have been set up, decisions about selecting and buying software need to be made. This chapter provides guidelines to help choose the software that's right for an organization. Because the need for sharing software among various workstations is a major reason companies choose to have a local area network, this chapter is filled with tips on getting the best software and buying it from the most reliable source.

DETERMINING HOW MANY WORKSTATIONS CAN USE SOFTWARE

Some manufacturers produce single-user software applications that will run in a LAN environment with the understanding and agreement that when such software is purchased, it will only be used by one workstation (or personal computer). The manufacturers' intention is to charge a fee for each workstation that uses the software. Technically, many single-user software programs on the market today may actually be used by more than one workstation; there may be less security and control available for the LAN and less customization for individual users than software used at only one workstation, however, because the same single-user software is being used. Some manufacturers may also add programming instructions specifically to limit the number of workstations that have access to the software. The best precaution is not to use single-user software as though it were multiuser software.

If an organization does purchase single-user software and then wants to allow more workstations access to it, the manufacturer or the software vendor should be consulted. There are four ways that manufacturers grant permission for more workstations to use such software.

First, some manufacturers require a separate software application package to be bought for each workstation, with each package costing the same price. The advantage is that each user would have his or her own manuals or documentation. The disadvantage is that this approach is generally expensive, especially if there are many individual users. Usually, only one set of software is installed with this type of purchase. By buying extra software application packages, the manufacturer is granting permission for other workstations to use the already-installed software.

The second way some manufacturers allow organizations to obtain permission to use software on more than one station is to require the purchase of a certificate or manual for each additional station. The certificate shows that the proper fees have been paid to access the software set already installed. This method is similar to the first except that the purchase of the entire software package for each station is not required.

The third method that software manufacturers use to allow permission for more than one workstation to use software is by the use of LAN packs. First, the single-user software application package is purchased; in addition, LAN packs are purchased to allow for more workstations. A LAN pack generally allows a group of users to be added. For example, a LAN pack of five would grant permission for five more workstations to use the software. This approach offers advantages to both software manufacturers and users. With LAN packs in use, there is more control of exactly how many workstations can use the software, making it more profitable for the manufacturer and offering more security for users. LAN packs also often allow users to customize their own environments; that is, if one user wants a blue screen and another wants a green one, each screen can be changed. Another benefit of LAN packs is their flexibility in allowing users to work with the same shared file. LAN packs, as of now, may be the most practical choice for an organization to use software at more than one workstation legally.

A fourth method of gaining permission is to purchase a corporate or site license agreement either directly from the manufacturer or through a value-added reseller (VAR), who represents the manufacturer. When a site license is purchased, the maximum number of users allowed to run the software is agreed upon, either in writing or through controlling within the software itself. Site license software would then be delivered to the company or organization by the VAR or the software manufacturer. Site license software packs are not commonly seen displayed on computer store shelves.

Software Metering

When selecting software for a LAN environment, the term *software metering* often emerges, especially in companies where security is highly regulated. Software metering involves counting how many users are logged into the network and are using a particular software application. Once the count has been taken, it is then checked against licensing information to see if the number of licensed stations running the software has been exceeded. Software metering is accomplished through special software that is loaded at the file server or administrator's workstation. Various companies sell add-on software metering programs.

Why Is Software Metering Important?

Suppose that an organization just purchased a software application with a licensing agreement for 10 people to use it at a time. As these users work at their stations, an eleventh person logs in and attempts to use the software. Even if the software application program does not start flashing red alert messages, the organization now has one user running the software illegally. Software metering alerts the administrator, who could then check to see if all the users requesting to use that particular software application are actually using it. For instance, if one user simply forgot to exit the program, the administrator can ask that user to exit so that another person can use it legally.

DECIDING WHERE TO PURCHASE SOFTWARE

Numerous places sell software. Some considerations that may help in the decision of where to purchase software are the following:

1. How long has the company selling the software been in business, and will it stay in business? Although number of years in the business is not the only criteria, it is a plus if the company has been in business for a while. Avoid shopping for software at going-out-of-business sales unless you already know about the software you are purchasing, plan on keeping it, and don't intend to have any questions for the software vendor.

2. How much does the software cost at this particular location? Although price is a big factor, make sure that a low price does not entail the sacrifice of service.
3. Does the person buying the software know anyone else who buys products from this particular source? Software should be bought from a store that has a good reputation. It's a good practice to get referrals.
4. What is the software supplier's return policy? Some stores take back software with no questions asked. Some will allow a specific number of days to try the software; after that time has expired, the software cannot be returned. Some give cash back, while others give in-store credit.
5. What type of support does the store offer? To compete for business, some stores require that their employees be knowledgeable in the use of various software applications. Ask or observe if the salespeople can answer questions or can help if a software problem develops.
6. What type of purchase plans are available? In working with software purchases for a LAN environment, the cost can vary depending on the number of workstations. Many companies, especially those with more workstations, have procedures for computer purchases. It is advisable to first check with the organization about how computer purchases are processed, and then find a store that is willing to cooperate with that process. Does the organization pay direct, with cash or check? Does the company require a purchase order? Do the payments need to be stretched over time?
7. Does the store offer any special training classes? To compete for business, some stores have training available. A nominal fee may be charged.

DETERMINING SOFTWARE'S USE

Before shopping for software, an inventory of what the software should accomplish is necessary. The following categories of software should be considered.

Word-Processing Software

Word-processing software allows a user to produce many documents, from simple letters to sophisticated publishing packages. Tasks that currently require editing, correspondence, and so forth, as well as upcoming projects, should be listed. When shopping for any software, poll the people who will actually be using it about their needs.

Spreadsheet Software

Spreadsheets allow for mathematical calculations in a column format. In addition, such software allows graphs to be created to depict the numbers and calculations.

Database Management Software

Database management allows for the management of records. It allows a user to produce reports and labels based on the records. Many database management software packages have the capability of allowing a company to set up a menu system from which to choose options.

Desktop Publishing Software

Desktop publishing involves the use of graphics, special layouts, and special type fonts. Desktop publishing software is highly useful if a company produces its own advertisements, announcements, newsletters, and other written materials. Newer word-processing software applications overlap in this area in that they also have some publishing capabilities.

Accounting Software

There are numerous choices in accounting software. As the word *accounting* implies, this category of software allows a company to manage its financial records. Although database and spreadsheet software have accounting capabilities, accounting software applications are generally already set up for financial purposes. With database or spreadsheet software, the user or company's programmer/operator must set up the financial system before it can be used.

Modem Software

Computerized dial-in bulletin boards, on-line services, and the Internet are all popular methods of communicating via a computer. Modem software enables one computer to call out to another through the use of a special device called a modem. Special software is required to operate or control a modem. Modems sold on the market today usually come packaged with sample software.

Integrated Packages

The field of integrated packages is the hot area in software development today. Integrated packages combine different categories of software such as word processing, spreadsheets, and database management from one vendor and sell it all together. Software vendors are usually involved in pricing wars to attract customers so that a user buys all the packages from the "winning" vendor. Advantages of this strategy for customers are price savings, compatibility among packages, one source to contact for support, and neat packaging.

Computer-Aided Design and Computer-Aided Mapping Software

Computer-aided design (CAD) and computer-aided mapping (CAM) software allow a user to design blueprints using a computer. These software programs are popular with architects and engineers.

Education Software

Many excellent educational software programs, from learning how to speak another language to learning how to cook, are available for use on a computer. Before shopping for this kind of software, make an inventory of the users' and company's needs to save time, confusion, and money.

DECIDING WHAT SOFTWARE TO BUY

The following steps should be helpful when looking for software, especially when all the programs look good. The following should help narrow down your choices to just a few.

1. Check the inventory list before shopping. Which software alternatives have the capability to meet all or most of the needs or features that you originally wrote down? If the software cannot do what you need it to do, keep looking until you find one that does. Otherwise, you may become frustrated and waste time and money.
2. Check out the software manufacturer just like you checked out the store from which to buy the software. How long has the software manufacturer been in business? How long has it been producing this type of software? Does the manufacturer offer any guarantees? Are there any customer-support phone lines? If so, is it toll free or not? Does the software manufacturer charge a consulting fee to answer your questions? If so, how much? Do you know anyone who has purchased software manufactured by this company? Ask the store salesperson which software applications produce the most sales.
3. Check training and support materials. How can you learn to use this particular software? Is the software difficult to learn? Are there any classes for this software in your area? Are there any magazines or newsletters that support this particular software application? How many books are available on this particular software?
4. Check if the software will run on your computer equipment. Do you have enough random-access memory (RAM)? Do you have a large enough storage space (hard drive)? Do you have a fast enough central processing unit (CPU) (586, 686, . . .)? If needed, will your monitor support special graphics? Do you have the right operating system (DOS, Windows, . . .)? Is it for stand-alones, single users? Is it network compatible or NetWare aware?

FINDING FURTHER INFORMATION ON SOFTWARE

With software constantly changing, it's difficult to stay current on all the features and capabilities available. Some resources are available to help stay in the lead on these issues, however, such as publications and other users.

Magazines

There are numerous magazines written for computer users. Several such magazines test various software, report main features, and compare software applications currently available. Several software publishers refer to these tests and reviews on their software packages. In addition, many software publishers advertise in the magazines and give information about acquiring demo disks of their products.

User Groups

Scattered throughout the United States are various user groups that meet to discuss various computer issues. Some groups are general in nature and address a variety of software choices, while others are more specialized. Because user groups normally are not in the business of selling software, they often provide more straightforward answers to your questions than manufacturers and suppliers.

Bulletin Board Services

Several software manufacturers have bulletin board services (BBSs) set up where users can dial up via modem and retrieve information on their products. Some charge for this service.

The Internet

The Internet allows users around the world to exchange information via modems and satellites. The Internet has an overwhelming amount of information regarding computer hardware and software. Many software manufacturers, libraries, schools, and businesses have accounts on the Internet and have set up information centers commonly called web sites that users can access.

Computer Stores

Local computer stores are also a resource for answering questions. Find out which software applications are recommended, and which ones produce the most sales.

Libraries

Most libraries carry computer books, and many will track down books for patrons. It's wise to find software applications that have books and documentation available for users.

Software Manufacturers

Most software publishers supply literature, customer support, and/or fax help. Call a particular manufacturer to see what's available.

SUMMARY

Selecting software is not always easy. But by following a few simple guidelines, the task is quite manageable. The needs of the users and the company should be determined before shopping begins. Vendors or stores that sell the software, as well as the software manufacturer, should be checked thoroughly. Many resources, such as publications and other users, can help answer questions.

EXERCISES

1. Define the following:
   a. single-user software
   b. software metering
   c. LAN pack
   d. return policy

    e. purchase plan

    f. categories of software

    g. integrated package

    h. user groups

    i. bulletin board service

    j. Internet

2. What do the following mean?

    a. RAM

    b. CPU

    c. BBS

3. Why is selecting the right software important in a LAN environment?
4. What determines how many workstations can legally use the software? What are the four ways manufacturers grant permission to use their software on the LAN?
5. What are some things to keep in mind when deciding on where to buy software?
6. What categories of software are available? List the software applications with which you are familiar and the category of each.
7. How can you decide among three or four alternative software applications?
8. Where can you find more information regarding a particular kind of software?

SPECIAL PROJECT

In the following project, you will investigate the software set up on the network you are currently using. You will also explore and practice the software selection process. After completing this project, you should have a greater understanding of the software currently residing on the network. You should also be comfortable selecting software and selecting where to buy software.

1. In prior labs, you discovered which directories are entrusted to you. Now that you know your trustee directory assignments, list the directories, what type of application is contained (if any), and to what use you would put the application.
2. Which software applications mentioned in step 1 can be used by more than one user at the same time?
3. For each software application listed in step 1, can you think of another software application that could also meet the needs of the organization?
4. Write down which company actually manufactured each application listed in step 1.
5. List the names of computer stores in your area that might carry the software application that you are using and the ones mentioned as alternatives in step 3.
6. Pick one of the vendors mentioned in step 5 and answer these questions:
   How long has the company selling the software been in business, and will it stay in business?
   How much does the software cost at this particular location?
   Do you know anyone else who buys products from this particular source?
   What is this vendor's return policy?

What type of support does the store offer?

What type of purchase plans are available?

Does the store offer any special training classes?

7. Pick one of the software applications listed in step 1 and find magazine articles about it.

8. Look through local trade magazines for user groups that meet to discuss any of the applications mentioned in step 1. Find as many as possible.

9. Do any of the organizations mentioned in step 8 support or encourage a particular bulletin board service or Internet address?

10. List the libraries in your area that have or can obtain computer books.

SERVER INSTALLATION

Server installation has definitely gotten easier with the more recent versions of NetWare coming on CD-ROM. However, before you can actually start with the installation of Net-Ware 4.11, there are a number of preparatory steps that have to happen first. Basically there are four phases: (1) preparing the hard drive, (2) recognizing the CD-ROM drive, (3) identifying the network interface card (NIC), and (4) installing NetWare 4.11. We will explore each of these phases in the sections that follow. Keep in mind that installations vary greatly depending upon the hardware and software configurations desired.

PARTITIONING THE HARD DRIVE

Using OnTrack Disk Manager™ allows for larger drives to recognize the entire drive space. Follow the directions compatible to your disk drive. Make sure that they are ones supported for your drive. As an example, the following instructions have been provided for partitioning a drive using OnTrack Disk Manager.

1. Boot the computer with a DOS floppy boot disk. (DOS disk #1 will work.)
2. Remove the DOS boot disk, and put in the OnTrack Disk Manager disk.
3. At the A:> prompt, key in "DM" and press Enter.
4. Select "Advanced Disk Installation" from the menu that appears.
5. Hold down the Alt key and press the letter C to specify that you want to remove current partitions and data.
6. Select option C to define your own partition. For the first partition, allocate approximately 100 MB. This will be our boot-up partition. This is the portion of the drive that will contain the boot upfiles and also our NetWare start-up files. When prompted for the size, type in 100 MB. By the way this first section, or partition is also referred to as the primary partition.
7. There will be some space left over on the disk drive. Press enter to leave the remaining amount alone. Notice that the remaining amount will go into what is called an "extended partition." An extended partition is the space on the disk drive that remains after creating the first (or primary) partition. Since Netware prepares this as a non-DOS partition, it is best to not allow DOS to do anything with the extended partition.
8. Select Save and Continue.
9. When prompted with the question "Use Fast Format?" press "N" for no.
10. You are about to erase all data on this disk! Are you sure you want to continue? Yes, press enter.

11. You will be prompted to put your DOS boot disk in A:.The partitioning process will take a few minutes to complete. You may choose to use this time constructively by reading through the remaining steps of server installation; otherwise, take a break. After the partitioning process is complete, you will be prompted to remove the disk in drive A: and restart your PC. Congratulations on completing the partitioning process.

FORMAT DRIVE C:

Even though OnTrack Disk Manager formatted the drive after partitioning it, you will most likely want to format the drive again using the DOS version that you are most comfortable with. Put the DOS disk containing the FORMAT command in drive A:. From the A:> prompt, indicate that drive C: should be formatted.

```
A:\>FORMAT C:/S
```

Special note: /S in the preceding command indicates that you want drive C: to contain the system files so it can boot up.

SPECIAL DOS FILES

In order to prepare for common tasks, there are a few DOS files that you may want to copy over from the DOS disk. Follow these steps:

1. First, create a directory on the hard drive to hold the DOS files. You may choose to just install all of DOS. However, since this would take up space, we will concentrate on the needed files.

```
C:\>MD DOS
```

2. Next, change to this directory.

```
C:\>CD DOS
C:\DOS>
```

3. Next, put the DOS disk #1 in drive A:.
4. You may view the directory at this time.
   Switch to the A:\> prompt.

```
A: (enter)
A:\>DIR/P
```

Special note: The /P indicates that you would like the system to pause after each screen full of information.

5. Use the **COPY** command to copy over key DOS files.

```
A:\>COPY EDIT.COM C:
A:\>COPY QBASIC.EXE C:
A:\>COPY MSD.EXE C:
```

6. Next, take out DOS disk #1 and put in the DOS disk containing MSCDEX.EXE. It is most likely on DOS disk #3. Once again you may use the directory DIR command to verify the contents of the disk. Copy the MSCDEX.EXE file from the floppy disk.

```
A:\>DIR/P
A:\>COPY MSCDEX.EXE C:
```

7. Next, switch your prompt back to C: and verify the contents of the C:\DOS directory.

```
C: (enter)
C:\DOS>DIR/P
```

You should have three files in this directory: EDIT.COM, MSD.EXE, and MSCDEX.EXE. EDIT.COM is useful for making changes to text files and batch files. EDIT.COM in some DOS versions requires QBASIC.EXE to reside in the same directory. QBASIC.EXE loads automatically when EDIT.COM is used. MSD.EXE is Microsoft Diagnostics, which allows you to check settings on your computer. Some key settings you may wish to check are Computer processor (under the Computer category), available memory (under the Memory category), and which Interrupts (IRQs) are in use (under the IRQ Status category). Finally MSCDEX.EXE is required for many CD-ROM devices. Setting up for CD-ROM device recognition is discussed in the next section.

CD-ROM DRIVER

Next, it's important to have the system recognize the CD-ROM device in order for it to read the IntranetWare CD. Find the driver disk that came with your CD-ROM. Put the disk in drive A:. Next, run the INSTALL.EXE program (or the appropriate one for your CD-ROM drive).

```
A:\>INSTALL
```

Follow the directions on your screen that are applicable to your particular CD-ROM drive.

If you are asked for the location of the MSCDEX.EXE file, type in **C:\DOS.**

If you are asked if you want the AUTOEXEC.BAT and CONFIG.SYS files updated, reply "yes."

Remove the disk from drive A:. Once you reboot your PC, the CD-ROM device should be loaded. If not, you may need to refer to the manual that came with your CD-ROM drive and/or call the technical phone support relevant to your particular device.

EDIT CONFIG.SYS

You will need to increase the number of files and buffers allowed for the server. This is accomplished by adding a couple of lines to the CONFIG.SYS located in the root directory of C:.

```
CD..
C:\>EDIT CONFIG.SYS
```

You will notice a DEVICE line placed in your CONFIG.SYS file from the CD-ROM installation program. Go below the DEVICE line and add the following:

```
FILES=100
BUFFERS=80
```

You may now save and exit the CONFIG.SYS file. (File, Exit, Save file? Yes) Please note that you must reboot your computer before the new changes will go into effect.

THE NETWORK INTERFACE CARD (NIC)

There are a wide variety of network interface cards on the market today, making it a little cumbersome to explain the installation process. Please refer to the installation instructions that accompanied your network interface card. The steps provided here are for one generic card.

For this illustration, we are working with a generic Ethernet NE2000 compatible NIC. The first thing we want to do is to plug in the card following the directions given in the card's users guide. Here are some key things to note about installing an NIC:

1. Make sure the computer is off and not connected to an electrical source before installing the NIC.
2. Make sure to discharge the static in your hands by touching a grounded metal object. The nonpainted portion of the computer's inner casing may be used for this purpose.
3. Be careful when handling the NIC. The backs of the board are very sharp and could cause injury to your hands if not handled properly.
4. Find an empty slot in the computer appropriate to the type of card you are installing. You may have to remove the slot cover in order to insert the new card.
5. When you insert the NIC into the slot, make sure it's fully seated (in all the way). The card should be straightly aligned.
6. Now you are ready to test it. At this point you may want to cover the computer to remind yourself that you have the power of the unit on. However, wait to close it tightly and replace all the screws, just in case the card is not working correctly.
7. Follow the instructions provided with your NIC regarding Interrupt settings if applicable. The particular Ethernet NE2000 (AE-200PNP) compatible card in our example needs to be set to not use jumpers before it will work properly.

Setting to not use jumpers, we need to do the following:

1. Copy the files provided from floppy to a subdirectory in the C: drive. In this case we will make an NIC driver directory first.
2. One of the executable files when ran allows for specifying jumperless. So, we can run the executable and specify jumperless.
3. Note any special instructions specific to NetWare given with the user manual provided with your NIC. For example, this card states that after we get the server program running, we will have to use a particular LOAD command to have the NIC driver loaded into the server's memory.

```
LOAD PNPSRV Frame=Ethernet_xxxxx
BIND IPX to PNPSERV Net=xxxxx
```

If your NIC comes with a software that detects its Interrupt and I/O Base settings, this information may come in handy later. Write down the settings given. With the card used in our example, it has been determined that Interrupt = 5 and the I/O Base = 260H, and the operating mode is set to Jumperless.

We will come back to this later.

INSTALLING INTRANETWARE 4.11

Boot up the computer and place the IntranetWare CD in the drive. Switch to the prompt for the CD-ROM drive (most likely E).

```
C:\>E: (enter)
```

1. Run the INSTALL.BAT file.

   ```
   E:\>INSTALL
   ```

2. The first screen to appear is the "NetWare Install" menu. Select the line you can read! For most of us, we would want to choose the one that says the following:

   ```
   Select this line to install in English
   ```

3. Next, you will see the "NOVELL TERMS AND CONDITIONS" page. You will want to read this part carefully, and make sure you are in compliance with what is stated there. By "pressing any key to continue" you are agreeing to the terms and conditions.

4. "**Select the type of installation desired**" is the next menu screen that appears. You will select "**NetWare Server Installation.**"

5. You will then be prompted to "**Choose the product you want to install.**" Select "**NetWare 4.11.**"

6. "**Select the type of installation you are performing**" is next. Since we want more than one volume name, choose "**Custom installation of NetWare 4.11.**"

7. Next, you are prompted for "Server name." For this example, we will use SERV1. Keep in mind that often organizations choose to have several servers. We will make this our first one.

8. The Internal network number is next. IntranetWare will make a suggestion for what to put here. It is recommended that you overwrite that selection with a commonsense number. This is the ID number that this particular server will be known as. For our example, enter the number "1."

9. The server boot files will be placed on the hard drive next. Accept the default by pressing Enter.

10. We will accept the defaults for the "Country Code" screen by pressing Enter. If you happen to be in a different country, however, arrow up to "Country Code" and press Enter to select your country.

11. "**Do you want to modify, add, or delete any special startup set commands?**" Select "**No,**" and press the Enter key.

Note: If we really want to modify the startup set commands, we can do that later after the installation is complete. If you have to abort the install at this point due to error, then you would need to start back at the beginning of the server installation steps.

12. "**Add commands to AUTOEXEC.BAT to load SERVER.EXE?**" Select "**No,**" and press the Enter key.

13. "**Choose the Server Drivers—Network Driver**" is the next place it stops. You may find the one for your network interface card on the list provided. If so, select the appropriate one. In our example, recall earlier that we copied over the appropriate files for the NIC into a directory on the C: drive. Press INS to install an unlisted driver. Then press F3 to specify a different path.

14. Once the NIC driver has been loaded you will be asked to "**Save parameters and continue.**" Press **Enter** to accept.

15. "**Do you want to select an additional Network driver?**" We will select "**No**" for now. We can always add more drivers later if needed.

16. Next, you see a summary of the drivers loaded. For our example, we have a CD-ROM driver and network (LAN) driver loaded. For "**Driver Actions,**" select "**Continue Installation.**" We will proceed with the installation.

17. When prompted for "**Protocol Selection,**" select "**Continue with Installation.**" (IPX has been selected as the default.)

18. Next, you should see "**Create NetWare Disk Partitions.**" From this menu, select "**Manually.**" Since we would like more than one drive volume name, we are required to do this ourselves. Selecting "Manually" results in the system defining the whole partition (or available drive space) as one volume and naming it SYS:.

19. From the "**Disk Partition and Mirroring Options,**" select "**Create, delete, and modify disk partitions.**" The steps that follow will allow us to customize our partition setup.

20. From the "**Available Disk Drives**" screen, press Enter on "**Device #1.**"

21. From the "**Disk Partition Options**" screen, select "**Delete any disk partition**" and press the Enter key.

22. From the "**Available Disk Partitions**" screen, select the second option, "**2 DOS Extended Partition.**" Be careful not to delete the first partition or make changes to it. Remember the first partition is our DOS boot-up partition that contains our driver and server start-up and load files. Confirm the warning; yes, you want to delete for the second partition.

    Note: A partition can be thought of as a divider. You are requesting that the physical hard drive be divided into more than one logical unit. This is similar to taking a huge physical room in a building and putting up a folding partition wall. The folding partition wall gives the illusion of there being two rooms when there really is only one. Similarly, partitioning allows us to have logically multiple hard drives, where physically there is really only one. Get used to hearing the word "logical." This is the key word to indicate the illusion sense. In the text, we refer to logical drive mappings.

23. Now indicate the type of partition to set up under "**Disk Partition Options.**" Select "**Create NetWare disk partition.**" By now you may be thinking, "Wait a minute! Are we going around in circles? Partitions were set up using Disk Manager earlier." Yes, this is correct. Disk Manager created partitions automatically for us. However, we need the first partition to be a DOS partition. We need the second partition to be a NetWare partition. Remember, DOS and NetWare are two separate operating systems. You can think of them as two separate languages, similar to having English in partition one and Spanish in partition two.

24. For "**Disk Partition Information,**" take the default by pressing F10.

25. Next, we are finished with defining the partition, so select "**Return to previous menu.**"

26. To "**Continue with installation,**" press Enter twice.

27. Press F3 to modify the space assigned to SYS:, then press Enter. For the "**Disk segment size**" associated with volume SYS:, change the number displayed to 500, and press F10 to save. Remember, we would like to have more than one volume. SYS: is

the volume that holds system-related files, public command line utilities, and so on. We normally do not store our day-to-day software applications and data files under SYS:.

28. Arrow down to the line that says "**free space**" and press Enter.

29. You are now prompted with a question, "**Make this segment a new volume.**" Press Enter to accept.

30. For the "**Disk segment volume name,**" type in **VOL1,** and press F10 three times to save and continue. When prompted to "**Save volume changes,**" select "**yes.**" Our software applications and data will reside in the VOL1: volume.

31. Press Enter to accept defaults for the CD-ROM drive.

32. Next, the NetWare operating system files will be copied. This may take a few minutes depending on the speed of your computer.

33. It will stop and prompt you "**Is this the first NetWare 4 Server?**" Select "**Yes.**"

34. Next, you will see "**Enter a name for this Directory tree.**" For our example, type in **ABC_CO.**

35. You will now want to select the appropriate time zone for your area. For example, "**United States of America, Pacific Time.**" Accept the defaults for "**Time Configuration**" and press F10 to accept.

36. In answer to the prompt "**Specify A Context For This Server And Its Objects,**" do not get too elaborate. For "**Company or Organization,**" fill in **ABC_CO.** You will be prompted to supply a password. Retype the password to confirm your selection. You just indicated the password for the ADMIN account. Remember the knowledge of the ADMIN password carries with it a great amount of responsibility. Keep this password in a secure place where nobody else can see it or find it.

37. When prompted "**Save Directory Information and Continue?**," reply "**Yes.**"

38. Next, the system will display a summary of what you just entered. This is a good point to stop and write this information down. It will be needed later as you work with your server.

```
Directory tree name: ABC_CO
Directory context: O=ABC_CO
Administrator Name: CN=Admin O=ABC_CO
```

39. You will now be prompted for the license disk. **Insert the disk labeled "NetWare license.**" This disk indicates how many licenses you are granted. The license counts govern how many simultaneous network connections you can have at any one time. One user logging into the network counts as one network connection, thus using up one license count.

40. Find the license disk, place it in drive A:, and press the Enter key. You should see the message, "**The Server Connection License was successfully installed from the directory path A:.**" Press the Enter key to continue on.

41. On the next screens you will be prompted to edit the STARTUP.NCF and the AUTOEXEC.NCF files. Continue through these two sections by pressing F10 to accept them as they are. When prompted to save them, select "**Yes.**" Remember, these files can always be edited later. Keep the installation steps as simple as possible to lessen the likelihood of there being a need to abort the installation.

42. Next, you should see "**File Copy Status (Main Copy).**" This step may take several minutes depending on the speed of your computer. You may be tempted to go out of

the room and take a break at this point. If you choose to leave the server, just remember the security rules early in the game. Never leave a server vulnerable to others who may alter or view the contents of the hard drive or damage the server itself. Although the server does not have any software applications or data on it yet, you are already establishing your personal habits and routines regarding security. Make security a habit from the beginning so that it becomes second nature.

43. You should see the screen that says "**Other Installation Items/Products.**" Bypass this by selecting "**Continue Installation.**" You can come back to this section later after the installation is complete if warranted.

44. Congratulations! You should see "**The server installation of NetWare 4.11 is complete.**" Go ahead and press the Enter key.

45. Now you should find yourself at the system console's colon prompt.

    `SERV1:`

46. You may now bring the server down. Hold on! Be careful not to simply press the off switch! You will DOWN the server and then EXIT to DOS.

    `SERV1:`**`DOWN`**
    `SERV1:`**`EXIT`**
    `C:\>`

    Now you may power off the computer.

FOR FURTHER LEARNING

MAGAZINES RELATING TO NETWORKING

NetWare Connection Magazine
http://www.nwconnect.com
NetWare Users International
http://www.novell.com/nui
Network Computing
Home page: http://www.networkcomputing.com

MAGAZINES RELATING TO COMPUTERS IN GENERAL

Byte
http://www.byte.com
Christian Computing
http://www.gospelcom.net/ccmag
Data Communications
http://www.data.com
Information Week
http://www.iweek.com
InternetWeek
http://www.internetwk.com
PC Computing
http://www.zdnet.com/pccomp
PC Week
http://www.zdnet.com/pcweek
Windows Magazine
http://www.winmag.com

INTERESTING WEB SITES ON THE INTERNET

Amazon.com

http://www.amazon.com

Compaq

http://www.compaq.com

Digital Equipment

http://www.digital.com

Evangelical Christian Credit Union

(author works here)

http://www.eccu.org

IBM

http://www.ibm.com

Intel

http://www.intel.com

Intel Corporation

http://www.intel/com

McAfee Associates

http://www.mcafee.com

Microsoft

http://www.microsoft.com

Novell

http://www.novell.com

Prentice Hall

http://www.prenhall.com

Symantec

http://www.norton.com

Velasco Home Page

http://home.earthlink.net/~velasco

ERROR MESSAGES

BAD COMMAND OR FILE NAME

The "Bad Command or File Name" error message is commonly displayed after a user has accidentally keyed in a command, such as WHOAMI, with spelling errors.

DIRECTORY COULD NOT BE LOCATED

The "Directory Could Not Be Located" error message normally comes up if a user is trying to change to a directory that does not exist or if the user has not been assigned trustee directory rights to the directory.

FILE CANNOT BE COPIED ONTO ITSELF

The "File Cannot Be Copied onto Itself" message usually occurs when a user is using the NCOPY or COPY command incorrectly. The copy commands require the user to specify the source (where the file is coming from) and the destination (where the file is going). This error message normally occurs if the same directory path and file name were entered as part of the command.

INVALID DRIVE SPECIFICATION

The "Invalid Drive Specification" message indicates that the workstation is unable to connect to a particular drive letter. If this message occurs while attempting to attach the workstation to the network, the error is usually associated with either cabling or connection problems. To rectify the problem, check the cables and connections for the workstation encountering the error message. If an entire string of workstations is encountering this error message, check the connections leading to the hub. Check to ensure that the power to the hub is working properly. If all stations are encountering this message, check the terminators, if any, on the backbone, the main cable running throughout the network. If all else fails, check the file server itself.

     If the "Invalid Drive Specification" message is not a result of cabling or connection problems, perhaps the drive letter to which the user is attempting to switch or reference has not been assigned. For example, if the user is at F:\> and is trying to switch to P:\> without having a map assignment to P:, the drive P: is unknown to the system and thus is invalid.

PATH/FILE ACCESS ERROR

The "Path/File Access Error" message is commonly encountered when attempting to save by using the DOS EDIT command. This message is conveying to the user that the system is not allowing a WRITE instruction to occur. This happens if the user either does not have enough rights assigned to the particular directory, if the particular files already exist and contain an attribute flag of read-only, or if the user's work disk is write protected.

THE COMMAND LINE SYNTAX IS INVALID

The "Command Line Syntax Is Invalid" message indicates that the user has a typing mistake in the command just entered.

YOUR CURRENT CONTEXT IS ABC_CO.CONSULTANTS; THE USER DOES NOT EXIST IN THE SPECIFIED CONTEXT; ACCESS HAS BEEN DENIED

The "User Does Not Exist" message occurs when logging in. If the system cannot find the particular account by the name that the user is entering, this error message appears on the screen. This could be the result of keying in the login name incorrectly or of not having the context set to the right container.

YOUR CURRENT CONTEXT IS ABC_CO.CONSULTANTS; ACCESS HAS BEEN DENIED

The "Access Has Been Denied" message, when not accompanied by the "User Does Not Exist" message, indicates that the password has been entered incorrectly when logging in.

GLOSSARY

Access Control   A right that allows a user to control who has access to a particular directory. The user can also change the IRF. If a user has access control but no supervisory privileges, and if an IRF is placed on the directory, the user cannot change the IRF back without the help of an administrator or someone with supervisory directory rights.

Attach   What happens when the workstation is identified as part of the network by the file server. Attaching occurs even before the logging-in process. A user can be attached, but not actually logged into, the network.

Backbone   The main cabling running through the entire local area network.

BBS   See *Bulletin board service.*

Bridge   A method of using special hardware and software to allow two LANs to connect together.

Bulletin Board Service (BBS)   An electronic bulletin accessed via modem. Many public and private organizations have bulletin boards into which users can dial with their modems and obtain information or assistance.

Bus Topology   The physical layout or arrangement of cabling for the LAN in which workstations are normally connected in a straight line, one after the other. The ends of the lines are capped off with what is referred to as a terminator; this marks the end of the bus.

Cabling/Cables   The wires (cables) used in physically connecting all the workstations and the file server to the network.

Cache   Fast-speed RAM that allows for faster processing of key data. Items used most often are placed here.

Carrier Sense Multiple Access/Collision Detection (CSMA/CD)   A particular access method regulating how data are sent on the network. The workstation's NIC must look to see if the channel (cable path) is busy before sending any data packets to the file server. If more than one workstation sends data packets at the same time and there is a "data collision," the network detects this, and the workstations' NICs will resend.

Centralized Processing   A method of processing applications and user requests at a central location. This type of processing is commonly found in mainframe environments.

Central Processing Unit (CPU)   The main processing unit of the computer, often referred to as the "brain." It receives commands and instructions and carries out the requests.

Client   The platform that requests data. See *Host.*

CLU   See *Command line utility.*

Command Line Utility (CLU)   Executable programs produced by Novell. For example, user CLUs are located in the PUBLIC directory. User CLUs include MAP, SEND, NDIR, and FLAG.

Concentrator   A central meeting point. Most commonly, it is an intelligent wiring center with sophisticated network management capabilities that can run multiple cable types and topologies simultaneously. A concentrator allows workstations to be tied into the backbone of the network.

Container Login Script   The script that executes first after logging in. Created by the administrator, it is normally associated with an organization or department and usually follows the hierarchical structure of the company.

Containers   Logical divisions of NDS, used for grouping and organizational purposes. Three types of containers are country, organization, and organizational unit.

Context   A position within the NDS tree structure that specifies the path to take to locate a particular leaf object.

CPU   See *Central processing unit.*

Create   The right required by a user to be allowed to make a new file.

CSMA/CD   See *Carrier sense multiple access/collision detection.*

Current Context   The position in the NDS tree at which a user is currently located when logged into the network.

Decentralized Processing   A method of processing applications and user requests at a local workstation location. The actual work processing takes place at the workstation by that workstation's CPU. This type of processing is commonly found in LAN environments.

Dedicated File Server   A computer that constantly acts as a servant to the workstations by sharing resources and serving files.

Default Login Script   If a user does not have a personal login script, the default login script, which is built into the LOGIN.EXE executable file, will run in lieu of it.

Disk Duplexing   Part of SFT II. Two hard drives exist in the file server. Each drive is connected to the motherboard by the *same* controller card, and identical information is written to both drives. If one drive goes out, the other drive keeps operating. To the end user, it is as if nothing happened. If the controller card fails, however, neither drive will function.

Disk Mirroring   Part of SFT II. Two hard drives exist in the file server. Each drive is connected to the motherboard by a *separate* controller card, and identical information is written to both drives. If one drive or its controller card goes out, the other drive and controller keep operating. To the end user, it is as if nothing happened.

Disk Operating System (DOS)   A local operating system widely used today. It controls the operation and function at the workstation level.

Disk Subsystem   A device that allows for expansion of the storage media. When the file server's hard drives are no longer sufficient to support the needs of the network, a disk subsystem allows for adding more disk drives or other storage devices.

DOS   See *Disk operating system.*

Downsizing   An organization's attempt to save financial resources by cutting back on personnel, unneeded equipment, or plants of operation.

Dumby Terminal   Workstations that do not contain a CPU for processing applications and programs as opposed to the stations that are dependent on another unit's CPU to do the actual processing. Dummy terminals are commonly used in mainframe environments.

FAT   See *File allocation table.*

File Allocation Table (FAT)   FAT keeps a record of the addresses (locations) of files stored on disk.

File Maintenance (FILER)   FILER is a NetWare menu utility that allows for the management of files and directories.

FILER   See *File maintenance.*

File Server (FS)   The computer that contains the network operating system and controls the overall operation of the LAN.

File Server Mirroring   Part of SFT III. A method of recovering operation during a power outage or hardware problem that involves the file server. If one of two file servers that are working side by side goes down, the other keeps operating. Because both servers are doing everything identically, to the end user it looks as if everything is running normally even if one server goes down.

FS   See *File server.*

Gateway   A method of using special hardware and software to connect dissimilar platforms, such as a LAN and a mainframe, together.

Home Directory   A data directory for private use. It is common for each user on the network to have his or her own home directory. See *Shared data directory.*

Host   The platform providing data. See *Client.*

Hot Fix   Part of SFT I. If the file server receives an instruction to write something on the disk, after it does so, it will read it to confirm that the operation was successful. If not, whatever the server was trying to write to the disk is relocated to a different area of the disk because the first area has a bad spot. The bad spot is then marked as unusable.

Hub   A central meeting point, usually a wiring box to tie workstations into the backbone of the network.

Hybrid Topology   Various other topologies are integrated together to best meet the needs of the installation site.

Inherited Rights Filter (IRF)   A way to block certain rights from trickling down to lower subdirectories.

Interconnectivity   The connecting of computers on more than one platform.

Internetwork Packet Exchange Open Data-Link Interface (IPXODI)   The communication protocol that governs how packets of data are dispersed through the network interface cards.

IPXODI See *Internetwork packet exchange open data-link interface.*

IRF See *Inherited rights filter.*

LAN See *Local area network.*

LAN Driver A software program that controls the operation of the network interface card (NIC). This software normally comes when the NIC is purchased. The manufacturer of the NIC, rather than Novell, provides the LAN driver.

Leaf Object An individual item on the network located inside of a container object. Users, groups, disk volumes, and printers are common examples of leaf objects.

Link Support Layer (LSL) LSL acts like a switchboard operator or mediator between IPXODI and the LAN driver.

Local Area Network (LAN) Computers connected together allowing for the sharing of hardware and software resources, the sharing of data, and communicating together.

Local Operating System (LOS) The local operating system, such as DOS, is responsible for controlling, operating, and carrying out instructions at the workstation level.

Login Restrictions These particular restrictions govern the login process. Common login restrictions include account disabled, account has expiration date, and limit concurrent connections.

Login Script Commands placed in a sequential order that execute upon logging into the network. Four types of login scripts are container, profile, user/personal, and default.

Login Time Restriction The restriction that governs the time periods that a user can log into the network. It does not govern when the user must log out. If a user logs in during the last two minutes of his or her allowable time, he or she can remain logged in indefinitely.

LOS See *Local operating system.*

LSL See *Link support layer.*

MAN See *Metropolitan area network.*

Map A way to give directions on how to get from one directory to another. A user can set up a map drive to get to a directory more quickly.

MB See *Megabytes.*

Media Another word for cabling.

Megabytes (MB) A measurement commonly used for accounting for disk storage. The number of MB

is equal to the number of kilobytes divided by 1024. The number of kilobytes is equal to the number of bytes divided by 1024. Each character on the computer requires approximately 1 byte of storage.

Menu Utility Executable programs produced by Novell. For example, user menu utilities are located in the PUBLIC directory. Examples of user menu utilities are FILER, NETADMIN, and PCONSOLE.

Mesh Topology A particular layout or arrangement of cabling in which each computer, including the file server, is connected. The connections are point to point.

Metropolitan Area Network (MAN) MANs represent the networking or tying in of LANs from surrounding cities in a metropolitan area. MANs are common with organizations that have branch offices located near each other.

NDS See *Novell Directory Services.*

Network Address Restriction A restriction that governs on which workstation(s) a user is allowed to log in.

Network Administrator Person who oversees the day-to-day operation of a network. By setting up and managing user accounts, controlling security, creating comfortable work environments, making sure that printers are set up and working, maintaining preventative backups, and monitoring network performance, an administrator makes sure that users can work on the LAN easily and efficiently.

Network Drive Map See *Map.*

Network Interface Card (NIC) A card that attaches to the motherboard inside the computer; considered part of the hardware group. Externally, cabling attached to the NIC allows the computer to be physically linked to the network. The NIC controls the physical aspects of sending and receiving data on the network. All workstations and the file server must have an NIC to reside on the network.

Network Operating System (NOS) The operating system associated with the file server. It is responsible for the controlling and processing instructions at the file server level. NetWare 4.1x is an example of a NOS.

NIC See *Network interface card.*

Nondedicated File Server A computer that acts as a file server only part of the time. The rest of the time, the computer doubles as a regular workstation.

NOS See *Network operating system.*

Novell Directory Services (NDS) A system for tracking all the resources on a network; a global, distributed hierarchical database. It is organized in an upside-down tree fashion with the "roots" of the tree at the top. A container is usually found off the roots.

Open Data-Link Interface The industry standard calling for networks to be flexible enough to support a variety of workstations that may be logging into the same network.

Organizational Unit A branch of the NDS tree, which normally represents the organization's divisions or branch structure. Organizational units are classified as container objects, and they may contain other container objects or leaf objects inside of them.

Password Restriction Different options that an administrator can use to control password security. These options include require password, minimum password length, force periodic password change, limit grace logins, and require unique password restrictions.

PDF See *Print device file or printer definition file.*

Personal/User Login Script See *User/personal login script.*

Polling A particular access method regulating how data are sent on the network. The file server will check with each workstation, one by one, to see if there are any requests or commands that need processing.

Print Device File or Printer Definition File (PDF) A special file that specifies configurations and instructions for a selected printer.

Print Queue A waiting line for print jobs that are waiting to print.

Print Server A computer designated for managing the printers.

Profile Login Script The script that executes after the container login script. It is usually assigned to a group of users, such as managers, clerks, or programmers. This script crosses department barriers.

Purge Deleted Files Permanently deleting one or more files so as to make them unsalvageable.

Queue A waiting line. See *Print queue.*

Queue Operator A person assigned to manage the print queues.

Queue Users People assigned to use a particular print queue.

RAM See *Random-access memory.*

Random-Access Memory (RAM) Temporary storage that goes away when the computer is turned off. This storage area is used during the processing of various commands. Maps are set up in RAM.

Read The right assigned to permit a user to see the contents of the file.

Rights The level to which a user or group of users has access to a given file or directory.

Ring Topology Workstations connected in a circular pattern with the file server also attached to the circle. The ends of the circle usually connect to the file server or some other central device.

Salvage Deleted Files An option that allows a user to bring back files that have been previously deleted as long as the files have not been purged. See *Purge deleted files.*

Search Drive Map Pointers set up in the workstation's RAM that allow for quick finding and executing of .EXE, .BAT, and .COM files. If a search drive map already points to a particular directory, executable files located in that directory may be called up at any prompt, without changing the directory containing those files.

Service Mode Indication about how forms are changed for different print queues.

SFT See *System fault tolerance.*

Shared Data Directory A directory containing data for use by more than one user, as opposed to a home directory. See *Home directory.*

Shielded Twisted Pair (STP) A form of cabling that offers a small amount of resistance to electrical interference. Very similar in appearance to a phone cable.

Software Metering Counting how many users are logged into the network and are using a particular software application. Once the count has been taken, it is then checked against licensing information to see if the number of licensed stations running the software has been exceeded.

Star Topology Workstations connected in a star pattern with the file server also attached. The file server sits in the center, and each workstation connects to a hub or concentrator connected to the file server.

STP See *Shielded twisted pair.*

System Fault Tolerance (SFT) Different techniques and features that help keep a LAN up and run-

ning in the event of hardware problems. See *Disk duplexing, Disk mirroring, Hot fix,* and *File server mirroring.*

System Files   The files required to boot up a system initially. Commonly found files for workstation boot up include IO.SYS, MSDOS.SYS, and COMMAND.COM.

Terminal Emulation   A special computer card and software that allow a personal computer to emulate or act like a dumby terminal for purposes of communicating to the host computer in a centralized processing platform.

Token Passing   A particular access method regulating how data are sent on the network. A logical token (box) is passed throughout the LAN from workstation to workstation. As long as the token is empty, the workstation's NIC can put a command or request in it. If it's already full, the NIC must wait for the next token pass.

Topology   How cables are arranged or the cable layout.

Tree   The graphical representation of the network structure corresponding to the organizational layout of container and leaf objects making up the network.

Trustee   The person or account holder entrusted to use a particular directory or file.

Uninterruptible Power Supply (UPS)   A battery backup hardware device (often software driven) that allows the computer to continue running in case of a power outage or electrical spikes. UPSs vary greatly in price and features. They are commonly attached to the file server, but some companies even have them on workstations.

Unshielded Twisted Pair (UTP)   A form of cabling that offers a small amount of resistance to electrical interference. It is very similar in appearance to that of a phone cable.

UPS   See *Uninterruptible power supply.*

User/Personal Login Script   The script that executes after the profile login script (if there is one) when logging in. It is customized for the particular user logging in.

UTP   See *Unshielded twisted pair.*

Variable Replacement   A system option used in login script commands that accommodates data items (variables) that are unknown or vary when the user(s) logs in. Sometimes the options for commands used in a login script may need to be changed depending on who logs in, on what computer, and when. Variable replacements accomplish this by allowing flexibility in the construction of the command. Variable replacements are preceded by a percent sign (%).

Virtual Loadable Module (VLM)   An executable file that allows a workstation to attach to the file server (network); it also allows a workstation to request different types of services.

Volume   The divisions of the file server's hard drive (or disk subsystem). It can contain NetWare software directories such as PUBLIC, SYSTEM, MAIL, LOGIN, and ETC. The volume may also contain software applications and data that users may be sharing.

Volume Space Restriction   An option that allows the amount of disk space that a user can have on the file server's hard drive or disk subsystem to be limited.

WAN   See *Wide area network.*

Wide Area Network (WAN)   A network that allows for LANs from a wider distance to connect together through the phone or satellite media. WANs are commonly used among organizations that have branch offices in different states.

Workstation (WS)   The computer at which a user sits to complete work. In a distributed processing environment, such as a LAN, the workstation's CPU usually does the actual processing of applications.

Write   The right assigned to permit a user to change the content of a file.

WS   See *Workstation.*

INDEX

Account disabled restriction, 198
Account restrictions, 197–200
Accounting software, 236
Actions for User menu, 95–100
Adapter, 6
Admin, 84
ADMIN, 170
ADMIN account, 3, 91–92
    creating, 3, 91–92
    equivalent, 3
    setting up an, 91
Assigning drive maps using Windows Explorer, 31–32
Assigning rights, 36
Assigning security access for, 84–85
Assigning users to groups, 83–84
Assignment, 84–85
    of security access, 84–85
    of trustee rights, 84–85
*, 41
Attachment, 115–116
ATTRIB command, 44, 45
Attributes, 45
    directory search, 125
    file search, 125
AUTOEXEC.BAT file, 114
Automating a menu, 226–228

Backbone cabling, 61
BACKUP command, 44, 45–47
Backups, 204
Base band coaxial, 7
Bridge, 11, 12
Broad band, coaxial, 7
Bus topology, 8, 9

Cabling, 7
    coaxial base band, 7
    coaxial broad band, 7
    fiber-optic, 7

shielded twisted pair (STP), 7
unshielded twisted pair (UTP), 7
CAPTURE command, 150, 173
Carrier sense multiple access/collision detection (CSMA/CD), 8
CD (change directory) command, 41, 43
Centralized processing, 6, 11
CHKDSK command, 44
Client, 12
CLS (clear screen) command, 41, 42
CLU (command line utilities), 137
    CAPTURE, 150, 173
    controlling printing with, 149–150, 151
    FLAG, 125, 145, 147–149
    LOGIN, 137
    managing directories with, 141–145
    managing files with, 145–149
    MAP, 26, 27, 30, 109, 218
    NCOPY, 145–146
    NDIR, 145
    NLIST USER, 139, 140
    NMENU, 145
    NPATH, 138
    NPRINT, 152
    NVER, 138
    PSC (print server control), 152
    PURGE, 147
    RENDIR, 143
    RIGHTS, 143, 145
    routine, 137–138
    SEND, 109, 141
    SETPASS, 138
    SYSTIME, 138
    WHOAMI, 115, 139, 140
Coaxial cables, 7
Collision, 8

COMMAND.COM file, 6
Command line utilities (CLU), 137
    controlling printing with, 149–150, 151
    managing directories with, 141–145
    managing files with, 145–149
    routine, 137–138
Communicating on network, 139–141
Communication access methods, 7–9
Communication protocol, 7–9
COMP command, 44
Computer-aided design (CAD) software, 236
Computer-aided mapping (CAM) software, 236
Concentrator, 61
Conditional instructions, 217
Confirm,
    deletions, 127
    file copies, 127
    file overwrites, 128
Connectivity, 3
Container login script, 211–212
Containers, 61, 93
Context, 58, 59, 61–62
    changing current, 172
    changing the, 93–95
    verifying and changing, 62
Context sensitive format, 84
COPY command, 41, 42
Copying multiple files in Windows Explorer, 21
Copying one file in Windows Explorer, 18
Crash, 8
Creating login script, 214
Current context, 61
CX command, 61–62

Data collision, 8
Data packets, 7–8
Database management software, 235
DATE command, 41, 42
Decentralized processing, 11
Default context, 59
Default drives, changing, 217
Default login script, 213–214
Deleted files, 126
    purging, 126
    salvaging, 126
DELETED.SAV directory, 32, 35, 126
Deletions, confirm, 127
DELTREE (delete tree) command, 47
Desktop publishing software, 236
Differential backup, 46
DIR command, 41, 42
Directories, managing with CLUs, 141–145
Directory folder, creating in Windows Explorer, 17–18
Directory information, view/set, 122–123
Directory pattern,
    exclude, 125
    include, 125
Directory rights, 36
Directory search attributes, 125
Directory structure, 32–33
Directory trustee assignments and LAN security, 201
Disk duplexing, SFT II, 205
Disk miroring, SFT II, 205
Disk operating system (DOS), 41–48
DISKCOPY, 44
DISPLAY filename command, 217
Distributed processing, 6, 11
DOC directory, 32
Documentation for printer, 159
DOCVIEW directory, 32
DOS editor, 47
DOS PATH command, 114–115
Dot matrix printers, 183
Downsizing, 11
DRIVE G command, 217
Drive mapping, 26–27
Drive maps, assigning using Windows Explorer, 31–32
Drives, 112–115
    logical, 26

mapping, 112
physical, 24
search, 27–28
Dumb terminals, 6, 11

EDIT command, 44, 47–48
EDLIN command, 44
Education software, 236
Effective rights, 144
Electrical interference, 7
Electronic mail, 2
ERASE command, 41, 42
ETC. directory, 32, 97
Ethernet, 8
Exclude,
    directory pattern, 125
    file patterns, 125
EXEC command, 225
Executing a menu, 225
EXIT command, 217
Expiration date on account, 199
External bridge, 11
External DOS commands,
    ATTRIB, 44, 45
    BACKUP, 44, 45–47
    CHKDSK, 44
    COMP, 44
    DELTREE, 47
    DISKCOPY, 44
    EDIT, 44, 47–48
    EDLIN, 44
    FDISK, 44
    FORMAT, 44, 48
    GRAPHICS, 44
    LABEL, 44
    MIRROR, 44
    MODE, 44
    MSBACKUP, 45–47
    MSD, 48
    RESTORE, 44
    SYS, 44
    TREE, 44
    UNDELETE, 44
    UNFORMAT, 44
    XCOPY, 44

F1 function key, 100
F5 mark key, 121, 124, 126
F10 select key, 121
FDISK command, 44
Fiber-optic cabling, 7. *See also* Cabling
File, specifying to print, 176
File copies, confirm, 127
File maintenance (FILER), 119

File patterns, exclude and include, 125
File search attributes, 125
File server, 4–5
#filename command, 217
FILER (file maintenance), 119, 124
FILER menu utility, 36
Files, managing, 121–122
    with CLU, 145–149
FIRE PHASERS command, 215
FLAG command, 125, 145, 147–149
Flags, 45, 46
FORMAT, 44, 48
Forms, Service Modes for, 181–182
Full backup, 46
Function keys,
    F1, 100
    F5 Mark key, 121, 124, 126
    F10 Select key, 121

Gateway, 11, 12
Grace logins, limiting, 200
GRAPHICS command, 44
Groups,
    assigning users to, 83–84
    creating, 81–83

Hardware, 3
    benefits of sharing, 3
Help, 100
Help key, 100
Home directory, 114
Host, 12
Hot fix, 204–205
Hub, 61
Hybrid topology, 10

Include,
    directory pattern, 125
    file patterns, 125
INCLUDE command, 217
Incremental backup, 46
Information sources for software, 237–238
Inherited rights, 144
Inherited rights filter (IRF), 97–100, 144
Ink-jet printers, 183
Integrated package software, 236
Interconnectivity, 11–12
Internal bridge, 11

Internal DOS commands,
CD, 41, 43
CLS, 41, 42
COPY, 41, 42
DATE, 41, 42
DIR, 41
ERASE, 41, 42
executing, 218
MD, 41, 42–43
PATH, 28, 41, 44
RD, 41, 43
TIME, 41, 42
TYPE, 41, 42
Intruder detection, 61
IO.SYS file, 6
IRF (inherited rights filters),
97–100, 144

LABEL command, 44
LAN components, 4–7
file server, 4–5
dedicated file server, 5
nondedicated file server, 5
LAN driver, 7
local operating system, 6
network interface card, 6–7
network operating system, 5
workstations, 6
LAN driver, 7
LAN pack, 233–234
LAN security, 3–4, 91, 197
directory trustee assignments
and, 201
passwords and, 202
safeguarding, 203–204
troubleshooting, 203–204
LAN troubleshooting, 60–61
LAN versus other platforms, 11
Laser printers, 183
Launching Windows Explorer,
16–17
Leaf objects, 92
Limit concurrent connections,
199
Local area networks (LAN),
definition of, 3
hardware resources, 3
software resources, 3. *See also*
Software
Local operating system (LOS), 5, 6
Local printer, 157
versus network printer, 157
Locating login script, 214
Logical drive, 26–27, 112
purpose of, 112–113

Logical drive mappings, life span
of, 28, 30
Logical drive names, 113–114
LOGIN, 137
LOGIN.EXE, 33
LOGIN.EXE screen, 116
LOGIN directory, 32, 33, 97
Login name as security, 59
Login process,
customizing the, 63–73
for network, 58–59
Login restrictions, 198–199
Login script, 113, 137
container, 211–212
creating, 214
default, 213–214
locating, 214
profile, 212, 214
user/personal, 213, 214
Login script commands, common,
214–218
conditional instructions, 217
DISPLAY filename, 217
DOS, 218
DRIVE G, 217
EXIT, 217
#filename, 217
FIRE PHASERS, 215
INCLUDE, 217
MAP, 218
sounding alerts, 215
WRITE, 215
Login script files, 211–214
LOGIN SERV2/USERXX, 138
Login shortcut, placement of,
70–73
Login time restrictions, 200
LOGIN/NS command, 137
Logins, limiting grace, 200
LOGOUT command, 138
LOGOUT SERV2, 138

MAIL directory, 32, 35, 97
Manage files and directories,
120–124
Managing,
according to search patterns,
124–125
files, 121–122
files with CLU, 145–149
objects, 92–93
subdirectories, 121
MAP, deleting, 30
MAP command, 26, 27, 30, 109,
218

MAP command line utility,
141–143
Mapping of drives, 112
Maps, 26–32
deleting map assignments, 30
life span of, 28, 30
logical drive maps, 27–28
network drive maps, 27–28
search drive maps, 27–28
using the NEXT option, 30–31
MD (make directory) command,
41, 42–43
Media, 7
Menu, actions for user, 95–100
advantages of using, 223
construction, 224
executing a, 225
requirements for running, 223
sample, 224–226
Menu construction, 224
Menus, netware, 222
rights required to create, 222
Mesh topology, 10
Messages, 111–112
sending to group, 111
sending to users, 111
set receive, 111–112
MHS directory, 32
Microsoft diagnostics (MSD), 48
MIRROR command, 44
MODE command, 44
Modem software, 236
Moving files in Windows Explorer,
22
MSBACKUP command, 45–47
MSD, 48
MSDOS.SYS file, 6

NCOPY command, 145–146
NDIR command, 145
NDS (NetWare Directory Ser-
vices), 59, 61–63
tree, 78–88, 91
NDS (Novell Directory Services),
214
NDS tree, moving in, 120–121
NETADMIN (network administra-
tion), 197, 198
account, 91
NETUSER options, 109, 110, 111,
113
and drive mapping, 113
NetWare, *see also* Novell NetWare
NetWare administrator (NWAD-
MIN), 76–77

NetWare client, 55
  creating workstation diskettes, 55–56
NetWare Directory Services (NDS), 59, 61–63
  tree, 78–88, 91
Netware menus, 222
Network, administrating the, 76
  communicating on, 139–141
  login process for, 58–59
Network address restriction, 200
Network drives, 28
Network interface card (NIC), 6–7
  address, 200
Network Neighborhood, 63–70
Network operating system (NOS), 5, 28, 30. *See also* LAN components
  component of LAN, 5.
Network printer, 157
  versus local printer, 157
NEW FOLDER, 36
NEXT option, 30
NLIST USER command, 139, 140
NMENU command, 145
Notepad, 24
Novell Directory Services (NDS), 33, 61, 214
Novell NetWare, 55
  security in, 59
NPATH command, 138
NPRINT command, 152
NVER command, 138
NWADMIN (NetWare administrator), 76, 159, 197

Objects, 59
  managing, 92–93
  selecting, 95
Organizational unit, 61. *See also* Novell Directory Services
Organizational unit objects, creating, 78–80

Parallel printer, 180–181
Parent, 93
Partitions, 24
Password, 59
  allowing to change, 199
  forcing change of, 200
  LAN security and, 202
  minimum length for, 199–200
  requiring, 199
  requiring unique, 200
  restrictions, 199–200

PATH command, 28, 41, 44
PATH versus search mapping, 115
PCONSOLE (print console), utility, 110, 173–177
Physical drives, 24
Platforms, 11
Polling, 8
Print devices, 170–171
  edit, 171
Print forms, 171
Print job, 157
  configuration, 173
  edit configuration, 172–173
Print parameters, changing, 177–182
Print queue, 110
Print queue user, 158
Print server, 157, 159, 180
Print server control (PSC), command, 152
Print utilities, 170
PRINTCON utility, 172–173
PRINTDEF utility, 170–172
Printer, 158–159
  management, 159–166
  setups, 159–166
Printer documentation, 159
Printer port, 110
  assigning for network use, 110
Printer queue, 157, 158, 175
  creating leaf objects for, 159–166
  ID, 179
  information, 175–176
Printers, local versus network, 157
Printers screen, 180
Printing, 109–110
  controlling with CLUs, 149–150, 151
Profile login script, 212, 214
Programmable read only memory (PROM), 6
PROM (programmable read only memory), 6
Properties of files in Windows Explorer, 22–24
PSC (print server control) command, 152
PUBLIC directory, 28, 32, 35, 97, 119, 137
PURGE command, 147
Purge deleted files, 126

Queue Operators, 179
Queue Users, 179
?, 41

RD (remove directory) command, 41, 43
Renaming a file in Windows Explorer, 22
RENDIR command, 143
RESTORE command, 44
Rights, 36 *See also* Effective rights; Inherited rights; Trustee directory rights
  assigning, 36
  assigning with directory information screen, 123–124
  directory, 36
  effective, 144
Rights available in NetWare, 87–88
  viewing or editing, 97
RIGHTS command, 143, 145
RIGHTS SERV command, 143–144
Ring topology, 9

Safeguarding LAN, 203–204
Salvage deleted files, 126
Sample menu, 224–226
Search drive mappings, life span of, 28, 30
Search map, 114
Search mapping versus PATH, 115
Search pattern, manage according to, 100–102, 124
Security access, assigning, 84–85
Security in NetWare, 59
SEND command, 109, 141
SEND/A command, 141
Serial printer, 180–181
SERVER.EXE, 5. *See also* Network operating system
Server list (SLIST), 33
Server mirroring, SFT III, 205
Service Modes for forms, 181–182
SET command, 223
  automating a, 226–228
Set default options, 127
SETPASS command, 138
SETPASS SERV2/ command, 138
SFT I, 204–205
SFT II: Disk mirroring and duplexing, 205
SFT III: server mirroring, 205
Shared processing, 6. *See also* Centralized processing
Shielded twisted pair (STP), 7
Single-user software, 233
SLIST.EXE, 33

Software, 3
 accounting, 236
 benefits of sharing software, 3
 computer-aided design (CAD),
   236
 computer-aided mapping
   (CAM), 236
 database management, 235
 desktop publishing, 236
 education, 236
 integrated package, 236
 modem, 236
 selecting and buying, 233
 single-user, 233
 sources of information about,
   237–238
 spreadsheet, 235
 where to purchase, 234–235
 word-processing, 235
Software installations for Windows
   Explorer, 17
Software metering, 234
Sounding alerts, 215
Space restrictions, 200
Spanning volumes, 24
Spreadsheet software, 235
Star topology, 8, 10
Status of printer, 178
Subdirectories, managing, 121
SYS command, 44
SYS:VOLUME partition, 33
SYSTEM directory, 32, 35, 97
System fault tolerance, 204
System files, 6
 COMMAND.COM, 6
 file names, 6
 IO.SYS, 6
 MSDOS.SYS, 6
SYSTIME SERV2, 138

Terminal emulation, 11, 12
Terminator, 9
TIME command, 41, 42
Token passing, 8–9
Topology, 9–10
TREE command, 44
Tree formation, 59
Troubleshooting, 60–61
Troubleshooting of LAN, 203–204
Trustee assignments, 84–85, 97
 adding, 87
 changing, 86
 viewing rights of, 97
Trustee directory rights, 201–202,
   222
Trustee rights,
 assignment of, 84–85
 viewing of, 85–86
Trustees, 84, 85, 97, 123
 assigning with directory infor-
   mation screen, 123–124
Twisted pair cables, 7
TYPE command, 41, 42
Typeless naming, 62

UNDELETE command, 44
UNFORMAT command, 44
Uninterruptible Power Supply
   (UPS), 204
Unshielded twisted pair (UTP), 7
User accounts, creating, 91–92, 95
 changing, 95
User leaves, 80–81
USERLIST command, 109
User/personal login script, 213,
   214
USERS directory, 36

Value-added reseller (VAR), 234
View Volume Information, 126
Virus protection program, 203
Virus threat, 202–203
Volume/space restrictions, 200
Volumes, definition, 5

WAN (wide area network) environment, 138
WHOAMI command, 115, 139,
   140
WHOAMI/ALL command, 139
Wide area network (WAN) environment, 138
Windows Explorer, 16–24
 assigning drive maps using,
   31–32
 copying multiple files in, 21
 copying one file in, 18
 directory folder, creating, 17–18
 launching, 16–17
 moving files in, 22
 properties of files in, 22–24
 renaming a file in, 22
 software installations, for, 17
Word-processing software, 235
Wordpad, 24
Workstations, 6
 installing NetWare client at,
   56–57
 preparing the, 55–59
WRITE command, 215
Write protection, 203

XCOPY command, 44